The Psychological World
of the Teen-ager

THE
PSYCHOLOGICAL
WORLD OF
THE TEEN-AGER

*A Study of Normal
Adolescent Boys*

DANIEL OFFER

With the collaboration of MELVIN SABSHIN

and the assistance of JUDITH L. OFFER

Basic Books, Inc., Publishers

NEW YORK   LONDON

Third Printing

© 1969 by Daniel Offer
Library of Congress Catalog Card Number: 73–78465
Manufactured in the United States of America

THIS BOOK IS DEDICATED TO THE STUDENTS, THEIR PARENTS,
AND THE TWO SCHOOLS WHOSE CONTINUOUS SUPPORT
HELPED MAKE THIS STUDY POSSIBLE.

Preface

Who are the youth of today? How do adolescents react to the everyday events of their lives? What are the future goals of a high-school student? It is taken for granted that in as large and diverse a country as the United States, youth will not be represented by a single or even a number of patterns of development. There will be different types of adolescents whose paths through the high-school years, though multidetermined, will take many different forms. It is crucial that we become aware of all types of teen-agers, and realize that there are many routes from childhood to adulthood.

We have chosen to work with a group of adolescents because of our interest in the psychology of the teen-ager. It is in high school that the student begins to separate from his parents and develop his own identity. The high-school years have always been known for their influence on the molding of the future personality of the human being. It is during these years that the adolescent acquires values of his own and begins the long process of finding himself.

Psychiatrists, as well as other social and behavioral scientists, have concentrated on studying the extremes. Individuals showing high degrees of pathology, disturbance, and deviancy have been studied extensively. From these studies investigators drew conclusions about the bulk of the adolescents whom they had not studied. It seemed natural to them that the "normal" teen-ager would manifest the same psychological patterns as the clinically disturbed.

We have tried to establish communication with one group of adolescents. Our subjects were primarily middle-class suburban high-school students. The study of adolescents who function within the middle range of adjustment seems to us the clearest method for observing what is representative of the greater teen-age population, individuals who are not always easily visible to society at large. An understanding of a group of suburban teen-agers can add dimension to our entire theoretical understanding of the phenomena of adolescence.

In our attempt to probe the psychological world of the suburban teen-ager, we have obviously selected a group who did not suffer from economic, social, or educational deprivation. On the contrary, we worked with subjects who came from intact families who usually were economically secure and who felt that their hopes would be realized rather than thwarted.

The material in this book has been carefully collected during the four years we spent in two suburban high schools. It is a psychological study and as such is subjective as well as objective. We used our methods and rating scales but we never forgot that our own values and personalities were crucial in our relationship with the adolescents. We believe that the teen-agers cooperated as enthusiastically as they did, not only because they felt that the scientific aims of the project were important, but also because we represented to them an opportunity for a dialogue with a distant though sympathetic and understanding adult.

The book is divided into four parts. In Part I, "Method," we describe the overall design of the project, which includes the selection process, the interviews, and our approach to the problem of data analysis. In Part II, "Results," we present our findings, using both statistical and interview data. Part III, "Discussion," is devoted to a theoretical integration of our findings in relation to the existing relevant theories of adolescence. Finally, in the appendixes, we include questionnaires and scales used in this research, as well as a detailed description of the method.

DANIEL OFFER

Chicago
March 1969

Acknowledgments

The Modal Adolescent Project began in 1961. We are grateful for the support given the research by the United States Public Health Service: First, with Mental Health Career Investigator Grant No. 4870 of the National Institute of Mental Health, 1961–1964. Second, with Grant No. 08714 of the National Institute of Mental Health, 1964–1966. Third, with Grant No. 02571 of the Child Health and Human Development Institute, 1966–1969.

It is important to stress that this research has been made possible by the active collaboration of many investigators. David Marcus, a psychiatric colleague, has been on the project from its inception and has been invaluable in his capacity as a psychiatric interviewer. Marlene Simon has undertaken the survey interview with the subjects. Joanne Miller has interviewed all the parents and has performed part of the ratings. Also, R. Polsky has done some of the ratings. Sara Lee Futterman has administered all the psychological tests to the subjects. Herman Diesenhaus has served as an extremely valuable methodological consultant.

At different stages we were fortunate in being helped by the following colleagues: Danuta Ehrlich, Kenneth Howard, William Simon, Brahm Baittle, James Masterson, Jr., Gerald Vogel, and Arnold Goldberg. Roy R. Grinker, Sr., the director of the Institute for Psychosomatic and Psychiatric Research and Training of Michael Reese Hospital, has advised us throughout the years and encouraged us by his own example as a research psychiatrist. Little in this book will be new to him as the normal adolescent project has been growing up within earshot of his office.

The construction of the Self-Image Questionnaire and the selection of the modal sample were performed at the National Opinion Research Center of the University of Chicago, under the guidance of William Simon. The data analysis was carried out at the Institute for Juvenile Research, using the IBM 1620 Model II, under the direction of Kenneth Howard and Herman Diesenhaus.

We would also like to thank Audrey Williams, our secretary, who cheerfully typed and retyped the manuscript through its many stages. The manuscript was proofread by Hadassah Baskin and Raye Korshak.

Parts of the results have been published in the following journals:

(1) *Archives General Psychiatry*, 9:5, Nov. 1963: "The Psychiatrist and the Normal Adolescent."

(2) *American Journal Psychiatry*, 121:9, March 1965: "Clinical Evaluations of Normal Adolescents."

(3) *American Journal Psychiatry*, 123:12, June 1967: "Research Alliance vs. Therapeutic Alliance: A Comparison."

(4) *Adolescence*, 1:4, 1967: "Studies of Normal Adolescents."

(5) *Archives General Psychiatry*, 17:3, Sept. 1967: "Normal Adolescents: Interview Strategy and Selected Results."

We are grateful to these journals for the permission to reprint sections of the results.

Contents

PREFACE   vii

ACKNOWLEDGMENTS   xi

PART I / METHOD

1. *Inception of the Modal Adolescent Project*   3
2. *The Method in Overview*   10

PART II / RESULTS

3. *The School Environment*   27
4. *The Home Environment*   46
5. *Rebellious and Antisocial Behavior*   69
6. *Heterosexual Behavior*   78
7. *Response to Special Crises*   89
8. *Affects and Their Vicissitudes*   96
9. *Psychological Testing: Thematic Apperception
    Test, Rorschach Test, and WAIS Vocabulary
    Scale* (BY PAUL R. SINGER)   110

PART III / DISCUSSION

10. *The Nature of the Relationship: The "Research Alliance"*   147
11. *Adolescent Turmoil*   174
12. *The Adolescent and His Parents: The Bridge Between the Generations*   193
13. *Coping Behavior of the Modal Adolescent*   209

PART IV / APPENDIXES

APPENDIX I   The Self-Image Questionnaire   227
APPENDIX II   The Interview Schedules for the Modal Adolescent Project   247
APPENDIX III   Selected Questions and Answers Collected in the Second Interview   262

BIBLIOGRAPHY   267
INDEX   279

PART I

Method

1

Inception of the Modal Adolescent Project

The purpose of the Modal Adolescent Project was to examine the relative influences of internal psychological and external environmental factors on the functioning of typical adolescents over a significant period of time. We were interested in studying the behavior of a selected group of adolescents in order to assess their relative strengths and weaknesses. We also wished to examine the kinds of psychological problems they have, their methods of coping with them, and, if they were not successful in their struggles, the reasons behind their failures. We aimed at obtaining information concerning our subjects' overall psychological experience in order to assess whether the developmental processes of adolescence are uniquely disruptive or are akin to other developmental stages.

In this book we describe the origin, development, and results of the project. The focus will be on adolescence proper, the years from fourteen to eighteen. We started the project when the subjects were beginning high school.

The data presented cover the high-school years. Although we

are continuing to follow our subjects in order to obtain a better understanding of the late adolescent years and the transition to young adulthood, we shall not report here on this later phase, since it seems to us that the problems of the young adult in our society are intrinsically different from the problems of the teen-ager. We shall, however, include relevant data on the study population from the first year after high school. We believe that this information will be helpful in evaluating our position con-cerning the adaptation of our subjects.

When we started our work with the modal adolescent, we were fascinated by the array of definitions of normality and mental health in the literature of the social and behavioral sciences. In the first volume derived from our research interests, *Normality: Theoretical and Clinical Concepts of Mental Health* (Offer and Sabshin, 1966), we have attempted to document the dilemmas facing any investigator doing research in the area of normality or mental health. We have also suggested potential solutions of the research dilemma. In the above volume we described four basic "functional perspectives" of normality:

(1) "Normality as health" includes the traditional medical-psychiatric approach, which equates normality with health and views health as an almost universal phenomenon.

(2) "Normality as Utopia," which is best typified by psycho-analysts, conceives of normality as that harmonious and optimal blending of the diverse elements of the mental apparatus which culminates in optimal functioning, something that is rarely, if ever, present in any individual.

(3) "Normality as average" is commonly employed in norma-tive studies of behavior. This approach is based on the mathe-matical principle of the bell-shaped curve and its applicability to physical, psychological, and sociological data.

(4) "Normality as process" stresses that normal behavior is the end result of interacting systems that change over time. In contrast to proponents of the other three perspectives, those who advocate this position insist that normality be viewed consistently from a standpoint of temporal progression.

In *Normality* we did not present our own definition of mental health, since we believed that such definitions should emerge from empirical research data. In the present volume we shall describe one group of adolescents in detail, in the hope that this description will help us come closer to a definition of mental health for at least one segment of our society.

Psychiatrists have been articulate in discussing *typical, average, modal,* or *normal** problems experienced by most, if not all, adolescents. There have been numerous discussions of adolescent development, and the literature is saturated with repetitive formulations of adolescent turmoil.† Frequently, however, these psychiatric formulations have been questioned from three overlapping perspectives. First, there is the classical issue of the validity of generalizing across cultural, ethnic, and class lines. To what extent can findings based on data collected from the middle-class American teen-age patients who represent the majority of the adolescent population seen by psychiatrists be transposed to groups of varying sociological, geographical, and temporal positions? Second, there is the question of making generalizations about modal behavior from work with disturbed adolescents seen in consultation rooms. To what extent can findings based on data collected from middle-class teen-age patients be transposed to nonpatient groups of the same sociocultural background? Third, there is the question regarding a value bias in favor of adolescent turmoil by mental-health workers. This bias is especially pertinent today, when teen-age unrest appears to have become part of major political movements. To be sure, clinical theorists who make generalizations about normative adolescent behavior have had contact with adolescents other than their patients. Their own past experiences, observations of their own children as well as those of

* These four terms will be used interchangeably in the book unless stated otherwise.

† "Adolescent turmoil" is defined here as "significant disruption in the psychic organization of the adolescent that leads to psychological disequilibrium and tumult resulting in fluctuant and unpredictable behavior on the part of the teen-ager."

others from similar social strata, and reconstructions of adolescent experiences in adult therapy are often utilized in discussing "typical" adolescent problems. Frequently, however, these latter observations are haphazard. There has also been the danger of focusing upon those observations which confirm the turmoil hypothesis. Thus, the remarkable paucity of studies by psychiatrists upon normal adolescent samples has been one resultant of their professional biases. Despite criticisms, the formulations of adolescence as a period of turmoil have been predominant in psychiatric literature. Those who questioned the turmoil hypothesis rarely utilized empirical studies.* Even more rare has been empirical investigation utilizing interview data over a significant time span.

Psychiatrists traditionally have functioned in a hospital and a consultation-room setting. Most of their clinical research methods have been geared toward such settings, which are relatively isolated from normative data. In these activities they have tended to assume that the behavior seen in patients reflects the common problems experienced by most people. Recently, however, there have been an increasing number of criticisms and questions about this extrapolation from consultation-room and hospital data.† Psychiatrists have asked what empirical evidence allows us to assume that the sample in our treatment facilities is representative of the total population. The fact that this question has come to the forefront simultaneously with the evolution of new roles and new activities by psychiatrists has given further emphasis to our study. To a significant degree, psychiatrists have moved out of their hospital and consultation-room settings and are now found in a variety of other areas of action. The move toward greater involvement in community psychiatry has afforded an excellent opportunity for new populations to be studied through utilization of a combination of older and newer methods.

* With the obvious exception of anthropological and sociological studies.
† The interested reader should turn to the proceedings of the Conference on Normal Behavior (1967), where these issues are discussed in greater detail.

In the process of extrapolation from psychopathology to normative theory, it has not been simple for psychiatrists to focus upon the adaptive in human behavior. This issue has been approached, of course, in treatment efforts when psychiatrists have studied the outcome of various therapeutic endeavors, asking questions regarding the difference between the patient at the beginning of treatment and toward the completion of successful treatment. In focusing upon this question it was necessary to construct a theoretical model that would permit a comparison between those two points in time. The question remains, however, whether our concepts of successful therapy are handicapped by the paucity of data that might permit us to compare patients at the end of treatment with the population to which they return at that time. Furthermore, there is always the nagging anxiety that psychotherapists might miss or underemphasize adaptive or coping mechanisms even at the end of treatment. Our theoretical concepts do not facilitate examination of the *nuances* of what is meant by "adaptation" and "coping" to the degree that is usually possible in studying psychopathology. In addition, psychiatrists are adept in perceiving coping behavior correctly but still clothing it in the garments of psychopathology. The psychopathological framework and language are difficult to give up even in research efforts on therapeutic outcome.

Pfeffer (1961 and 1963), for example, reported on a follow-up study of patients who had undergone psychoanalytic treatment, but he still focused on psychopathological evidence although through quite subtle processes. He interviewed the former patients in his office and utilized techniques close to ordinary analytic practice, thus bringing the subjects back to the psychoanalytic situation with which they were so familiar. In this setting there is a tendency for the former patients to resume their prior roles and hence automatically to regress, indulge in free association, and exhibit the less adaptive and more pathological parts of their psyche. Pfeffer did not concentrate on how their coping had changed since their treatment, nor did he comment on the metapsychology of their new adaptation. Such an approach has not been undertaken in as much depth and detail as have studies of the more pathological processes. Hence we were not surprised that his findings stressed the recurrence of a miniaturized transference neurosis as an indication of positive therapeutic outcome.

Psychiatry has begun to change at a rapid tempo in the recent past. The symbol of the psychiatrist is no longer the man in the white coat who comes to take the patient to some far-off asylum. This traditional symbol was rapidly altered for the middle and upper classes in the United States after World War II, although it persists in the lower classes. For the middle and upper classes, the symbol of psychiatry that began to appear in popular magazines, plays, and advertising media was a slightly foreign, bearded gentleman who sat behind the couch with pencil and notebook in hand. This symbol always involved the locale of a consultation room and rarely, if ever, involved the psychiatrist in action in a social agency, a school, or a community setting. The 1960's have brought on new roles that will ultimately change the symbol of psychiatrists at least to the extent of including these new activities in locales other than their offices (Caplan and Grunebaum, 1967). Indeed, our teen-agers were more willing to accept new symbols than their parents. Hence our young subjects originally were probably more comfortable with this new role model of psychiatry than we investigators were. Even though we were interested in studying normal teen-agers, we were still tied in many ways to our own role concepts and were not so flexible as the new generation in accommodating to change.

We believe that our investigation can serve as a prototype of a kind of study that will become increasingly common over the next few decades. Although we have discussed psychiatrists' moves in these directions, we should make it clear that we do not believe that psychiatrists are the sole or the best contributors to the understanding of adolescent psychology. There is an increasing literature on the adjustment of the typical adolescents stemming from the investigators in the sociobehavioral sciences. Our investigation of modal or typical adolescent boys is *one* contribution to an increasing literature of studies on normal adolescent populations. (See, as examples, Grinker, 1963; Grinker *et al.*, 1962; Silber *et al.*, 1961a and 1961b; Heath, 1965; White, 1963 and 1966; Masterson, 1967; Coleman, 1961; Friedenberg, 1959 and 1965; Douvan and Adelson, 1966.) We are mindful of and deeply committed to the multidisciplinary nature of these investigations including our awareness that the teen-agers themselves have a great deal to teach us. We are aware that all of the mental-health professions, as well as educators, parents, and others in the community, have significant perspectives regarding normal teen-age behavior that should be encompassed in a new description of normal teen-agers. We do believe, however, that the specific abilities and training of the psychiatrist will contribute to the integration of the new empirical data with models of psychopathology. We also believe that some of the methods, in particular the semistructured interview, that have been developed in the course of psychiatric work with disturbed people will become applicable for the collection of new valid data about the interior world of the adolescent as well as data about his external adaptation. It is our contention that psychiatrists can have little confidence in their broad generalizations from clinical samples without systematic empirical data obtained from populations other than those who come to our office seeking relief from emotional sufferings. The task of obtaining reliable and valid data of adequate depth and scope from a population that we seek out rather than from a population that seeks our aid presents complex methodological problems. This book presents some of our contributions toward the solution of these problems.

2

The Method in Overview

Selecting the Modal Adolescents*

The overall aim of the Modal Adolescent Project was to study intensively a representative group of modal or typical adolescent boys over the four years of high school. In our earlier book *Normality* (Offer and Sabshin, 1966), we have discussed the problem of selection of normal subjects in detail. We have based our selection on a statistical approach, normality as average, which is useful for group research and which we hoped would help us eliminate extremes of psychopathology or superior adjustment. We wanted to select the modal group from the widest possible spectrum of teen-agers living in a particular community. The selection of a group of modal or typical adolescents from a total high-school population was, then, the first problem that confronted us. A

* We are grateful to H. Diesenhaus for his methodological advice and help in writing this chapter.

natural choice was a high school attended by all the teen-agers in one community. We believed that two different high schools representing the range of the middle class would assure us a better sample than, for example, twice as large a group in one high school. It would also assure us of avoiding findings biased by the selection of a special school (for example, a private school).

Our need was to select as modal a group as possible. Since we were aware of the high percentage of psychopathology in volunteers that has been reported by Perlin *et al.* (1958) and Esecover *et al.* (1961), we were not interested in asking for volunteers. We wanted to make the selection ourselves. Therefore, we needed a reliable means to select our study population.

Our operational approach for the selection rests on two major premises. First, it is necessary to evaluate the adolescent's functioning in multiple areas, since in our own clinical experience we have often observed adolescents who can master one aspect of their world while failing to adjust in another. Second, the psychological sensitivity of the adolescent is sufficiently acute to allow us to utilize his self-description as a basis for a reliable selection of subgroups. We reasoned that if we were to construct a questionnaire ourselves and select our modal population on the basis of this new instrument, we would want our modal population to function relatively well in all, or most, of the areas selected. Accordingly, the items of the questionnaire were chosen to elicit the adolescent's overall self-description.

The findings reported by Rosenberg (1965) corroborate the above premise, although his work was not available to us during our initial search. Rosenberg found that the self-image of adolescents correlates significantly and positively with the image that important others have of him (for example, his parents or teachers). Early in our search through the literature we ruled out group projective tests. We believe that projective tests are particularly

---

* We were not impressed with the consistency of Symonds's (1949 and 1961) findings; also, R. D. Hess (1964) strongly advised against the use of projectives in adolescence as a *major* research tool.

difficult to use during adolescence, and hence we did not want to utilize them as a basis for a selection of subjects.*

Searching through the literature, we decided that there were two possible tests: the Minnesota Multiphasic Personality Inventory (MMPI) and the Bell Adjustment Inventory for Adolescents. We ruled out the latter because its emotional scale was undynamic and did not focus sufficiently on internal psychological processes. Finally, we gave serious consideration to the use of the MMPI, but decided not to use it and instead to develop our own Self-Image Questionnaire. Our major reason was that our interest was primarily the internal psychic state or feeling states of the teenager as related to the eleven areas described in Appendix 1. In other words, we were originally interested in psychological norms and we believed that the MMPI would select subjects mainly on the basis of how close they came to the social norm.* Currently, we believe that the distinction between social and psychological norms is somewhat artificial, and in retrospect cannot be defended as a scientifically valid criteria. Although the perception of social and psychological factors might differ within individuals, it seems to us impossible to tell, from a response of a number of individuals, which factor was the more crucial one. The social and psychological factors are so highly interdependent as to be considered one factor, the "social-psychological" factor.

In Appendix 1, the interested reader will find the background of the construction of the Self-Image Questionnaire, its reliability, and a discussion of the validity of the instrument. In addition we have listed the items and scales of the Self-Image Questionnaire together with the means and variances of the items for the total sample in the two high schools.

---

* Our decision could be open to criticism since our instrument does not have the thoroughness of the MMPI. At the time we constructed the Self-Image Questionnaire, the data from Hathaway and Monachesi (1963) were not available. Had they been available we might have chosen the MMPI as our selection device, although we still believe that the MMPI is oriented more toward uncovering psychopathology and less toward assessing the feelings and behavior of normal teen-agers.

The Selection Process: Step One

We were now ready for selection of the experimental group. The Self-Image Questionnaire was given to 326 freshman boys in the two suburban high schools chosen. In High School A, we administered the questionnaire to the total freshman male population $(N = 181)$. In High School B, we administered the questionnaire to one home room that included about a quarter of the total freshman male population $(N = 145)$. In both schools the questionnaire was administered during the study-hall period by Offer.

ADMINISTRATION OF THE QUESTIONNAIRE

We were introduced to the group by a school official. In High School A, the guidance director introduced us to the students. In High School B, the assistant superintendent introduced us. In both schools the school officials stayed in the room with us throughout the testing period. We told the students, briefly, that we were psychiatrists, and that we planned to study a specially selected group of teen-agers in order to understand better their psychological world. We told them that the results from such a study might help those adolescents who suffer from mental illness. We also told the group that adults have been pontificating for too long on what is right or wrong about the teen-ager, and how he should or should not feel. We stated that we thought it was time we found out from them how they felt about themselves, their families, and their world. At this point there was some mild applause.

We asked two students to help us with the distribution of the questionnaires, first reminding the boys that this was not an exam, and the group started to work. There were a few appropriate questions concerning printing errors. There was an aura of seriousness in the room interrupted only by an occasional wisecrack. Only one student in each school refused to cooperate, and only nine students failed to complete the questionnaire. The average student finished the questionnaire in forty minutes. The majority of the adolescents reacted very positively to the experience and reported that they enjoyed it.

The Selection Process: Step Two

In addition to administering the psychological questionnaire, we asked the schools to inform us whether any of our 106 modal students showed serious behavior problems in the school. Only three of these students, or approximately 3 per cent of the sample, were classified as exhibiting such behavior, and they were not included in our interview sample. This 3 per cent contrasted with the overall proportion of behavior problems as defined by the school, which was between 12 and 15 per cent. Here we have, then, an indication that the questionnaire was able to differentiate between groups of varying behavior in the high school. It is impressive to note that those students in our experimental group, on the whole, did not present behavioral problems in the schools. The percentage of honor students in the modal group selected was the same as in the total high-school population of both schools. In addition we asked the parents of the subjects selected to inform us whether their children had had psychiatric treatment or whether for any reason the parents believed that their children were maladjusted. No subject was classified as abnormal by his parent.

Characteristics of the Interview Sample

We believe that we succeeded in selecting adolescent subjects significantly different psychologically from disturbed adolescents seen in psychiatric practice. Since the rest of the book will be devoted to documenting the vicissitudes of this point in depth, we shall only present a brief description of the adjustment of our subjects. Only 7 of the 103 students, or about 7 per cent, had fairly severe emotional problems that became manifest in the course of our contact with them. Five of the students developed chronic problems with delinquency (they had police records). One had a problem with exhibitionism and voyeurism and one had a paranoid character. Over a period of four years none of these seven students needed to be hospitalized and none became schizophrenic or psychotic in any form. This finding of 7 per cent with moderately severe emotional problems could be contrasted with studies like the midtown New York City project (Srole *et al.*, 1963), where the authors found that moderately severe emotional disorders are seen in at least 25 per cent of the population. Despite the fact that Srole *et al.* studied a different population and that the study did not include any person under twenty years of age, the general epidemiological finding is of interest. There is, to our knowledge, no similar study on teen-age populations.

Out of the original 106 students who met the statistical criteria, 3 were dropped by us because they had behavior problems in the schools, 8 had refused to participate in the beginning, and another 14 subjects have since moved away from the community. We have lost only 8 students who began to participate in the project but then decided to drop out during the course of the last three years. Utilizing our Self-Image Questionnaire as one measure of adjustment, we have not found any significant difference between those subjects who dropped out, those who refused to participate originally, and those who stayed in the project.

We ended up, then, with 73 active subjects who participated in all aspects of the project throughout the high school years. Forty-one subjects came from High School A and 32 from High School B. The larger sample from the first high school can be ascribed to the fact that we tested a slightly larger population in that school. The percentage of students selected in each high school from the larger sample of students taking the questionnaire was identical. This book describes in detail our findings on the 73 subjects.

The Data Collection Procedure

Involving the Subjects

Once the students were selected in the spring quarter of the
freshman year, we contacted the parents by mail and asked for
their cooperation in the project.

One hundred and six students were selected on the basis of their
responses to this questionnaire. After the selection was made, their
parents received a letter on official high-school stationery describing
the purpose of the project and asking for their cooperation:

> DEAR MR. AND MRS.———————————:
> We are conducting, with the cooperation of——————————
> ————————High School, a study to determine what makes a normal,
> healthy adolescent tick; and we are asking for your cooperation. This
> project is sponsored by the National Institute of Mental Health.
> ——————————————High School has been selected because
> of its nationally recognized standards in education.
> The field of adolescent psychology is a challenging one which has
> been given all too little attention or imaginative thought. My re-
> search and clinical experience at Michael Reese Hospital and at the
> University of Illinois with emotionally disturbed adolescents has im-
> pressed me with the great need that exists to initiate a study of
> the normal adolescent. We believe that this study can provide us
> with a better understanding of the problems and challenges that
> confront the normal adolescent. This will be of great help to the
> teacher and ultimately to the parent in furnishing us with a con-
> structive guide in relating to the adolescent.
> The project will involve the following: a large group of freshman
> boys was given two questionnaires in the Fall of 1962. Subsequently,
> by statistical means, a group of normal adolescents was selected.
> Beginning with March 1963 we will give these students a few more

pencil and paper tests and interviews once every calendar quarter for a period of four years. As parents of those children who were found to be most representative of the normal adolescents you will be asked to evaluate the adjustment of your children. This will require only *one hour* of your time and will be done only once.

As parents of healthy, normal adolescents, your cooperation will make a significant contribution in this most vital area of attention to our children of high-school age.

I would like to add that the material will be kept strictly confidential and will be used only for scientific purposes.

Thank you.

Sincerely yours,
DANIEL OFFER, M.D.

The psychiatrists (Offer and Marcus) contacted the subjects by phone. We told the subjects or the parents that there was absolutely no relationship between the project and the school. When asked, we told the parents that those parents who did not want their children to participate in the study should say so, and we would not call on them again. We were encouraged by the fact that only one parent turned us down. Out of the 106 subjects selected, we were able to gain the cooperation of 98 in the beginning. In other words, eight subjects refused to participate in the project, and it is of interest to state that only one parent (the one who called us) did not approve of the project. The other seven who refused to participate were the teen-agers themselves; their parents told us over the phone that they had encouraged their children to go. We have often been told later, by the teen-agers, that the parents had encouraged the boys to go once and see what it was all about; if the boy did not like our project, his parents would let him drop out. It seemed to us in retrospect that this was an extremely helpful gesture on the part of the parents and probably increased our samples by at least 30 per cent. Another eight subjects dropped out of the project by refusing to continue to come to see us after one or two interviews, but none did so because he did not want to come to see us again after three interviews. Seventeen families moved away from these two communities in the four years of the project, to all four corners of the United States. We were able to continue to study three subjects whose families moved only to the nearby city or from one suburb to another. This left us with 73 subjects, who have all finished the high-school part of the project. All 73 had completed the interview schedule, although four did not take the psychological testing. Five others who did not complete the interviews did, however, take the testing.

The Interviews

There is a voluminous literature on the many variables that affect the responses obtained by an interviewer. The vast majority of the articles and books on this important subject are to be found in the social and psychological sciences. These works deal almost exclusively with specific research questions and not with clinical matters. (See, for example, Richardson *et al.*, 1965; Kahn and Cannell, 1957; Hyman, 1954.) As can be ascertained from reading these works, interviews are utilized for a great variety of purposes in the behavioral and social sciences. Massive amounts of data are collected by scientists who utilize the interview in their research. These interviews range from those conducted primarily for the purpose of therapy (psychoanalysis, psychotherapy, counseling) to others where the major focus is information gathering (clinical interviews for research purposes, psychological testing, social-science research, and the more straightforward polls). We can conceptualize a continuum of interviews. On the one extreme there is the clinical (therapeutic) interview and on the other there is the single interview conducted on the phone by nonprofessional workers where the only aim is to obtain information concerning areas that are more neutral psychologically (Which TV program do you enjoy most? Which soap do you buy?).

Most of the literature on research interviews deals with survey research in social psychology and participant observation in sociology. Recently there has been also some literature on the complexities of epidemiological surveys (for example, Srole *et al.*, 1963). However, even this careful evaluation of a variety of response sets that may influence data collection deals with the structured interview. An article by Krause (1965) discusses the relevant variables that may influence interview results and hence should be of interest to the investigator. The problem of obtaining maximum reliability and validity in research interviews is also discussed.

Richardson *et al.* (1965) examine the interview as a major tool for data collection in the social sciences. They present specific techniques utilized by interviewers and detailed examinations of interviewers' responses. According to these authors, the main task of the interview is to gather information; hence, it differs considerably from the usual social relationship. It is of interest to note that at no point in this book do the authors consider the nature of the relationship between the interviewer and the subject. They are clearly biased in the direction of the structured or standardized interview. Their focus probably stems from the tradition of utilizing this technique primarily for psychologically nonsensitive areas. Rosenthal (1966) describes sophisticated studies of experimenter bias in behavioral research. No comparable studies exist as yet in the area of clinical research. For psychiatrists, the basic model for the interview has been clinical in nature (that is, oriented toward disease or maladaptation). For example, Sullivan (1954) in his description of the clinical interview stressed the interaction between the expert and the client.

> The psychiatric interview is a situation of primarily vocal communication in a two-group, more or less voluntarily integrated, on a progressively unfolding expert-client basis for the purpose of elucidating characteristic patterns of living of the subject person, the patient or client, which patterns he experiences as particularly troublesome or especially valuable, and in the revealing of which he expects to derive benefit.

Sullivan, then, stresses the doctor-patient relationship. Grinker *et al.* (1961) basically agreed with Sullivan although Grinker visualized the relationship as being more of a process of transaction between two people. Grinker described

> Convex areas of two incomplete circles across which disturbed, misunderstood, and incomplete messages traverse in both directions . . . both therapist and patient strive to learn each other's language and test out its trustworthiness as an honest medium of communication.

This model of the clinical interview has to be modified considerably when working with "normal" (for example, nonpatient) populations, since the focus changes from one basically interested in uncovering psychopathology to one interested in discovering the psychodynamics. In all studies utilizing interviews over time, the nature of the relationship becomes crucial in the data collection. We believe that this is true both for interviews that are conducted for the primary purpose of data collection (that is, research) and for those that are conducted for the primary purpose of helping the patient. (The distinction between these two types of interviews will be discussed in detail in Chapter 10.)

Our main information-gathering device was the semistructured clinical interview conducted by a psychiatrist who interviewed each student six times throughout the remainder of the three high-school years.

TABLE 2–1

Chronological Summary of the Data-Collection Procedures

	Procedure	Time
1.	Administration of SIQ for Selection of Modal Group	Fall 1962
2.	First Psychiatric Interview: Introduction to the Study	Spring 1963
3.	Survey Interview: Background Information. Mrs. Simon, Interviewer	Summer and Fall 1963
4.	Second Psychiatric Interview: General Problem Areas	Winter 1964
5.	Third Psychiatric Interview: Affects and Relationship with Adults	Spring and Summer 1964
6.	Psychological Testing. Dr. S. L. Futterman, Psychologist	Between Fall 1964 and Spring 1965

TABLE 2–1 *(continued)*

Procedure	Time
7. Fourth Psychiatric Interview: Sexuality and Vocation	Spring and Summer 1965
8. Fifth Psychiatric Interview: The Study in Retrospect	Fall 1965 and Winter 1966
9. Interview with Parents. Mrs. Miller, Interviewer	Between Summer 1965 and Spring 1966
10. Sixth Psychiatric Interview: The High School in Retrospect	Spring 1966

NOTE: See Appendix 2 for a detailed description of the procedures. There were two psychiatric interviewers (Offer and Marcus) who saw the subjects for the entire series of six psychiatric interviews.

On the average each student was seen three times a year. Each psychiatric interview lasted about 45 minutes.

The second interview in the series of nine individual contacts differed from the six psychiatric interviews in that it was more structured. The interviewer came to the interview with a detailed questionnaire and followed the prescribed sequence. The answers were recorded directly on the questionnaire. The areas covered in this interview consisted of (1) developmental history, (2) child-rearing practices, (3) child's perception of his future life (socially, vocationally, familially), (4) relationship with peers, teachers, siblings, and parents, (5) the administration of a family-interaction scale, and, finally, (6) three early memories (see Appendix 2).

The fifth session consisted of a battery of individually administered psychological tests (Rorschach, TAT, and vocabulary subtest of the WAIS). The psychological testing averaged 80 to 90 minutes. The parents were interviewed during the junior year. We were able to see all but four mothers. One mother refused to be interviewed (although her son is still active in the project); three mothers had moved out of town by the time the parents were interviewed. The fathers proved more difficult: we were able to elicit the cooperation of 49 fathers as contrasted to 69 mothers.

From a methodological point of view we believed that it would be important to have two psychiatrists do the interviews. One of us (Offer) interviewed 85 per cent of the subjects, the other (Marcus) 15 per cent. Subjects were assigned at random. Each of us followed his own subjects throughout the years of the study. We took careful notes during each interview and dictated them soon afterward. The material was typed, and we exchanged impressions only after a particular cycle of interviews was over. All the ratings were done independently from the typed interviews. We analyzed the two sets of data and found no significant differences in the important variables. Although we were pleased by the high degree of reliability, it is important to state that the two psychiatrists went through psychiatric residency training together and are good friends who share a similar outlook on psychiatry.

The psychological testing was administered to the subjects as close to their sixteenth birthday as possible. These tests, like the interviews, were administered in the schools. The parent interviews were begun in the third year of the study. Neither Futterman nor Miller had access to the student interview material until the project was over. The psychiatrists likewise did not see the material from the parent interviews or the psychological testing.

Teachers' ratings were collected at the end of the freshman and junior years and were another independent source of information (see Chapter 4).

Analysis of the Interview Data*

The nine interviews provided a wide variety of data. Much of the information about demographic variables, developmental history, and attitudes was obtained in response to structured questions; the responses to these questions were easily coded or directly represented as a numerical value during the interview (this is especially true of the data from Interview 2). However, other information represented responses to open-ended questions or participation in

* A more detailed description of the data analysis utilized by us in this project can be found at the end of Appendix 2.

a semistructured discussion; these responses were more difficult to categorize and were rated from the transcripts. Another kind of interview data is the ratings made by the interviewer that are based on the entire sequence of his interaction with a subject up to the time of the rating (for example, the symptom-rating scales). In addition, both the subjects and parents filled out a questionnaire during the interview period (the Family Interaction Scale). An abbreviated version of the Self-Image Questionnaire was also completed by both parents, in which they were asked to predict their son's original answers. Several other sources of external data—the teachers' ratings as well as the psychological tests (Rorschach, TAT, etc.)—are included in the analyses. Throughout, we have attempted to combine presentations of statistical findings with illustrations from the psychiatric-interview material.

PART II

Results

3

The School Environment

The Two High Schools and Their Communities

High School A had a total student population of 1,800 and is in a town of 30,000* which is composed of a mobile population of middle and lower middle-class people. This suburb, which was built soon after World War II, has a remarkably homogeneous population; at the time of the study the school was 100 per cent white. Almost all the men work in the large city. This community is the more distant from the large city and has more of a "small-town" atmosphere than Community B. The high school was opened only five years before the study began. It had a fairly typical administrative organization, with a superintendent, a principal, and a guidance director. The superintendent was a strong person who was eager to give his school a national reputation. He was very popular in the beginning of his tenure, which almost coincided with the beginning of the project. Later he came under criticism from both the teachers and the Board of Education, and

* The statistical and socioeconomic data about the two communities are drawn from the Census Tracts report (1962).

he left his position in the last year of the project. Fortunately, the project was never directly associated with him so that his departure did not affect it significantly. Also, by that time we had developed a good relationship with both the principal and the guidance director so that we continued without any problem.

High School B had a total population of 5,000 and is located in a town of 80,000. The suburb is mainly a stable middle and upper middle-class community composed of professional and well-to-do businessmen. In addition, there is a small (about 10 per cent) segment of stable lower-class working people. The community had a Negro population of about 12 per cent at the time this study took place. This population distribution was reflected in the number of Negro students in the high school, which was 12 per cent at the time of the study. Although a large percentage of the professional and businessmen worked in the larger city, many of the lower-class people worked in the community itself. The school is an old and very well-established high school with a national reputation. Because of its excellence, many people from the larger metropolitan area move to this particular suburb when their children reach school age. The school itself is divided into four semi-autonomous high schools, each with a different principal and its own guidance counselor. There was one superintendent, who had been at the school for many years and was there throughout the project. The Board of Education is not so active as in High School A. Thus, Offer met twice with the Board of Education of High School A during the four years of the project, giving them progress reports; but he never met with the Board of Education in High School B, and was never asked any questions about the project.

The cooperation from the top administrative level in both high schools was excellent. We were provided rooms for the interviews in each high school. We spent one afternoon a week in each high school for about 3½ years for the purpose of interviewing our modal adolescents.

All interviews were scheduled after school hours; we started interviewing at 3:15 P.M., and we were usually finished by 6:30. There were a few amusing incidents at the beginning of the project. One time the janitor locked us out and we needed the guidance of our normal teen-agers to show us how to get in. In general, the cooperation of the school personnel was good. We did, of course, go through an initiation period. For example, the secretary would assign us a room in the guidance wing and when we would arrive at 3:15 in the afternoon she would look at us in surprise and say, "You mean the teen-agers are still coming to see you?" From time to time, the teachers would notice us in the hall and ask us whether we had a pass or what we were doing in the building. But these incidents were rare and they occurred only at the beginning of the project. Later when a new teacher who seemed particularly zealous in keeping his high school pure of intruders would ask us a question, we would tell him about our project and then ask whether he would like to cooperate or whether he would like to tell us anything about teen-agers. The usual reaction was, "You're doing a fine and interesting job but leave me out of it." We also encountered some problems with a few teachers who wondered whether our project was not harming the students. The wholehearted support of each superintendent was extremely important and helped us in overcoming any resistance by the school faculties.

In the beginning, we had a large number of missed appointments: out of an average of six appointments set for an afternoon, only two students would show up, and the others would not even call to cancel their appointments. The number of missed appointments decreased very slowly over the years, until at the end of the project about 80 to 90 per cent of our appointments would show up. We believed that the reason so many subjects "forgot" their appointments was that they were not sure of the relationship with us, and that as their anxiety increased they used other things they had to do as convenient pretexts for forgetting. When we became a little more meaningful to them, they would leave us a message or call us if they could not keep the appointment; this occurred frequently and we would then suggest another time.

During the first months of the project the subjects often brought other boys with them. The most extreme case was the boy who brought six of his friends with him for the first interview, apparently to protect him if necessary. When the subject left the interview they asked him, "Well, how was it? Is your head shrunken yet?" The subject was somewhat embarrassed at the question and, instead of answering it, introduced me to all of his friends and said that the interview was not really that bad. The incident might be seen as a sign of the multiple impact of our project on the social environment of the school. Our subjects were eager to share their experiences with others, and the friends were curious to meet the outsiders. As the project went on and the teen-agers grew older, they stopped bringing other boys to the sessions and instead would bring their girl friends and introduce them to the psychiatrists. We often were introduced to the girl friends as "This is my psychiatrist," spoken with a smile and not without a sense of pride.

We had no contact with the parents of our subjects until the third year of the project. Possibly for this reason we received very little publicity. When we did start to interview the parents, we got a few requests for interviews from reporters in the two communities. We granted one interview to each local paper and both were published. There was no visible reaction from the parents or from the schools concerning these articles. We did have some reaction from our subjects, who in general liked the statements we made about them and felt they were correct.

In retrospect, the fact that we received little publicity testifies that our study was not considered to be unusual. Although there was a basic difference between the two schools in their orientation toward the mental-health profession, this did not seem to affect us in any obvious way. High School A had no social workers, psychologists, or psychiatrists functioning in any capacity in the school system. When we finished our project, the Board of Education in High School A asked our opinion about hiring a part-time social worker. We outlined the possible functions of such a person, on the basis of our general professional knowledge plus our acquaintance with the school. The Board of Education rejected the proposal, which had been suggested by the guidance director and the principal, because it was "too expensive." In High School B, in contrast, there was a complete social-work department with five psychiatric social workers, a psychology department with one full-time psychologist and two part-time psychologists, and a psychiatric consultant who has consulted on special cases and spends half a day a week consulting with the social workers. Our good personal relations with the social workers at High School B helped our morale, especially in the beginning of the project. We did not feel quite so out of place there as in High School A.

We included subjects from two high schools because we wanted to explore whether or not there would be any major psychological differences between modal students in the two schools. We believed that our findings could have greater significance if a modest comparative technique was to be employed. As we have stated earlier, we found no significant difference between the performance of the two total adolescent samples on the ten scales of the SIQ. We next looked for differences between the two high schools in our modal group on other major variables. We found only the following differences between High Schools A and B:

TABLE 3–1

*Variables Differentiating the Modal
Adolescents from the Two High Schools*

| | HIGH SCHOOL | | | |
VARIABLE	A	B	TOTAL	χ^{2*}
Character structure:				
Compulsive	25	25	50	
Hysterical	17	3	20	
TOTAL	42	28	70	
				5.91
Religion:				
Protestant and Catholic	40	14	54	
Jewish and Other	4	15	19	
TOTAL	44	29	73	
				14.30

* Chi square with Yates correction, $df = 1$; $p < .05$ for both variables.

1. There were significantly more hysterical characters in High School A. The subjects were classified as to their character structure by the two psychiatrists at the end of Interview 5.

2. There were significantly more Jewish subjects in High School B than in High School A.

3. The students in High School B were rated by their teachers (in their junior year) as possessing less leadership ability and as being less creative than their peers in High School A. On the other three variables rated by the teachers, the two groups had no significant differences (see Table 3–8).

We did not expect the first finding. The second difference confirmed one of the demographic differences between the two communities. The third factor might point to a rating bias rather than cultural differences. There were no other significant differences between the schools on social class, class standing, minor delinquent acts, or other psychological variables we have studied.

Since these three differences were the only differences found, we believe that the high-school subgroups were so similar that they could successfully be considered as one group. Hence, from now on we shall not distinguish the two school subgroups but rather describe the boys collectively as the modal adolescents.

The Student-Teacher Encounter

It has been our experience, while working with disturbed adolescents, that school can be of central importance in the lives of these youngsters. It came as no surprise to find that the students ranked school and studying as their most important area of conflict. The majority of the students thought that the determination of their vocational and educational goals was the most difficult problem they had to resolve during the high-school years. Interestingly, relations with parents and sexual feelings were not rated as difficult or important problems by the majority of our teen-agers.

Students and teachers can help enrich each other's lives by stimulating the growth potential within themselves. It was there-

TABLE 3-2

Important Conflict Areas as Seen by the Adolescents Ranked from
Most Frequent to Least Frequent Response

		NUMBER OF RESPONSES
1.	Vocational and educational goals	53
2.	Impulse control	42
3.	Interpersonal relationships	35
4.	Growing up	23
5.	Relations with parents	16
6.	Handling sexual feelings	15

NOTE: Responses were in answer to the question "What are the three most difficult problems which an adolescent has to overcome during the high school years?" Responses were categorized as follows with greater than 80 per cent agreement between the two raters:
1. *Vocational and educational goal*—find one's interests; finish college; get school work done; not drop out of school; decide what to do as a career.
2. *Impulse control*—all those that do not specifically mention opposite sex, such as: avoid temptations; avoid drinking, smoking; juvenile delinquency; keep out of trouble; learn to control oneself.
3. *Interpersonal relations*—(those not specifically mentioning the opposite sex)— get along with adults; get along with parents; being understood; social life; avoid ridicule; get in with right group.
4. *Growing up*—face responsibility; develop personality; be an individual; stand up for oneself.
5. *Relations with parents*—wherever parents were mentioned in any way.
6. *Handling sexual feelings*—specific mention of sex; also, getting along with girls; getting dates.

fore of particular interest to us to investigate how the teachers and students viewed each other. Although we had collected feelings and attitudes of the students toward the teachers throughout this study, it was only in Interview 4, during the end of the sophomore year, that we explored this aspect in detail (see Appendix 2). We have not interviewed any teachers formally so that our data about teachers' attitudes are derived mainly from our own observations of teachers, from the students' reports of their encounters, and from the two sets of ratings done by the teachers.

Teachers' Ratings of the Freshmen

We designed the first set of ratings in order to obtain the teachers' impressions concerning the general functioning of their students. During the spring of the freshman year, the teachers were asked

TABLE 3-3

Frequency Distribution for Teachers' Ratings Made in the Freshman Year for the Modal Adolescents

	AVERAGE	BELOW AVERAGE	ABOVE AVERAGE	CAN'T SAY
1. Performance in school	46.6% (34)	27.4% (20)	20.5% (15)	5.5% (4)
2. Ability to follow rules and regulations	58.9% (43)	12.3% (9)	23.3% (17)	5.5% (4)
3. Amount of anger expressed	67.2% (49)	20.5% (15)	4.1% (3)	8.2% (6)
4. Number of friends	71.2% (52)	8.2% (6)	13.7% (10)	6.9% (5)
5. Parents' interest in school	76.7% (56)	1.4% (1)	15.1% (11)	6.9% (5)
6. Number of days missed because of illness	68.5% (50)	20.5% (15)	5.5% (4)	5.5% (4)
7. Emotional stability	71.2% (52)	9.6% (7)	13.7% (10)	5.5% (4)

to complete the seven-item scale on all the male freshmen who had taken the Self-Image Questionnaire earlier in the fall of the same school year. The ratings were done by the students' homeroom teachers. We wanted to find out whether (1) there were any significant differences between the teachers' ratings in the two high schools; and (2) whether a modal group, as determined by teacher ratings, would be similar to the modal sample selected on the basis of the Self-Image Questionnaire.

The next three tables will enable us to answer these questions. On Question 1, we can state that there were no significant differences between the two high schools on the basis of the teachers' ratings (Table 3-4). The rating behavior of the teachers from the two high schools differs. Teachers from High School A made no additional comments on *any* of the forms they completed, while teachers from High School B added comments on more than a

TABLE 3–4

Means, Variances, and t-Tests* for the Teachers' Ratings Made in the Freshman Year for the Two High Schools

VARIABLE†	HIGH SCHOOL A			HIGH SCHOOL B			
	Mean	Variance	N	Mean	Variance	N	t
1. School performance	1.88	0.60	171	1.72	0.60	131	+1.39
2. Following of rules	1.92	0.56	170	2.01	0.56	132	−1.04
3. Anger expressed	1.81	0.37	162	1.77	0.53	132	+0.46
4. Number of friends	1.84	0.35	167	1.88	0.41	132	−0.48
5. Parents' interest	1.98	0.48	171	1.84	0.58	123	+1.63
6. Absences	1.76	0.25	171	1.95	0.56	131	−2.58‡
7. Emotional stability	1.75	0.27	169	1.79	0.47	132	−0.61

* The variances for High School A on Variables 5 and 6 are much smaller than those for High School B and suggest restricted use of the rating scale by the teachers in High School A.
† Above average = 3; Average = 2; Below average = 1.
‡ $p < .02$, two-tailed test.

TABLE 3–5

Intercorrelation of the Teachers' Ratings Made in the Freshman Year
for the Two High Schools

	1	2	3	4	5	6	7
1. School performance		.66*	−.05	.22	.32	−.05	.35
2. Following of rules	302		−.07	.22	.28	.02	.48
3. Anger expressed	294	295		.22	.12	.23	−.05
4. Number of friends	299	300	295		.35	.24	.47
5. Parents' interest	295	294	286	291		.14	.23
6. Absences	303	302	294	299	295		.13
7. Emotional stability	301	302	295	300	293	301	

NOTE: *r* above the diagonal; *N* below. We have teachers' ratings on an average of 300 students compared to the 326 SIQ's. The difference is explained by the fact that the SIQ's were given at the beginning of the year and the teachers' ratings were completed at the end of the year by which time 10 per cent of the families had moved away from the communities.

* $p \leq .05 \approx .11$; $p \leq .01 \approx .14$; $p \leq .001 \approx .20$.

hundred of the individual forms! The comments were mostly psychological, ranging from "He is suffering from an inferiority complex and needs more masculine identity" and "I do not feel that John is getting the love and attention he needs from his parents and I think that this is affecting his school work" to "This student is working above his capacities [*sic*] and I am afraid that it is damaging him psychologically."

In both high schools when we intercorrelated the seven ratings done by the teachers (see Table 3–5), the intercorrelations were only relatively high. This suggests that the teachers did use the individual items as separate entities and did not use a common denominator in their ratings, such as "Is this student likable?"

To answer Question 2, we can say that if we had utilized the teachers' ratings as a basis for the selection of our modal sample, we would have ended up with a different sample. The teachers' ratings did not correlate with the Self-Image Questionnaire scores as highly as we had expected (see Table 3–6). Although we have to take into account the fact that there was approximately a seven month interval between the teachers' ratings and the students' self-descriptions, we had still expected a greater agreement be-

TABLE 3-6

Intercorrelation of Self-Image Questionnaire Scores and Teachers' Ratings
Made in the Freshman Year for the Total Sample

	TEACHERS' RATINGS						
	1	2	3	4	5	6	7
SIQ Score							
1. Impulse control	−.14*	−.11	.00	.01	−.10	.05	−.03
2. Emotional tone	−.11	−.06	−.01	−.13	−.09	.12	−.03
3. Body and self-image	−.07	−.02	.09	−.06	.00	.04	−.04
4. Social relationships	−.10	−.06	−.02	−.14	−.01	.01	−.02
5. Morals	−.19	−.18	.07	−.00	−.08	.07	−.07
6. Sexual attitudes	−.30	−.21	.18	−.05	−.04	.07	−.10
7. Family relationships	−.23	−.15	.00	−.09	−.11	.02	−.07
8. Mastery of external world	−.24	−.20	.08	−.11	−.17	.02	−.13
9. Vocational and educational goals	−.21	−.14	.05	.01	−.05	.07	−.00
10. Psychopathology	−.31	−.22	.00	−.11	−.20	.04	−.11
11. Superior adjustment	.11	.11	−.11	−.23	−.01	−.16	.01
TOTAL (10 Scales)**	−.28	−.19	.08	−.09	−.11	.07	−.09
N	302	302	294	299	294	302	301
SIQ Factors							
I: Emotional state	−.16	−.09	.04	−.09	−.04	.07	−.02
II: Mastery	−.31	−.22	.03	−.12	−.19	.03	−.12
III: Interpersonal relations	−.29	−.22	.14	−.03	−.09	.07	−.09

NOTE: See Chapter 1 for details. Low score on the SIQ scales represents high adjustment; high score on the teachers' ratings represents above average.

* $p \leq .05 = .11$; $p \leq .01 = .14$; $p \leq .001 = .20$.

** Scale 6 not included. Sexual attitude scale did not lend itself to factor analysis.

tween the self ratings and teachers' ratings in the corresponding areas. Many of the variables had essentially a zero correlation and were low even if there were a significant correlation because of the large sample size (a correlation of .20, significant yet accounting for only .04 of the common variance); this included also those variables which were included in the teachers' rating scale specifically for the purpose of comparing the two impressions, for example peer relationships as measured in the fourth scale on the SIQ and the number of friends (peers) as rated by the teachers. The majority of our correlations are not significant, which probably implies that the teachers in making their ratings stress aspects of the student's personality that differ from those stressed by the student when he describes himself. Had we selected a modal group based on teachers' ratings, we would have studied a different group of teenagers.* How different psychologically these two groups would have proved to be is an interesting though at present unanswerable question.

Teachers' Ratings of the Juniors

The second set of ratings, available only for the modal adolescents, was constructed by the schools themselves and was automatically filled out by each homeroom teacher on each student at the end of the junior year. The rating is all-inclusive in nature and combines the views of all the teachers concerning a particular student. It is used by the schools as part of their recommendations for college applications. This particular set of ratings had been used in the schools for many years and is carefully standardized. It is significant that for our group the ratings of the majority fall in the

* In a study by Harris (1959), the author selected a group of normal children and studied them and their mothers. He reports that the teachers preferred the children who were quiet and did not make any trouble. As a result, Harris's study was a study of students who fitted the teachers' concept of normality. Silber *et al.* (1961: A) also selected their sample mainly on the basis of teachers' ratings, though they were looking for a superior group of students.

TABLE 3-7

Frequency Distribution for Teachers' Ratings,
Made at the End of the Junior Year for the Modal Adolescents

	Number	Percentage
1. Leadership:		
1. Actively seeks leadership; accepted as leader, makes things go	1	1
2. Occasionally seeks leadership, or contributes in important affairs	8	11
3. Sometimes takes leadership responsibility, but is not accepted as leader	39	53
4. Cooperative, but seldom leads	15	21
5. Negative	5	7
6. N.A. (or no opportunity to observe)	5	7
TOTAL	73	100
2. Initiative and creativity:		
1. Actively creative; nearly always contributes something of his own	5	7
2. Shows originality in some areas; and is consistently self-reliant	15	21
3. Makes little or no creative contribution; does routine assignments	35	48
4. Conforms; no creativity or awareness of it in others	13	17
5. N.A. (or no opportunity to observe)	5	7
TOTAL	73	100
3. Social sensitivity:		
1. Deeply concerned; very responsive and sensitive to needs and feelings of others	5	7
2. Generally concerned and sensitive to needs and feelings of others	29	40
3. Somewhat socially concerned but varies in his response to others	27	37
4. Usually self-centered, but occasionally considers needs of others	7	9
5. Seems indifferent to needs and feelings of others	—	—
6. N.A. (or no opportunity to observe)	5	7
TOTAL	73	100
4. Responsibility:		
1. Thoroughly dependable; assumes much responsibility	10	14
2. Conscientious; but does not assume responsibility for others	27	37

TABLE 3-7 *(cont.)*

4. *Responsibility:*	Number	Percentage
3. Usually dependable but is not consistent	28	38
4. Fairly dependable, but must be reminded of obligations	1	1
5. Unreliable; neglects responsibility even when reminded	2	3
6. N.A. (or no opportunity to observe)	5	7
TOTAL	73	100
5. *Industry:*		
1. Eager and interested; seeks additional work	8	11
2. Prepares assigned work regularly; occasionally seeks additional work	21	29
3. Gets required work done; needs occasional prodding	26	35
4. Frequently does not complete required work; needs constant pressure	13	18
5. Indolent, seldom works even under pressure	—	—
6. N.A. (or no opportunity to observe)	5	7
TOTAL	73	100

middle of the scale in each one of the five ratings; this particular scale corroborates our selection of modal students. It is also of interest to note how few of our subjects fell in the superior range in each of the ratings; thus, only 15 per cent of our subjects fell within the superior range in the responsibility category, and only 7 per cent were rated creative by the teachers.

We have found when comparing the two high schools on the teachers' ratings that there was a significant difference in two variables: (1) leadership and (2) creativity. This finding is of great interest since these two ratings were done over the past three years by similar teachers (the homeroom teacher) who knew the subject well. Since our own ratings did not show any difference between the high schools, we would have expected the teachers' ratings also to show no differences. We believe that the observed differences may be attributed to the differences among the raters and their rating behavior rather than any basic difference in the students.

TABLE 3-8

*Means, Variances, and t-Tests for Teachers' Ratings
Made at the End of the Junior Year for the Modal Adolescents*

| Rating | HIGH SCHOOL A | | HIGH SCHOOL B | | |
	Mean	Variance	Mean	Variance	t
Leadership	3.05	.418	3.45	.899	−2.05*
Creativity	2.46	.571	3.31	.436	−4.83**
Social sensitivity	2.39	.664	2.72	.493	−1.80
Responsibility	2.38	.874	2.38	.601	0.02
Industry	2.56	.989	2.76	.690	−0.85

NOTE: High score on rating equals poorer performance.
* $p < .05$; two-tailed test.
** $p < .001$; two-tailed test.

Four out of the five teachers' ratings correlated significantly with our measure of social class as well as class standing. This finding is similar to that of Hollingshead (1949). It does suggest that the

TABLE 3-9

*Intercorrelation of Teachers' Ratings Made at the End of the
Junior Year with Social Class and Class Standing*

| TEACHERS' RATING OF: | INTERCORRELATION WITH | |
	Social Class	Class Standing
Leadership	.27*	.20*
Initiative	.22*	.41**
Social sensitivity	.02	.06
Responsibility	.23*	.53**
Industry	.21*	.59**
N	68	67

NOTE: High score on social class rating equals lower status, based on rating of father's occupation. High score on teachers' ratings equals poor performance.
* $p \leq .05$; ** $p \leq .01$.

teachers' attitudes toward the students may have been influenced by the students' class backgrounds. Although the opposite explanation—that students from the higher classes were indeed more able, etc.—is tenable, we are not in a position to say with certainty which factor was more important. Academic class standing is, after all, not an independent measure. It, too, might have been influenced by the factor of social class.*

The Students' View of the Teachers

It has been our impression throughout our interviews that the teachers who were respected the most by faculty and students alike were the coaches and the leaders in the sports activities. The teachers who were leaders of the intellectual courses, whether in literature, art, or science, were rarely mentioned as meaningful figures for the adolescents. A large proportion of the principals and counselors came from teachers who had been coaches or leaders in the various sports activities. The intellectual leaders might become chairmen of departments or go on to teach in college after they received their doctorates.

As far as the students are concerned the athletic coaches are almost the only teachers in the high-school environment who treat them as individuals. (Friedenberg, 1965, has described the same phenomenon.) The coaches often serve as confidants, helping many students overcome emotional hurdles. One student told us, "If it hadn't been for Mr. A [the basketball coach], I don't know whether I could have stayed in school. He was able to present me with the hard facts and convince me that it was for my own good to stay in school. Also, staying on the team was important for me, so I decided to stay in school." The opinion of the coaches was sought more often than that of any other teacher and was regarded as more valuable. The coaches usually used their important position well, although there were exceptions. Sports were highly valued in both high schools. The students often stated that to win

* We have observed the following on two of our subjects. Two students had the same grade average (C+) by the end of the junior year. One boy's father was a bank president. The counselor tried very hard to help him get into the best college possible. The other boy was a Negro and his father was a janitor. The boy wanted to go to college and study history. The counselor tried to persuade the boy to learn how to be a construction worker and then "you can make lots of money," say $125 a week in 1965. A similar story is told by Malcolm X in his autobiography (1964, p. 36).

a game was more important to their coach or to their school than how to win it or whether it was a good game. The competition that was taught to the students was dramatized by the following incident. One of our subjects was an extremely good athlete. He was not interested in sports, however, but in music. He was an excellent musician and refused to participate in one of the popular sports. The coach was highly disappointed in this student and made fun of him in front of the gym class. According to the subject's report, the coach went so far as having some of the big bullies of the class pin the boy against the wall and threaten to "cut your long hair and make you a real man if you don't join the group and fight for your high school." This incident was corroborated by other students we interviewed. The coach could not comprehend the fact that this student really did not want to participate in sports. We might understand the incident in the following way. The coach was probably sincere in his attempt to "help" the student. To the coach, sports probably represented masculinity. He reacted as if the student's refusal to accept his values was personally threatening to him. Therefore, the coach overreacted in the hostile way he did. However, the student was a person with strong convictions who had a group of his own friends and was not shattered by this specific experience or by the continuous depreciation. It was crucial that his parents were on his side and supported his decision.

The coaches also wanted to make sure that the students would "stay within the line." In racially mixed High School B, the coaches would give their classes a talking-to at the beginning of high school against interracial dating, delivered informally in the locker room, at the swimming pool, or on the basketball court. It was not a formal lecture in any way overtly condoned by the school administration or faculty, but it was given and was recounted to us in our interviews with some of our subjects. This particular approach to race relations was disliked by many of the students, yet it caused them to fear the consequences were they to date girl friends from a different race.

In trying to answer the question of the students' reactions toward the teachers, we obtained data continuously through the four years of the study and specifically in the fourth psychiatric interview. We asked each student to tell us what an ideal teacher would be like. The response was varied and is indicative of the obvious variety of teachers these students had. We thought that their description of an ideal teacher could also be seen as reflecting their attitude toward their own teachers and their relationship with them. What impressed us most in the students' descriptions was that the general attitude toward teachers was negative. Rarely did a student say that an ideal teacher would resemble his math teacher, or his biology teacher, or someone he had just seen that week.

The great majority of the students were critical of the teachers. The criticism ranged from the overt, as in "How should I know what an ideal teacher is like? I never had one," to the implied, as in "An ideal teacher is someone who can keep the class under control. He is interesting and makes the subject worthwhile. He lets the students think for themselves and allows you to have your own opinions. He also, of course, has no favorites." Infrequently we had such responses as "An ideal teacher is someone who never gives homework," "An ideal teacher is someone who lets you pass." The most frequent response concerned the teacher's knowledge of his own subject and ability to communicate it to the students: "An ideal teacher is someone who knows his subject," or "He is someone who can learn from his students and does not teach you a stereotyped course. He wants you to understand the subject and does not want you to just memorize a bunch of facts you forget the next day or after the exam." In addition the students wished that their teachers had a better sense of humor and would use it more often. Twenty-five per cent of all our subjects stressed this, stating that there is nothing worse than a dry and boring teacher. We had the impression that the students wanted to feel that learning could be enjoyable and that somehow they are conditioned to overlook this aspect of education.

The teachers did not serve as ego ideals for the students. For example, when the students were asked whom they admired most outside of their family, only 5 per cent gave teachers as examples. The most common expressions concerning teachers were, "They're all right," or "They should leave me [us] alone." We rarely noticed any enthusiasm during the interviews when students talked about their teachers. The students reported that when there was a lot of "kidding" between teachers and students, it would end with the embarrassed awareness of both the student and teacher that maybe they had come too close.

It has also been our general impression that the school environment is a tense one for both the student and the teacher. We observed that the students behaved much of the time in a stereotyped manner. They hurried from class to class and stood in line for almost everything, from library cards to interviews with their counselors. This was true especially in High School B, in which, because of its large size, it was sometimes physically difficult for the students to go from class to class in the allotted five minutes. Although the school does appear to stultify some of the student's individuality, it does not affect him as adversely as it might; he has learned to live with it. Harmony is not an attribute of the student-teacher relationships. The students often feel constricted in the school environment and cannot wait until they are finished (daily or in the long run). It impressed us how well the students adapt to high school despite the problems.

When the students are asked to look back on their high-school years (in their senior year of high school as well as in the freshman year in college), they do so with nostalgia. In retrospect, the majority of our subjects feel that they enjoyed the high-school years. They do find it difficult, however, to name a particular teacher who they thought helped them more than the others. They might go back to see the school, but almost never to seek out a particular teacher. Hence we feel justified in stating that our modal student does not value his relationship with any particular teacher, though he has obviously adapted well to the high-school environment in general.

4

The Home Environment

Characteristics of the Modal Group

In general, the adolescents we have studied seemed to be well mannered and had poise that was not characteristic of adolescents whom we saw in our clinical practice. They appeared relatively self-confident and handled the stressful situation of the interviews with remarkable ease as contrasted with the patient population to which we were accustomed. They related well, were curious about the life of the interviewers, and did not hesitate to speak when a question occurred to them. Many were very active physically and were leaders in the sports activities in their schools. This was not true of all of them, as we pointed out in our description of the students' attitudes toward the school.

DEMOGRAPHIC CHARACTERISTICS

Only one of our subjects was foreign-born. Only two subjects were Negro, there were no Oriental subjects, and the rest of the 71 subjects were white. There were 40 Protestants, 17 Jews, 7 Catholics, 1 Jehovah's Witness, and 8 subjects who stated that they had no religion at all. The geographic mobility of the subjects showed that the majority had been fairly stable. From an ordinal-position point of view, our subjects were similar to what one would expect from a random sample.

TABLE 4–1

Characteristics of the Modal Adolescents

Geographic mobility of subjects:

(1) Lived in the same community for past 8 years	27
(2) Moved once or twice in the past 8 years	41
(3) Moved more than twice in the past 8 years	2
(4) No exact information available	3
TOTAL 73 subjects	

Characterization of ordinal position:

(1) Only child	9
(2) Older of two children	15
(3) Younger of two children	10
(4) Oldest of three or more children	19
(5) Youngest of three or more children	6
(6) Middle child in three-child family	6
(7) Intermediate child in family of four or more children	8
TOTAL 73 subjects	

History of physical illnesses:

Serious physical illness (such as rheumatic fever, asthma)	Yes 12; No 57
Hospitalization (for any extended period)	Yes 3; No 66
Allergies (such as hay fever, eczema)	Yes 32; No 37

Initial adjustment to school was	Good 57; Fair 7; Poor 5
Major child rearing during first few years assumed by	Parents 65
	Relative 3
	Hired Help 1
TOTAL 69 subjects*	

* Only 69 subjects are represented here. These questions were drawn from the parents' interview, and we were not able to interview all the parents.

The subjects were remarkably free of serious physical illness. Only three of them had been hospitalized for any extended period, and two of these hospitalizations were for auto accidents. Minor physical problems were relatively high in our group, however; 32 subjects stated that they suffered from allergies such as hay fever or eczema. More than 90 per cent of our subjects were reared by their natural parents. When we first selected our group in 1962, only 2 subjects had lost their parents by death, and 2 subjects stated that their parents were divorced.

The low figure of parent loss in our sample (6 per cent) is particularly impressive when we compare it to findings obtained by other investigators from a variety of different populations. As the project went on, 3 other subjects' parents were divorced and 3 other subjects lost their fathers.

SOCIAL CLASS

The mean income in the two communities was $9,000.* In Community A the range of income was much smaller than in Community B. In the former, about 85 per cent of the inhabitants earned between $7,000 and $11,000 a year. In community B, although the mean was the same, the range was much broader, from $3,000 to $50,000.

Two possible indices of socioeconomic status were available, a nine-step rating of father's occupational level and an eight-step scale of father's educational attainment. The information was obtained from the subject as part of the structured second survey interview and was corroborated in the parent interviews or by telephone contact with the parents. The ratings were made through use of materials developed at the National Opinion Research Center. Frequency distributions and a comparison of the two high schools are presented in Table 4–3. The differences between the two high schools were not significant; there was a slight tendency for fathers from Community A to obtain a higher social-class rating on occupation and those from Community B to show greater educational attainment. The distributions for Community B were more spread out, reflecting the socioeconomic differences between the communities discussed in Chapter 2. The correlation for the 73 subjects between the two ratings was −.59, significant beyond the .001 level. We have chosen to use the rating of father's occupation

* U.S. Census Tract Report for Metropolitan Chicago (1962).

TABLE 4-2

Percentage of Disrupted Homes in Other Samples

INVESTIGATOR	N	POPULATION	AGE LIMIT	PERCENTAGE TO HAVE LOST ONE PARENT BY DEATH	PERCENTAGE DIVORCED
Metropolitan Life Brown (1961)	216	Controls Adult depressed	15 15	7 44	
Gibbons (1963)	200	Adolescent delinquents	17 to 20	19	26
Pollock (1962)	380	Patients seen in private practice	15	12	
				PERCENTAGE TO HAVE LOST ONE PARENT BY DEATH, DIVORCE, OR SEPARATION	
U.S. Census (1962)	—	Chicago suburbs Communities A and B	16	9	
Our sample (1962)	73	Chicago suburbs Communities A and B	14	6	

TABLE 4-3

Frequency Distributions, Means, Variances, and t-Tests for the Ratings of Social Class

FATHERS' OCCUPATION	HIGH SCHOOL A	HIGH SCHOOL B	TOTAL
1. Professional and technical	23	7	30
2. Managers and officials	6	11	17
3. Proprietors	1	1	2
4. Clerical	4	1	5
5. Sales	5	4	9
6. Craftsmen and foremen	1	1	2
7. Unskilled and semiskilled	4	0	4
8. Service	0	4	4
9. Farmers	0	0	0
N	44	29	73
Mean	2.56	3.24	2.84
Variance	4.34	5.83	4.97
			$t = -1.27$; $df = 71$

FATHERS' EDUCATION	HIGH SCHOOL A	HIGH SCHOOL B	TOTAL
3. Attended high school*	0	5	5
4. Completed high school	14	5	19
5. Attended college	10	3	13
6. Completed college	12	7	19
7. Attended graduate school	5	0	5
8. Completed graduate school	3	9	12
N	44	29	73
Mean	3.39	3.66	3.49
Variance	1.55	2.34	2.34
			$t = -0.73$; $df = 71$

* Categories 1 and 2 refer to educational levels below high-school attendance. These categories did not

as our index of social-class status in subsequent analyses. Sixty-six per cent of the mothers were housewives and did not work. The rest of the mothers worked in occupations ranging from professional and technical (11 per cent) to proprietary, clerical, sales, and service women (4 per cent).

Although in the beginning of the project we had eliminated those students who stated that they were in psychiatric treatment, we later found that five parents had had psychotherapy in the past or were having treatment at the time of the project. We also found that four additional parents had consulted someone once or twice concerning their children. We did not eliminate any students from the project because their parents were in treatment. In addition, three subjects, as we have mentioned previously, entered into treatment during the project. Also, one sibling of one of our subjects was receiving psychiatric treatment.

Although we did not find any major differences between the parents of High School A and High School B, we did note in general that the A parents were much more school- and child-oriented. The P.T.A. group was more active, was more involved in the school administration, and, when there were difficulties or problems in the school, many parents would attend the board meetings. In contrast, High School B gave more of an impression of a large and remote institution in which the individual parent had little interest. The P.T.A. group was not influential or very active and did not take a great interest in the happenings of the school. After our study was finished, however, when a new superintendent decided to institute a higher degree of school integration, the meetings of the Board of Education had a larger parent attendance.

Relationships Between the Teen-Agers and Their Parents

The amount of agreement in the pictures presented by both generations concerning the relationships between parents and teenage boys was striking. Both concurred that the most arguments and disagreements took place during the seventh and eighth grades. Once the student entered high school, the parents had fewer difficulties with the boys and new relationships were established (see also Chapter 5).

The great majority of the subjects (80 per cent) stated that their parents approved of their future plans, which in these cases usually meant going to college. Only two subjects felt that their parents definitely did not approve of their future plans. The others were not certain.

We found that the boys tended to feel close to one of the parents but rarely to both. Although 59 per cent of the subjects stated that they took after their fathers, not all of them reported feeling close to them emotionally, the majority feeling that their mothers understood them better in that respect. Very few indicated that they were equally close to both parents and just as few believed that they were close to neither parent.

On the other hand, the parents felt quite differently about their children. About a third of the parents told us that neither parent was close to the child; another third that both parents felt that the boy was closer to the mother. These data were obtained from interviewing the parents separately. Of the 49 sets of parents in which both father and mother were interviewed, only 5 per cent disagreed with each other. The feelings of the teen-agers and the parents obviously shift back and forth during the high-school years. We found the above overall data consistent for the group of the modal adolescents from year to year although it changes and different adolescents feel differently at various times. For example, toward the end of high school the teen-agers who earlier had felt closer to the mother, now identified more with the father and felt that they could talk more freely with him, while there was a feeling of estrangement or awkwardness near the mother.

We inquired into the students' feelings about their religion. Sixty per cent of the subjects said that their parents went to church once a week and wanted them to go along. Sixty-four per cent stated that religion had been helpful to them in the past. But in a different part of the same interview, when asked how often they went to church, only 37 per cent answered "every Sunday." The rest of the group were divided between those who did not attend church at all (20 per cent) and those who attended infrequently (31 per cent); 12 per cent did not respond to this question. In our follow-up interviews, during the junior and senior years, it was clear to us that in this particular group of teen-agers, religion was not of central importance. Even if the students did attend church, they rarely took an active part in church youth activities. When they were asked to describe their picture of the ideal world, God was not an active and organic part of it. Even for those students who were regular in their church attendance, about half considered it a chore rather than something very meaningful. Only 15 per cent of the group said that religion was meaningful and that they followed its dictates to the best of their ability. The 10 per cent who later attended denominational colleges came exclusively from these boys.

The vast majority (88 per cent) stated that they were generally disciplined reasonably and fairly. Some students (20 per cent) thought that their parents were too lenient with them, another 20 per cent felt their parents were strict, and 60 per cent stated that the discipline was variable and unpredictable. Physical punishment was used by 80 per cent of the parents and scolding by all. Interestingly, only 7 per cent told us that they were punished by a withholding of love. When we compared the adolescents' statements about father and mother as disciplinarians, we found, somewhat to our surprise, that the boys felt that their mothers were far more strict with them than the fathers (36 per cent vs. 20 per cent).

To gain a better understanding of the subjects' feelings toward their home environment, we asked them during the second interview, in their sophomore year, a set of ten open-ended questions about their home environment. Ratings were then made on each scale separately, and a second, independent rater was used to check the reliability of the ratings. The highest single group described the "nicest thing about my home life" as the emotional comfort. When asked to describe the "worst things about my home life," the highest single group did not talk about lack of warmth or empathy, but rather about the "physical environment" —such things as sharing rooms with siblings, being cramped for

TABLE 4-4

Frequency Distribution for Responses to the Sentence-Completion Test

Nicest thing about my home life is:	Number
(1) Physical comfort	8
(2) Emotional comfort	41
(3) Closeness with parents	15
(4) Closeness with sibs	3
(5) Increase in self-esteem	5
(6) Other (or no answer)	1
TOTAL	73

Worst thing about my home life is:	
(1) Physical discomfort	20
(2) Emotional discomfort	5
(3) Overt family conflicts	7
(4) Sibling rivalry	10
(5) Decrease in self-esteem	9
(6) Don't know	7
(7) Other (or no answer)	15
TOTAL	73

What would you like changed about home?	
(1) Physical setting	17
(2) Emotional environment	7
(3) Relations with parents	12
(4) Relations with sibs	9
(5) Dependence—Independence	5
(6) Nothing	14
(7) Other (or no answer)	9
TOTAL	73

Which parent do you take after?	
(1) Father	43
(2) Mother	15
(3) Don't know	1
(4) Both	8
(5) Neither	6
TOTAL	73

TABLE 4-4 *(continued)*

Father's best trait:

	Number
(1) Competence	17
(2) Intelligence and knowledge	5
(3) Relationship with subject	14
(4) Discipline	1
(5) Emotional understanding (also humor)	30
(6) Other (or no answer)	6
TOTAL	73

Mother's best trait:

	Number
(1) Competence	20
(2) Intelligence and knowledge	2
(3) Relationship with subject	12
(4) Discipline	3
(5) Emotional understanding (also humor)	32
(6) Other (or no answer)	4
TOTAL	73

Father's worst trait:

	Number
(1) Incompetent and unintelligent	3
(2) Relationship with subject	6
(3) Discipline	4
(4) Not understanding	16
(5) Impulsive	25
(6) Habits	8
(7) Nothing	6
(8) Other (or no answer)	5
TOTAL	73

Mother's worst trait:

	Number
(1) Incompetent and unintelligent	1
(2) Relationship with subject	10
(3) Discipline	5
(4) Not understanding	14
(5) Impulsive	20
(6) Habits	12
(7) Nothing	5
(8) Other (or no answer)	6
TOTAL	73

I enjoy most:

	Number
(1) Physical outlets (sports, work with hands, etc.)	40
(2) Mental activity (reading)	3
(3) Interpersonal relations (peers)	17
(4) Family relationships	7
(5) Other (or no answer)	6
TOTAL	73

TABLE 4–4 (continued)

I enjoy least:	Number
(1) Physical work	13
(2) School (homework, etc.)	21
(3) Mental activity (reading)	6
(4) Interpersonal relations (peers)	12
(5) Family relations	5
(6) Other (or no answer)	16
TOTAL	73

Definitions of Ratings for Sentence Completion Test

Physical comfort:	Place to rest; nice home; crowded house; many chores; crowded space
Emotional comfort:	Plenty of love; being punished
Closeness with parents:	Togetherness; listening to parents quarrel; parents don't know much
Closeness with siblings:	Companionship with siblings; fights with siblings
Increase in self-esteem:	Get a voice in everything; parents won't let me do things
Dependence—independence:	Mother nagging; wish parents approved of friends; "let me do what I want."
Emotional environment:	When only general terms are mentioned (e.g., togetherness or love) without specifying parents or siblings
Emotional understanding:	Description of parents' personality without specifying relationship with subject (e.g., humor, kind, understanding, good personality, friendly, happy)
Non-understanding:	Opposite of above; plus hardheaded, selfish, moody, worries too much
Habits:	Rubs nose; smokes; drinks; talks a lot
Discipline:	Lenient; punishes too much
Impulsive:	Gets upset; gets mad; yells
Intelligence and knowledge:	Learned; intelligent; smart; likes to learn
Competence:	Can do things; is good with hands; good cook
Relationship with parents:	Whenever parents are mentioned specifically; the same thing holds for siblings.

NOTE: These were open-ended questions asked by the interviewer during the second interview (sophomore year). The rating scale was based on the answer given. The reliability agreement between two independent raters was 82 per cent.

space, and having only one family car. Although problems in the home were described, one gets a strong feeling that the emotional atmosphere was positive. More than 90 per cent of the subjects planned to get married and have families similar to their own. It is of interest to note that the subjects who described the father's best trait as "emotional understanding" were not the same ones who thus described the mother's best trait. So again we can state that the teen-ager believes that one of his parents understands him, but almost never both.

As can be seen from Table 4–4, although the subjects were critical of their parents and often very critical of the relationship between mother and father, only a few were bitter toward the parents. One boy greatly resented his father's drinking. He was glad when his parents separated, though he had not felt particularly positive toward the mother either. Another teen-ager complained that his father always called him stupid. He said in one interview, "My dad says that you must have picked me so that the bright boys will stand out in contrast." In general the teen-agers did not express feelings of hatred toward their parents. They were not harsh in their judgment and did not claim that their parents were harsh toward them. The great majority of the group did not mention parents' drinking, beating, cursing, or lack of love or affection. Only three students actively complained about their parents. The most significant common feature is the lack of reports of physical or severe emotional trauma in the lives of our modal adolescents. These findings are in marked contrast to the interviews we have had with disturbed adolescents (Marcus, Offer, Blatt, and Gratch, 1966).

Again, when asked in the third psychiatric interview to describe the ideal parent, the teen-ager did not specify that he felt neglected, that the parents were not good providers, or that they were not reasonable most of the time. At times the subjects complained about a lack of consistency in discipline. They would have liked to have their own car, their own television set. They wanted their parents to be of more help with their school work. A few teen-agers complained that their fathers were more interested in their work than in them; again, however, the majority felt that the ideal parent was parallel to the parent they had described in reality. This finding is in marked contrast to the picture that the teen-agers drew about their teachers, where the ideal teacher did not resemble the teacher with whom they had experience in the high-school setting.

As we stated above, basically the teen-agers share their parents' values and reflect the middle-class values of the parents. The group is future-oriented; almost 90 per cent planned to go on to college. Nonetheless, they do not have a flair for study; only 4 per cent mentioned reading or studying as the activity they enjoyed most.

This was not an idealistic group. For example, when asked in the second psychiatric interview what they would do with a million dollars, the vast majority stated that they would use it for personal purposes. They would invest it, save it, or spend it. Only 19 per cent mentioned that they would give a significant portion to charity. They described their goals, pleasures, and frustrations in terms of their immediate environment. Here again, probably, they

TABLE 4–5

*Three Wishes: Ranked from Most Frequent Response to
Least Frequent Response*

---

(1) *Academic achievement* (also intelligence): get good grades; get through college; intelligence; be smart.
(2) *Success* (also good job): be successful; have a place in society; lead a good life.
(3) *Wealth:* to be rich; etc.
(4) *Interpersonal relations:* get along with everyone; be popular; raise a good family; have lots of friends.
(5) *Happiness:* stated as such.
(6) *Athletic achievement:* stated as such.
(7) *Altruism or idealism:* help others; make others happy; no more wars.

NOTE: Responses were in answer to the question: "If you had three wishes which could come true, what would they be?" Agreement between two raters was greater than 80 per cent.

share their parents' way of life. Although the teen-agers had opinions on the larger issues of our time (the war in Vietnam and civil rights), they were not going out of their way to work for a cause. Only four subjects planned to volunteer to join the armed forces so they could fight in Vietman; the rest would go if drafted but preferred to stay out of it. No one said that he was going to burn his draft card, and only one subject told us that he thought of doing so but decided against it. Only two subjects were sincerely interested in civil rights. The rest of the subjects had a distant interest in these issues. Most of the white students did not have Negro friends and, although sympathetic to the Negro cause, many expressed the widespread belief that the Negro "has gone too far." After the 1966 riots, in the first post-high-school interview, many felt that more police force was necessary.

We inquired whether there was any relationship between the ordinal position of the subject and whether he considered himself the parental favorite. Although there was a slight tendency for the firstborn to see himself as either the father's or the mother's favorite, it was not statistically significant. We are therefore unable to make a definite statement about our group, although our data do seem, to a minor extent, to perpetuate the myth of the firstborn boy's being the parent's favorite. In the interviews the students could cite both advantages and disadvantages for the various ordinal positions. One told us: "Being the oldest, you can boss everybody else around, but then, your parents boss you around more than they do the others." Another said: "Sometimes it is lonely being the only child, but I like having my own room. I wouldn't like to share it." In answer to the question "Do you feel you are spoiled?" none seemed to think that they themselves were spoiled. If anybody was spoiled it was the youngest sibling—that is, if the youngest was not the one being interviewed.

When asked during the second psychiatric interview, "If you were alone on a desert island and you could have one person to join you, whom would you want?" more than 50 per cent of our subjects stated, in the freshman year, they would want their boy friends to join them. Only 12 per cent said they would want their girl friends to join them, and 26 per cent of them stated that they would want one of their immediate family members. The rest gave a variety of responses, from teachers to relatives. With the exception of the boys whose families had recently moved to the suburbs and who consequently still lacked friends, in general our subjects had good relationships with other teen-agers. They were popular socially or at least had a few close friends in whom they could confide. The goals they were striving toward were very appropriate in the sense that they fitted very nicely into the cultural milieu in which they were living and were almost always in accordance with the parents' expectations. The adolescents moved rather steadily toward increasing independence from the parents. While occasional examples of residual dependent behavior were noted, especially in regard to ties with their mothers early in adolescence, we wish to emphasize steady progress from this position during ages 16 through 19.

The Parent Interviews

As we have stated in Chapter 1, we interviewed 69 mothers and 49 fathers, toward the end of the junior year. (See Appendix 2 for the parent-interview schedule.) In addition to the 49 fathers we interviewed, 12 others returned the two questionnaires. Three fathers died during the first three years of the project and there were 3 divorces (the subjects lived with their mothers). In all, we had information from 61 fathers and no information from 12. The coding of the parent interviews and their analysis did not yield significant results because for each item we had a large number (up to 30 per cent) of "No answer" responses. We did not plan the structured part of the interview as carefully as we did their children's. As a result we have no relevant statistical information concerning the parents. We have, however, accumulated interesting interview material from the parents and present some impressions of the overall sample.

In attempting to draw a "profile" of the parents in this study, the first thought that occurs, after a reading of the interviews, is that there are more similarities than differences. And the first comment would have to be on the gratifying cooperation we received from the parents. The parents were contacted by phone and interviews were arranged during evenings and weekends. Most of them took place in the high schools, but on occasion they were conducted in community centers, churches, or the public library. We never interviewed parents in their own homes. Only one mother definitely refused to come for an interview. Sixty-nine of the mothers came—most of them with their husbands—on time, at the first date set, and often during torrid weather or snowstorms. The other three mothers had moved out of town by the time the interviews took place.

They came out of a high degree of involvement with their sons —not, initially, out of interest in the study. The overwhelming majority approached the interview anxiously and immediately asked, in one way or another, "What's wrong with my son?" or "What can you tell me about my son?" After a description of the purposes and methods of the study was given and the parents were reminded of the original letter together with emphasis on the need for confidentiality, most of the parents relaxed visibly, relieved to understand that ours was a study of "normals." They were then quite ready to share their views and to describe their sons to us.

Most comments on our study were vague, some negative. Some expressed doubt that the study could really accomplish what we hoped, either because the sample was "too special" or "you can't possibly define 'normal.'" Most of them, when asked what they thought about the study, said something like "Oh, I'm sure it's a good thing, but I don't know much about it," or "I really haven't given it much thought." One mother expressed the opinion of a very few when she said: "I'm not too happy about ———— being called normal, because I don't think normal people can be very creative." A larger number agreed with the mother who said, "I'm so relieved to know he's considered normal."

Although most of the parents couched their comments on the study in rather wary terms, they tended to describe their sons' attitudes more positively. Some said they thought their sons were "thrilled to be chosen" for the study; the majority agreed more with the mother who said: "He seems to enjoy it more than going to the doctor or dentist; I'll put it that way." No parents thought involvement in the study had hurt their sons, and several believed it had helped them.

All this by way of saying that the parents cooperated with us

willingly and well, even though they began with a hazy understanding of the study. It should be added, however, that later the
parents became more fully involved. For example, two years after
the parent interview, all the parents were telephoned for information on college addresses. Without exception, these calls elicited
warm and interested responses and questions about the progress of
the study. In the late spring of 1967 a detailed follow-up questionnaire was mailed, with a letter, to the parents. Within the first four
weeks 55 out of 73 had completed and returned the questionnaire.
In the following three months all but 4 families had returned the
follow-up questionnaire, including the 12 families who had moved
away from the Midwest.

In summarizing the general pattern or tone of the parent
interviews, one could say, first, there was the initial cooperation
—they came. Then, in the first few moments, while interviewed
together, they were mostly stiff, wary, anxious. After discussion of
the study and a better understanding of it, there was a more
relaxed attitude. Each parent was then interviewed separately
while the other filled out questionnaires in another room. It was
here that the majority of the parents opened up most freely. The
only "drawing back" point, for most, came when we introduced
questions about their own adolescence. It was not possible, in the
scope of one interview, to get them very far into this earlier
period. When we asked, "What do you recall about your own
teen years?" we got descriptions of the town, the family, the
social pattern, but very little of the *feelings* of those years. One
mother said, "Oh, what a terrible question!" Another said, "Oh,
that's not fair!" Many said, "I don't remember much about it."

The major problem encountered in the parent interviews was
that there was not time in the hour to establish just the right
"alliance" for any very revealing discussion. Time was nearly
always a problem, and the interviews, we felt, seemed too brief to
all concerned. On the other hand, if initially we had asked the
parents to give us more than an hour, it is quite likely that more
would have refused cooperation. The question also comes up
whether it is possible to develop a good relationship with adoles-

cents *as well as* their parents. The problem is especially germane in situations where the families are not seen conjointly, as is the case in family therapy. It is also possible that had we started interviewing the parents and the teen-agers at the same time, we would have been unable to develop a meaningful relationship with either. Obviously we cannot answer these questions and can only hope they will be taken up afresh.

In the parent interviews, after an initial discussion of the purposes of the study, we asked each parent alone to describe his or her son. Here again we come up with the strong sense of similarity in the responses. Four reported real concern or disappointment. The overwhelming majority, however, expressed approval of their sons, and those things which they saw as problems were minor, by their own admission. Although the comments of the parents are remarkably similar, there are slight but interesting differences in emphasis between mothers and fathers. The mothers tended to simplify, to see their sons in terms of good and bad and thoughtfulness to others. These are typical remarks: "He's a good boy. He listens to us, knows the difference between right and wrong"; "I think he's kind and good—not bad"; "Generally he is what you'd call a good boy. He is obedient, thoughtful to us and the rest of the family. He always wants to please us." The fathers tended to analyze their sons' personalities a little more finely: "I think he is a boy who has a sense of responsibility and fairness and a keen sense of justice"; "He is hard-working and conscientious, assumes responsibility, and is fairly capable of making his own decisions"; "Well, I like his enthusiasm. He's aggressive, but not overly so. He's a pretty good student too."

We find these statements repeated by the mothers and fathers over and over again with minor variations, throughout the interviews. It is apparent that the parents in this group adhere to similar value patterns—they praise their sons for being (or else they wish they were) conscientious, responsible, studious, obedient, and sensitive. This is hardly surprising, considering the sample, which is almost entirely suburban middle class.

We find a similar thread of sameness running through the parents' accounts of their own adolescent years. Most of the parents, particularly fathers, said their own families had been affected by the Depression, were less affluent, harder working. Nearly all said their sons had more things, more knowledge, more opportunities— and they were glad of that. But there was a strong hint, as many of these parents talked, that their sons were not better off, despite the things and opportunities. The suggestion was that one *should* have to work hard for rewards, that it all should not come as easily as it does to today's young. There was some nostalgia, too, as expressed by one father: "I grew up in the Depression and everybody worked to keep the family business going. We were a large and closely knit family. I had a good time." Or this from another father: "In my day the world was small and there was more mystery to things—there were still kids—you know."

There were those who felt, unambiguously, that things were better for their youngsters. As one mother put it, "It's a better, wider world." Another aspect, which many of them commented on, was the greater freedom in relations with adults. It was summed up by the mother who said, "He's permitted a say. I wasn't allowed a say."

There were even more, however, who said, "I feel sorry for kids today." And the reasons for feeling sorry were expressed thus:

"I think there's a difference because they know more and are pushed more. Our parents didn't partake of our activities—we were on our own more and were children longer, it seems to me. There's more pressure on them now in every way."

"Everything is harder on our youngsters now. The pressures are far greater in every way."

"I don't think they are basically different, but I think they're not as happy. They have more of everything and are not as happy. There's also a faster pace—more pressure."

Recollections about their own adolescent years led easily to general comparative statements about then and now. And, although almost all the parents saw differences in the environment, the way of life, the opportunities, the pressures, hardly any of them felt that teen-agers are basically any different. As one of the more articulate fathers summed it up: "I think fundamentally there's no difference. There are some accidental manifestations of difference, like more intense education, earlier maturation, etc., but generally the response of teen-agers to good and bad is, as always, dependent on the parents."

One very noticeable difference between then and now, according to most of the parents, has to do with the place of the automobile in the teen-ager's life. Most of the fathers volunteered that they had driven a car, if at all, very rarely and usually at a much later age than their sons did. Many of the parents felt that their sons were deliberately delaying dating until they could drive. And a great many of them expressed concern that the car makes life much different and more dangerous. They were concerned not only about car accidents but also about sex and about independence.

A mother said: "And now they have cars—and that presents more problems. I had a bicycle, and you can't do too much wrong on a bicycle." Another mother said: "We didn't have cars—we had to go everywhere on a yellow bus. That way there was not so much trouble either." And a father: "They have to have a car or they won't go anywhere. They don't know about other modes of transportation."

Communication Within the Family

We administered two separate instruments to each parent, the Family Interaction Scale (see Appendix 2) and a modified form of the Self-Image Questionnaire. The former was a derivative of the Osgood-Semantic differential designed to elicit the degree of open communication in a family. The latter was used to assess the degree of agreement of both parents regarding the self-image of their sons. (Hence, we were testing for the comunication between parents as well as the ability of the teen-ager to communicate his feeling about himself.) The statistical analysis of both instruments revealed a high degree of congruence. We found no significant subgroups within the parent sample. These results stand as verification of the good communication between members of the family. We obtained different results when studying communication patterns in disturbed adolescents and their parents. These findings should be evaluated especially in contrast to the study of communication in disturbed families (see Marcus, Offer, Blatt, and Gratch, 1966). It was further evident in the interviews themselves that the family members could freely discuss differences as well as similarities. We were constantly impressed by the frequency with which one parent tended to say the same thing—in almost the same words—as the other parent, when discussing their children or their relationships with them.

The same agreement holds when we consider the values held by the parents and the sons. There was no basic difference expressed by the majority of parents or of sons. The previously mentioned parental emphasis on honesty, goodness, productivity, and cooperation seems to have been accepted by the subjects, with little or no rebellion. Although it was not a question that we consistently asked in the interviews, a number of the mothers volunteered the opinion that their sons had given them more trouble or seemed more unhappy at twelve or thirteen than in the present (high-school) years. (See Chapter 5 for further discussion.)

Likewise, when we talked about the sons' relationships with siblings, a common response was that things had improved lately. Very few parents felt there were any serious problems between siblings; all of them reported quarreling and competition, but did not seem perturbed by it. As one mother put it: "I guess their relationships are normal—they love one another one minute and can't stand each other the next."

From the parent interviews, the teen-agers emerge pretty much as action-oriented, ambitious to have things and do as well or better than their fathers, but not as intellectuals, not liking to read or study. This area is one minor area in which parents frequently expressed dissatisfaction. Most of them mentioned a desire to see their sons study harder or read more, to "broaden" themselves. A great many of them said, "They have to know so much more nowadays," or "It's a very competitive world."

The parents' relations with the school or community were not probed systematically. Many of those interviewed volunteered some comments, though, and these were about equally divided between praise of the community and disapproval of it.

Many mothers—not fathers—commented with some vehemence about the pressures put upon their sons by the school. They felt that there was great pressure to achieve academically, and also in sports. They felt that this emphasis on sports was detrimental to the boys because it caused an extra burden of stress and anxiety. One mother implied that the fathers contributed to the stress: "All the fathers are very involved too, and they are out there at the practices looking over the fence—and I think there's just too much push, push, push."

Some traumatic incidents had occurred in several of the homes before the time of the parent interview, and we were able to get some glimpses of how the family coped with them. One mother told of years of problems—serious illness of two of the children (including our subject), separation from her husband, then reconciliation, and more severe marital discord. As she spoke, two things emerged: her apparent strength, and her admiration for her son's success in coping with "the whole mess." She had sought counseling help for him when he was upset; and, she said, "There was always good, wide-open communication between all the children and me."

Just prior to the parent interview, this particular family had been through alcoholism, bankruptcy, and divorce. The mother had had major surgery. She seemed amazingly in control for one who had been through so much. She was greatly concerned about the children and how all this would affect them. She told of conversations with her son, and she said he had asked her permission to leave town. Again, we got the sense of effective communication within the family.

In another family, an older brother of our subject had been seriously crippled in a major accident. After some discussion of this, the mother was able to talk quite objectively of the subject son and of the family pattern as a whole. We got a strong sense of vitality, of carrying on, within this family.

In two other cases it was the fathers who spoke with enthusiasm of how well the sons had coped with the mothers' emotional illnesses and the resultant strain on the families.

What came through in each of these interviews was the sense that communication was fairly good and that it did not break down during severe trauma. This thread of open communication channels seems to run through our observations of most of the families in the study.

5

Rebellious and Antisocial Behavior

Most of our subjects did not participate in overt antisocial behavior. They were not delinquents, defined here as having a police record. The defiant or rebellious behavior that they did manifest was directed toward the parents, and with rare exceptions toward the schools. They did, however, admit to often having the *urge* to act in a manner that would get them "into trouble." During the Second Psychiatric Interview (see Appendix 2), which took place in the sophomore year, the adolescents were asked to describe the three most difficult problems a teen-ager faced. Ranking their answers, we found that they considered controlling their "antisocial tendencies" as number two on their list (see Table 2–2 for details). We often heard statements like: "The teen-ager has to be careful not to get involved with the wrong crowd"; "I have to learn to control my temper"; "I remind myself that I should not drop out of school even though the classes bore me." But how successful were they in curbing their aggression?

Rebellious Behavior

In our subjects, rebellion manifested itself most clearly in early adolescence, at ages twelve and thirteen. They described themselves as "getting into fights with our parents" over seemingly small and insignificant issues. At that period they broke the rules of the house constantly. For example, they refused to take the garbage out, dressed differently, came home late, did not make their beds, or went out with the wrong crowds. In our group, the boys did not go to church as often as their parents did. Rebellious behavior carried over to their interaction with schoolteachers, church workers, and other significant adult males. It did at times spill over to overt delinquent behavior (see below), but the delinquent behavior was not extreme and most of the overt behavioral forms of the rebellion disappeared by the time the teen-ager entered high school.

However, some of the rebellion lingered on, being manifested in group situations and when the teen-ager had access to the parents' car at age sixteen. Arguments also continued over clothes and hair styles beyond thirteen or fourteen. These observations were confirmed by interviews with the parents.

The rebellion was characterized by chronic disagreements (lasting one to two years) with parents and schoolteachers, which were more or less intense at different times over issues that seem small or undramatic. There were usually no great pitched battles over crucial or world-shaking issues. But the adolescents did consider the differences crucial and the parents did not regard the disagreements as insignificant either. Nearly all the parents stated that the early adolescent years (twelve and thirteen) were the most difficult time they had in raising their children.

Our adolescent subjects showed a certain degree of conformity to each other in behavior, values, dress, recreation, consumer consumption, and so forth. But this conformity to each other did not make them any less rebellious at home. On the basis of our definition of rebellion, the objects of rebellious behavior are authority figures; yet conforming ritualistic behavior with groups of boys of their own age did not rule out defiance to parents and parental substitutes. Rather, they went hand in hand. We had evidence that the teen-agers maintained the same middle-class values as their parents. The reader is referred to Chapter 4 where we discuss the high agreement on the Family Interaction Scale among all the members of the family. We found that the subjects had the same class biases, claimed allegiance to the same religious denominations as their parents even if they tended to drop out of church attendance, and intended to follow in the footsteps of their fathers' occupations, either the same or class-related ones.

The subjects who were concerned with stopping world conflicts were often those who were most concerned with controls for themselves. For example, one boy who fought a lot and was proud of his fighting skill used up his first of three wishes to wish for peace in the world. When asked what he would do with a million dollars, he said: "Buy a car and a swimming pool, and put the rest in the bank." His wish for peace was not strong enough to enlist his financial support! Another boy, whom we present because he was the exception rather than the rule, stated that his three wishes were: (1) peace in the world, (2) eternal happiness, and (3) to have lots of money for himself. The first wish is interesting because it comes from a boy who liked to fight and was proud of his fighting ability. One of his grandfathers had been a prizefighter.

According to Erikson (1959), a psychosocial moratorium is provided by each society to allow a period of time for the adolescent to experiment with, play around with, and test various roles before he commits himself to a certain role, or style of behavior. It seems as if rebellious behavior is one area wherein the adolescent is free to try his wings, and where in our society, for example, the family and school are willing to give him time by permitting, within limits, some breaking of rules and regulations. We shall illustrate the above with the following example: During high school, the individual rebellion ceased to a great extent, and took on a more systematized and institutionalized form. In the two high schools 50 per cent of the modal students were active smokers at any one time. Because of their habit and that of their peers, they, like the teachers who smoked, wanted to smoke during the lunch hours. But, unlike the teachers, the students did not have a lounge where this was permitted.* Therefore, they developed the following arrangement with the school, in which they did not really defy the rules openly and yet did not accept them either. In one of the high schools the students would cross the street, stand within half a block of the school, and smoke during their lunch hour. In the second school many students would smoke in the washroom while one of their peers watched out for the teacher who was on patrol that particular day. When the teacher came near the washroom the student would whistle a particular tune and all the cigarettes would be flushed down the toilet. The teacher would go into the washroom which, of course, was full of smoke, but he could not catch any of the students smoking. He then simply asked all of them to leave. The interaction was repeated many times each day. Such accommodations may be passed down to the next younger generation of adolescents, developing a tradition. The adolescents' rebellion and the school's method of coping with it will then become ritualized and institutionalized for succeeding generations of adolescents. As we can see from this example, this practice was not only an institutionalized form of rebellion; it also provided the teachers and parents (that is, "the authorities") something that they might smile about and possibly be proud of. No policeman has arrested the teen-agers for it. Here is a different example stressing the stepping-through of an accepted boundary: One of our subjects told us that he was telling a friend, within earshot of the football coach, that he had just smoked a cigarette. The coach immediately turned to him and told him that he would not let him play on the team for the whole season. The subject was sad about the incident and pleaded with the coach to change

---

* The visitor to the school is struck by the enjoyment those teachers who do smoke get from being able to do so by going to the teachers' lounge for their coffee and smoke. We have observed that teachers were especially prone to tell their colleagues and friends that they were going to the teachers' lounge to smoke when there were students around who could hear their statement.

his mind. The coach did not. When the student told the incident to us he added, "I probably asked for it because I knew exactly how he felt about smoking."

Delinquent Behavior

Our subjects varied in their rebellious behavior as described above. In some, the ability to control their impulses was less developed. In our sample, 25 per cent of our subjects stated in the Second Psychiatric Interview that they had participated in at least one delinquent act as defined above. Fifty-two per cent of our subjects told us that they had known or associated closely with people who had been involved in delinquent acts. The delinquent acts performed by our subjects consisted of stealing (money, goods from stores, and, on rare occasions, cars), throwing Coke bottles on major highways, vandalism, and serious physical fights. Other, milder patterns included overturning of dozens of garbage cans after a particularly exciting football game. Most of our subjects who did participate in delinquent acts abandoned this particular form of behavior after one or two trials. Hence we note that only 3 per cent of our sample had chronic difficulties in controlling their impulses. Two of the three delinquent boys eventually underwent psychotherapy for their problems. Although we did not refer them to treatment initially, once the parents asked for our advice we responded accordingly. The third delinquent boy did not receive any psychiatric treatment.

The Case of Lester

We turn now to the case example of Lester, who demonstrated rather well some of the difficulties of many of our subjects in controlling aggression and rebellious feelings. His case will also show to some extent how this particular boy learned to curb his aggression.

Lester was thirteen years old when his parents moved to the suburb from the big city. He was a short and stocky boy, eager to please the interviewer and proud of his athletic achievements. One major reason for the move was to allow Lester to benefit from the better school system in the suburbs. Lester did not see the move in similar perspective. He was now far away from his friends and was not yet part of the group in his new environment. He missed his old friends and would go back to the old neighborhood (which took almost an hour by public transportation) whenever he could. His performance in school was poorer than before and although he was passing all his subjects, his parents were concerned with his academic standing. When his parents found out about his trips to the old neighborhood, they strictly forbade them. Nonetheless Lester, who was now fourteen years old, continued to go. A few months later he got into a violent fight with a member of the old clique, fracturing one of the other boy's bones. The fight had to be stopped by the police, who told Lester that they would not tell his parents if there would be no recurrence and he would "stay out of trouble." The parents are still not aware of this particular incident. Lester learned from his experience and was motivated to drop his old friends and develop more appropriate friendships in his new environment. For Lester the rebellion was over.

Lester was given the psychological tests at age sixteen, approximately two years after the fight. We shall present a summary of the psychological-testing results in order to ascertain whether Lester had indeed developed inner controls. It is important to stress here again that the interview ratings and the psychological-test analyses were obtained independently, without any cross-communication between the psychiatrist and the psychologist.

At the time Lester took the psychological tests he appeared to be greatly concerned about anything he did that was wrong, virtually dividing his actions between good and evil. Despite the considerable superego pressure to be a good boy and to stop doing bad things, he was literally preoccupied with doing bad. On the one hand, there seemed to be some anxiety connected with being good, as though being good prevented him from easily discriminating himself from his father. There was also the feeling that he would not be doing bad things for very long, that basically he was a good person, and that things would turn out well.

Though of only average intelligence, Lester was a very imaginative, creative youngster. He was down to earth and stuck to the concrete issues, but managed to solve problems in new though realistic ways. He looked freshly on what he had learned and combined discrete fragments of knowledge in novel ways to solve new problems.

Though eager for relationships, he often expected them to be tenuous. He felt that when he was close to somebody, somebody else might easily intrude on the closeness and separate them. This attitude, at least in part, seemed to reflect some of the complexity of his relationships with his mother and father. There was resentment toward his father as an intruder, but a very strong pull to take from him and be like him. He ambivalently tried to hurt his father, to rub salt on his wounds, but then would feel not only guilty but also anxious lest this behavior would push his father farther away from him. He looked toward his mother as a control, but felt that he had less need of her, since he should now be able to use his own resources.

He was an introspective youngster, who kept most of his feelings to himself. There was little opportunity for release of feelings or for validating how he saw things. Since he was quite reactive to affective stimulation, he would fill up but could allow himself no safety valve. He was thus a rather uncomfortable youngster, but one whose pragmatic concentration and resourcefulness allowed him to get what he wanted to function productively.

The case of Lester was presented to illustrate how this particular teen-ager coped with his aggressive impulses. In early adolescence

Lester was rebellious toward his parents and the defiance spilled over to delinquency. One had the impression that Lester had to rebel openly once or twice before he would learn that there were other more appropriate ways in which he could channel his aggression. Though at age sixteen he still struggled with what to do with his aggressive ("bad") feelings, he now demonstrated to himself and others that he was capable of coping with these feelings and impulses on his own. In other words, Lester had begun to develop inner controls that were aiding him in mastering his own aggression.

The Relationship Between Rebellious and Delinquent Behavior

Lester demonstrated both rebellious and delinquent behavior. What is the relationship between the two forms? The relationship between juvenile delinquency and adolescent rebellion is an important one. Although the two have attributes in common, rebellion need not be delinquency. Rebellious acts that remain within the confines of the home and are acts of defiance clearly and solely against the rules of the home should not be confused with delinquency. Only when rebellious acts involve violations of the law and ethics of the society at large can they be said to constitute delinquency.

When we asked one of our subjects what made him stop his delinquent behavior, he replied: "You get older. You have better judgment. You don't do things for fun if you know they are wrong or if you know they can hurt other people."

More than 90 per cent of our subjects believed that delinquency in high school was caused by parents who did not care about their children. Too much freedom associated with too little love was blamed for juvenile delinquency. The desire for money and the lack of attention given by teachers to the poorer students were added reasons for the dropout problem.

Channeling Aggression

The modal teen-ager learned to channel his aggression in the following ways. First and foremost, he learned from his own experience that delinquent "acting out" is an antisocial act that has negative consequences, both externally and internally. The antisocial behavior is not only legally curbed by getting him into trouble, but it is also something that by and large violates his internal standards. Hence he attempts to channel his impulses in a different direction. His manner of accomplishing this includes his being very active in sports. A large number of our students stated that they thought of sports as one of the more important areas where they could be aggressive and could express themselves physically. In general, it was true of our subjects that they were action-oriented and preferred to channel their feelings into action. Besides participating in sports, many of our subjects were active in various social clubs and other groups in the high school: a debating team, a Latin club, even church groups, although the latter choice was far in the minority.

Only two subjects from our group were actively interested during the high-school years in the various social-action groups of our times. These two students were able to control their aggressive impulses and did not report being involved in any form of delinquent behavior. In the vast majority of our sample, we did not notice any dissatisfaction with the existing social order. They did not experiment with drugs. The problems of civil rights, peace, or social justice were not part of our subjects' immediate world. These issues were almost always observed from a distance.

6

Heterosexual Behavior

Obtaining Data about Sex

It is probably safe to say that the whole area of sex is one of conflict for all middle-class, adolescent American males. The teen-ager
must learn to interpret the maze of adult double standards, implicit and explicit peer communication, and family values. He has
to balance what he learns from external sources with his own internal feelings and impulses. His personal experiences will be the
final pathway by which he tests his own feelings and fantasies
against the external world. It is, at times, extremely hard for the
teen-ager to separate fantasy from actual experience. On the one
hand teen-agers have the tendency to brag; on the other hand we
find that some teen-agers are unwilling to talk freely and openly
about such personal matters as sexual feelings. A skeptical person
may rightly question the validity of our data in this area. Based on
the general nature of our relationship (see Chapter 10 for details),
we trust that we were not led far astray from the real life of the
teen-ager.*

---

* See Chapter 10 for a discussion of the relationship between the reliability
of the data and the nature of the interview relationship.

If we had asked our teen-agers about sex in the first interview, most likely we would have elicited a guarded and/or superficial response. On the other hand, not asking teen-agers about sex at some time during a later interview could be equally damaging. Sex is an area which is highly charged emotionally for teen-agers. Our subjects would have felt that we were insincere if we had not discussed their sexual feelings with them. After all, we had claimed that we were studying the problems of the "normal" teen-ager! Frequently, when we asked a teen-ager about his sexual feelings and experiences, there would be a definite sigh of relief in our subject and he would say, "I wondered when you would ask me these questions." Still, the subjects were usually anxious when discussing sex with us. They frequently blushed, looked the other way, and on two separate occasions refused to discuss the subject altogether.

Within the context of our interviews (see Appendix 2), we obtained data concerning dating patterns and sexual behavior three times: during the survey interview and the Fourth and Sixth Psychiatric Interviews. During the Fourth Psychiatric Interview we explored in depth the feelings of the adolescent toward sex.

Our experiences, as we shall illustrate below, were very different from the one that Friedenberg describes (1965, p. 126):

> In my experience adolescents rarely discuss sex with adults unless adults insist on it. Even though sexuality is central to adolescents it would have demeaned my subjects if I had tried to engage them in a discussion of it. For the first time in the high school experience of many of them, they were being seriously consulted. Sex, to American adolescents, is seldom a serious topic; it is either clinical or comical. They would not have been shocked at all if somebody doing research on adolescence had turned out to be another Kinsey-type shrinker avid to count their orgasms and stuff like that. But they would not—and quite rightly—have mistaken such a preoccupation for an interest in them. Conversely, I was interested in them as *functional* human beings; that is to say, as they saw themselves on their own terms.

In our opinion Friedenberg's statement accepts the purported opinion of the adolescents too literally. If he had only *tried* to broach the subject with his adolescent subjects, very likely he would have arrived at different conclusions. Our data seem to indicate that it is possible to be interested in the adolescents as functional human beings and including sexuality as part of their functioning.

Dating Behavior

A significant number of our subjects (45 per cent) had not gone out with girls by the end of the freshman year. The number of adolescents who dated increased slowly in the next two years so that by the end of the junior year 77 per cent of our subjects were dating. It is important to note, however, that most of the teenagers dated irregularly and did not seem either to relish the experience or think that it is important for teen-agers to date. At the same time (junior year) those who did not date (23 per cent) did not feel abnormal or self-conscious because they had not gone out with girls. According to our subjects, if anyone felt that teenagers should date, it was the parents and especially the mothers.

A typical example of many of our subjects' attitude toward girls was the student on the football team who, by the end of the sophomore year, had never dated and felt that he was not missing anything. As far as he was concerned, he would have plenty of time for "that sort of thing" in college. But even while he was expressing his indifference, his level of anxiety went up; when this was pointed out to him, he stated that he simply did not understand girls and wanted to be left alone by them.

We noticed a striking difference in our subjects when we interviewed them toward the end of their senior year. By then 95 per cent were dating, and girls had begun to occupy a much more prominent place in their lives. The change was dramatic. It was not limited to the fact that most of the teen-agers were dating. More significantly, almost all our subjects, including the football player mentioned above, looked forward to their dates and enjoyed their relationships with the girls. At this point the few teen-agers who did not date stated openly that they wanted to date, but lacked the courage.

The dating experience is not a critical one for the adolescent in the first two years of high school. Although many teen-agers do not "think much about girls" in the first two years of high school, they are very conscious of them. "I stay away from girls because I am too young, and we don't understand each other." If the interviewer presses the teen-ager and asks, "How do you know you don't understand one another?" the reply will be quick and definite: "I know." It was striking to the interviewer to note how often, right after they had talked about how they do not date and had given a "rational" explanation for it, they unconsciously brought their mothers into the picture. The teen-agers might then tell us about their conflicts with their mothers or how much they liked their mothers.

Many of the teen-agers complained that their mothers (and at times also their fathers) teased them about their anxiety concerning girls. It was almost as if the more embarrassed the adolescent was about girls, the more he was teased by his parents. For example, one subject told us that he liked his mother much more than his father. Next he said that he thought he probably would not marry; he never thought about sex and never daydreamed about girls. He was the only subject to say that he probably would not marry. Other comments of his indicated that his negative responses were due to a fear of his inexperience. He feared growing older and the possibilities of failures in new experiences. His mother, he reported, enjoyed "joking" about his lack of interest in girls. Her jokes made him uncomfortable. His parents may have tried too rapidly to turn a serious problem for the boy into something that could be handled by laughter.

As the teen-ager matured, his interest in girls increased. It was toward the latter half of the high-school years that the involvement became meaningful emotionally to the majority of our subjects. It was as if their curiosity about girls enabled them to overcome their fear of girls. Although the anxiety that they described while learning how to ask a girl out was considerable, according to their own evaluation, the satisfaction that they received was worth it. In the beginning a major reason for dating is a social one. They shared their experiences with their peers almost immediately after they brought the girl home. The minute dissection that goes on among the boys telling each other what they did, right or wrong, is extremely helpful and suggestive. They try to do better next time, not so much because they enjoy kissing or petting, but so they can tell their boy friends. As their anxiety diminishes in their relationships with girls, they begin to enjoy the encounter more, and eventually can look forward to a date simply because they like the girl, and want to share their experiences with her and her alone.

In our sample, we found that there was a tendency for those subjects who did the most dating in the junior year to be poorer students academically during the same year. Our data therefore

TABLE 6-1

Pearson-Product Moment Correlations (r) *Between Dating Behavior in the Freshman and Junior Years and Selected Variables*

DATING BEHAVIOR VERSUS	FRESHMAN		JUNIOR	
	r	N	r	N
Delinquency	−.10	64	−.01	66
Class standing	.10	65	.28**	66
Emotional experience	.13	70	.21*	72
Emotional expressiveness	.09	70	.06	72
Relationship with interviewer	.09	70	−.08	72

NOTE: Dating behavior was rated as: 1 = none, 2 = some, 3 = a lot. The original scale for classifying dating behavior in the freshman and junior years had four steps: (1) Never goes out with girls, (2) Dates only in groups, (3) Has had two or more single dates, (4) Is going steady. The scale was redefined as: (1) No dating, (2) Some dating, and (3) A lot of dating, by combining original Steps 3 and 4, since only two subjects in their freshman year and seven in their junior year were going steady and they were not the same subjects. Delinquency scored as: 1 = active participation, 2 = association, 3 = none. Class standing was scored by quarters: high score = poorer school performance. The last three items were psychiatric ratings. High score = poorer performance.
* p ≤ .05; ** p ≤ .01

show a tendency for the honor students to come from the non-daters, while the active daters were less academically inclined.

Sexual Behavior

Almost all our subjects (more than 94 per cent) had reached puberty by the end of the freshman year in high school as measured by the fact that their voices had already changed. During the freshman year, among the small group that dated actively, kissing and necking were the prominent ways of expressing affection. Our data would agree with Reiss (1961), who reported that the majority of teen-agers are conservative and restrained in their sexual behavior. During the junior year 30 per cent of the subjects were active daters, defined here as those who were going steady or had gone on more than one single date. Half of the active daters had experienced heavy petting. Ten per cent of the total subject group had sexual intercourse by the end of the junior year. No subject admitted participating in overt homosexual behavior. The subjects did state that they masturbated and denied having any unusual problems associated with it. We did not collect any data concerning fantasies during masturbation.

Finally, 80 per cent of the subjects approved of premarital sexual intercourse but only after high school. The main conscious reason that the teen-agers gave for not engaging in sexual intercourse in high school was the fear that the girl would get pregnant.* It seems that most of them think that anything goes, except intercourse, not because intercourse was wrong but because it was dangerous.

Talking about intercourse was like circling around the mulberry bush. The students, if sufficiently at ease, would be pressed by the interviewer for more exact responses. The student would retract the statement he had just made concerning, perhaps, the probability of intercourse leading to pregnancy and then close the con-

---

* In this regard, it is of interest to note that in a study on pregnancy during early adolescence, Barglow *et al.* (1968) found that the vast majority of the girls who did get pregnant had not believed that it could happen to them.

versation with an irrational, "Well, I don't know why. That is just the way it should be," or "Adults know what they are doing, teen-agers don't." Are you sure? "No." When told that pregnancy need not be the outcome of intercourse, the most frequent response was, "Well, in high school we're not mature enough to handle it." Too much sexual closeness was frightening. "We just are not ready for it" was repeated over and over. Statements about a certain maturity level being necessary for intercourse are replacing fear of pregnancy responses as the latter lose their realistic value.

Almost all the subjects (more than 90 per cent) said that they daydreamed about girls, but only a small group (25 per cent) stated that their reveries included anyone they knew personally. In the latter case it was often an older woman. (Incidentally, almost all the subjects thought that their mothers were very attractive— not always corroborated by our follow-up interviews of the parents!) The teen-agers who did not date by the junior year daydreamed about girls in the abstract: movie stars, heroines from fiction, or even young and attractive new teachers. The object of their fantasies was rarely a teen-age girl they knew personally.

The Case of Al

Al was one of our typical subjects. Well developed physically, Al was on a varsity team and was very proud to tell the interviewer the many details and complexities of his sports activities. He was an excellent student and his plan was to go into engineering after he finished high school. During his freshman and sophomore years, Al had no interest in girls. He belonged to the group that had not gone out yet on single dates and felt that this was the way it ought to be. Al started dating girls in the beginning of his junior year. He told us that he felt it was a major accomplishment for him and he was proud of it. Al was shy with girls, was not sure that he was liked by the opposite sex, and described himself

as "full of nervousness" before a date. Toward the end of the
junior year he talked about his difficulties in getting dates. He
was not going steady and had no definite tastes in girls. He was
less anxious now about asking girls out, but was not sure what to
do once he was out on a date. Al claimed that his mother helped
him when she told him that girls are just as afraid of boys, and
he should realize that and not worry. She also told him that girls
need courting and wooing, and he figured out that he had to "do
a good public-relations job and then I will be in business." When
asked about his own sexual experience, he replied: "People in high
school should have certain drives; even though contraceptives do
exist, people should not go too far because they are not mature
enough and cannot handle it. After high school sexual intercourse
is OK." When he was asked how far he felt was "safe," Al answered: "Far enough so they can handle it." When pressed, he
gave the examples of kissing and necking. In a later interview,
toward the end of the senior year, Al was much more comfortable
when talking about his dating and sexual experiences. Although he
had not experienced sexual intercourse, he felt comfortable in the
presence of girls.

Al was given the psychological testing a few months before his
junior-year interview described above. Al was described thus by the
psychologist:

> A very bright, imaginative young man, introspective and sensitive
> to what goes on within himself, but awkward, ill at ease, and blun-
> dering in social situations. His orientation is away from practical
> considerations, and although he spends a great deal of energy mull-
> ing things over and ruminating, he is unlikely to consider the social
> implications or consequences when his feelings get stirred up. He is
> a boy who knows himself well, is able to articulate this knowledge
> with ease, but who tends to bluster his way through encounters with
> other people. Al wants to be seen as a person in his own right and
> places considerable value on self-assertion. He is a youngster with a
> rich inner life and allows the richness and complexity open rein in
> his contacts with others. Although polite and interested in pleasing
> others, especially adults, he does not take orders easily; rather his

wide range of interests and his flexibility allow him to do things that are personally gratifying to him in order to please others. Problems result, however, and he becomes quite uncomfortable because he has incorporated a need to live up to his mother's expectations of him.

Al makes very quick decisions about what he is supposed to attend to in situations and what is irrelevant, and sometimes these decisions, though rigid, are arbitrary. Once the decision is made, he sees relationships between aspects of a situation very quickly and is able to use a highly abstract attitude to define these relationships. He does not often seek consensual validation of his ideas, and the result is sometimes high-powered intellectually but somewhat eccentric, or at least idiosyncratic. He seems to have been recently made aware of this and is somewhat anxious that he will be rejected by peers for his eccentricity or for his need to assert himself.

There is a great deal of concern right now about sexuality and his feeling that he doesn't know what to expect of himself in relation to girls or of girls in relation to him. Al is largely afraid he will be too soft with regard to girls and that this will leave him open to be taken advantage of by them. He sees his very strong orientation around being an individual in jeopardy, and although he is drawn to dating, feels that this kind of involvement will take something away from him. He is resolved, however, to take the risk but conceives of it as a risk—and is somewhat anxious.

Al has a striking capacity for intellectualization. When he is angry, he feels anger—but lest it not be acceptable, he communicates the feeling in very abstract, intellectual terms. There is a Pollyanna quality to this, too—and what one sees in part in the blustering described above is a conception of his that "Gee whiz, things are bound to turn out well for the good guys or the little guys."

Sexual Education

Although there was obviously a wide divergence in the experience that different adolescents had with both dating and sexuality, almost all of the boys exhibited marked curiosity about our findings. The students wanted to know in detail what our findings were concerning dating and sexual behavior. They were anxious to feel that they were "within the normal range." This observation strengthened our feeling that for many young teen-agers the discussions with other boys about their dating and/or sexual experiences are more important than the experiences themselves.

Other questions that were put to us less frequently had to do with venereal diseases and prostitution. In turn we asked our subjects to tell us the reasons behind these questions. If one appeared to be a "theoretical question," we answered it in general terms, citing statistics and telling about medical aspects of venereal diseases. On rare occasions, the questions were more specific and personal. For example, one student asked us whether it was true that a man gets syphilis after intercourse with a prostitute. It became apparent very quickly that the subject believed that that was indeed the case. We were able to relieve him of much of his strong anxiety, especially after we found that the sexual encounter that had aroused his fear had taken place three months earlier. Four students reported having had sexual relations with prostitutes by the end of the junior year. They all felt somewhat guilty about the experience and stated that they did not enjoy it.

In regard to sexual education, our impression was that this particular group of students had received very little straightforward information concerning sex from either their parents or teachers (including religious teachers). Sex education had not been given, and although many thought it should be, none felt they had profited from anything they had been told by teachers or parents. Here is a typical example of their dissatisfaction: "In sixth grade the athletic director showed us [boys] a movie about mating; the birds and bees movie. The athletic director was giggling just like the rest of us. When the movie was over, he asked if anyone had any questions. One boy asked a question concerning girls. The class roared and that was the end of that. Later my mother told my father to tell me about girls. He took me aside and said: 'You know all about girls, don't you?' I said: 'Sure, Dad,' and that was the end of that. In church they told us that we would get sex education in school. No one really told us anything. *Everyone was passing the buck.*" We heard the same kind of dissatisfaction in different variations, many, many times. In their struggle with one of the most important aspects of their growing up, the students received very little help from the adult world.

Conclusion

We found that the modal teen-ager moves slowly in the direction of heterosexuality. Our subjects were physically well developed. The individual psychodynamics vary, but we can safely say that in general the modal adolescent has been limited in his range of sexual experiences.

7

Response to Special Crises

During the high-school years, our 73 subjects have had their share of expectable traumatic events. Thirteen have experienced major life crises. Among these, four had lost their fathers; three of our subjects' parents were divorced during the boys' high-school years; two subjects have had serious, life-threatening injuries; and one saw his brother crippled for life.

We would like to give two examples that illustrate how the teen-agers attempted to master these crises. But first we want to stress that none of the teen-agers in this group developed clinical syndromes as a result of the trauma. They were not part of the group of seven subjects whom we found to be clinically disturbed.*

---

* An exception is one subject whose mother died shortly before his first appointment with us. Reacting strongly to her death, he canceled the appointment and refused to make another. All attempts to get him to come back failed, despite the fact that his father encouraged him to cooperate.

The Case of Dave

Dave was a pleasant-looking teen-ager who related with ease to the interviewer. He was rated an average student by the teachers, and had great hopes of going to college and becoming a physical-education major. His grades were slightly above average and Dave stated that he and his parents were satisfied with his performance. Dave was quite genial, a good mixer, went out with girls relatively early (starting in the freshman year), and in the sophomore year was going steady with his girl friend. He was on the football team and was very proud of his athletic achievements. In general, Dave impressed the interviewer as a person with relatively few psychological conflicts who functioned well within his environment.

Dave was examined by the psychologist when he was sixteen years old. He noted that Dave was a young man of average intelligence who, though cautious in his dealings with people and reluctant to present himself as different from others, was fairly free, assertive, and spontaneous. The psychologist's interview notes follow:

> Within the limits of what is acceptable, he does what he wants and what he feels is right. From time to time he pulls back from this position, lest he be considered an oddball or lest he hurt the feelings of people close to him. Then when his needs are threatened, he becomes anxious and solves the problem temporarily by becoming critical of extraneous or irrelevant aspects of the environment. As he becomes more sure of himself and of the response he elicits from others his freedom increases. Part of the reason for this moving back and forth is that sometimes, when he feels pressure, he acts on the basis of poor judgment and gets himself into some difficulty.
>
> Although Dave is concerned about his confusion as to whether he is a child or an adult, he does know that behavior based on the confusion or out of a need to assert his adulthood is of little value. He is sensitive to the fact that adults have reasons and that it is important for him to understand what they are experiencing. The impression he gives is that of a youngster ready to feel put down by adults but ready also to reflect on this feeling and test out its reality.

He probably then bends over backward and is likely to take the initiative in settling the problem.

He expects relationships to be transient: people get angry and part, people die and thus leave, children grow up and leave their parents. He makes light of his anxiety around separation—he plays it cool—but the preoccupation about separation is real and almost omnipresent. What seems very important to Dave is that once a separation takes place, you've got to go about your business, and if you do this, then things are bound to turn out well. He does not deny the sadness about separation—he accepts it as an expectable part of life and feels that out of the separation arises an opportunity to function independently.

Right now the general picture is that of a very conscientiously controlled young man, but one able to function constructively, independently, and assertively. He is tuned in to his feelings, and on reflection is able to change his course of behavior to one that is most practical for himself and others. He is somewhat limited in his interests and what he allows himself to get involved with, but does not move away from the challenge of new experiences.

During his junior year, a few months after the interview recounted above, Dave had a serious injury and was unconscious for several hours. Fortunately for him, he was within a few blocks of a hospital. Even luckier for him, the appropriate specialists happened to be present at the hospital at the time.

When I (Offer) saw Dave six weeks later, Dave was smiling and didn't seem greatly different from his usual self. Since I was not living in the community, I was not aware of what had happened. The boy had a kind of sly smile on his face, and I assumed he wondered when I was going to ask the obvious question. Since the question was not coming, he finally said, after I had asked him several routine questions like "How are you?" and "Anything new in your life?": "You know, Dr. Offer, I was supposed to die."

This shocking statement did catch me off balance, not without some pleasure to Dave. He then told what had happened and said, "You know, I'm going to have a substitute put in here. It's kind of a funny feeling to have part of you missing. I guess I can't be as active in sports as I used to be. I love football but I guess

I'll have to give it up. Maybe I'll have to become an intellectual like you."

What was dramatic was that Dave felt, "Well, I had a bad break. I can't blame anyone. It's just the way things are. I'll have to make the best of it." He changed his interests and knew that he could not have the kind of career he originally wanted to have. The crisis changed Dave's outlook on himself and may have caused him to make the leap from childhood to adulthood sooner. He adapted rather well.

The Case of Larry

The second example is that of Larry, whose father died during his junior year. Larry had been a jolly, slender boy, who always related well, had many jokes to tell, and liked to stay and talk for a long time. It was easy to develop a relationship with him throughout the years, and he always seemed to us to be a good-natured and not very serious person. He had many boy friends and would have someone waiting for him to "walk home with him" after the interview. He did not date in the first two years of high school; when asked about his opinion of girls or sex, he would respond with a joke. He seemed to alleviate whatever anxiety he had with jokes. He thought that life was fun. He had no specific plans except that he wanted to go to college.

Larry had his psychological testing when he was sixteen years old. He was described thus at the time:

> Larry is a very bright, imaginative young man who is unsure of himself and his abilities. The feelings of inadequacy are real, but Larry is able to use them for the support he needs. He is a very reflective young man who evaluates all aspects of a situation in determining what it means to him. This does not preclude spontaneity and an ease in expressing his feelings. He is able to see relationships within disparate elements of situations and to use these relationships constructively in dealing with the situations.

Larry is interested in getting close to people and sustaining relationships. When his anxiety rises with people, he does not move away but rather deals directly with the situation, adding a strong element of humor. His easy access to humor makes the mechanism of undoing a very constructive way for him to handle difficult situations. He jokes and meets the situation head-on, and thus the experience of anxiety comes to be minimal.

Despite a tendency to impulsiveness, control is a very important value for this young man. The impulsiveness tends to be limited to gross attitudinal statements on feelings; as far as specific behavior is concerned he is thoughtful, weighing consequences and unlikely to act on the basis of a lapse in judgment. He has to work to maintain this kind of control, and some limitation to his gratifications results. However, Larry is not a limited, bound-up young man; he is strongly oriented to what is real in the world and how his needs and feelings might best fit in with that reality. For example, he belittles and becomes impatient with adult authority talking down to him. His solution is to sit quietly, make the adults feel they have some impact, and then compromise. But the compromise is not spoken—they are to think he has done what they want.

Although cautious with others, Larry is honest with himself. His defenses of undoing and compromise are strong and work well, and he is not an anxious young man. Rather he meets the world quite comfortably, sometimes with his fists up; but since part of that is in his wit, people don't hit back. His ability to look over situations, to keep seeing what's involved, leads to a constant re-evaluation of what he is doing and its effect, and this in turn shows up in an attitude of general flexibility.

When Larry was seventeen years old, his father died suddenly of a heart attack. In his fall interview of the senior year, Larry told us about the death of his father. He seemed much more mature than in the past, and he had also gained some weight. He said, "My father died last July from a heart illness. He was fifty years old. My mother is forty-eight. I was unprepared for his dying, as was my mother. He had never been sick before—and here, all of a sudden, he was gone. He supported us well but left almost no money. I worked all summer to support my mother and myself. We had a financial problem since my father was not very good with money. I just could not understand it. I am still a little bitter about his dying. Most of my friends have their fathers. We're going to move to New York or Boston, we haven't decided yet. We feel that we'll have more chance there." Larry was asked whether there was anything worrying him at present. He said, "Of course I miss my father and I miss the guidance that someone like him could give me, but I also worry about financial problems. I want to go to school; I have to go to school and yet I also have to help support my mother. I'd like to tell you that I moved from the lower quarter academically to the upper half last year. I really am doing well although I'm under much more stress; but, on the other hand, my social life has been very minimal and I haven't been able to go out as much as I like. You might like to hear, Dr. Offer, that I have a new hobby, chess playing. Maybe I think that in the East they do it more."

The subject stated that he would miss the project and would miss the relationship with me, and he said that he hoped I would write to him and tell him how the project was doing. In parting he said with a big smile, "I want you to know that I'm not moving to New York just to get away from you." It is of interest to add that this subject has continued in the project although he is now living on the East Coast. We last heard from him after he had finished the first year of college.

It was our impression that Larry handled the loss of his father in an adaptive way (Wolfenstein, 1966, describes a similar case). There was no evidence that the father was overidealized, and hence Larry could express ambivalent feelings toward him. Larry accepted the finality of the loss and mobilized all his resources to help the acute (realistic) situation. We did not observe any regressive pull on this subject. A full comprehension of the meaning of Larry's father's death to him is beyond the scope of this study. Whether he actually mourned his father we do not know. But we can state unequivocally that Larry adapted as well as could be expected. Follow-up study of two years later supports this view.

Concluding Remarks

These two examples are not unique. They illustrate the way in which our modal adolescents coped with situations of extreme stress. They were not always as successful as these two cases suggest. Nonetheless, it has been our distinct impression that our subjects were able to cope with the stressful situations that came their way and to make the best of the situation. The subjects did not ignore or spend most of their energies denying the reality of the trauma. They were flexible enough to be able to change their goals when the situation required it. Their actions, which were almost always goal-directed, were propelled by a relatively strong ego that allowed for change and adaptation—even in midstream. This kind of ego resiliency, which we will discuss in greater detail in Chapter 13, was what made it possible for them to change their life styles and eventually derive their pleasures from newly created sources.

8

Affects and Their Vicissitudes

The Experience of Affects

The affects of anxiety, depression, shame, guilt, and anger are crucial in any stage of life. Our everyday life experiences elicit these affects and they are handled differently by each of us. Affective responses depend on many variables, from a genetic (biological) predisposition to the ability to cope, strength of ego, and the cultural modes for the outlet of feelings. We have not followed our adolescent subjects daily or even weekly, and hence there are limitations in our knowledge of the more rapid cycles of affect in our subjects. However, our cumulative observations of our 73 subjects did enable us to observe trends and consistent modes of handling affect among them. We have conducted more than 600 psychiatric interviews with our adolescent sample. Hence, we had the opportunity to talk to our subjects under many different circumstances. We will illustrate the kind of affective states which our subjects manifested with select examples from our interview material, as well as by the more structural rating scale.

We asked the students in our Third Psychiatric Interview, which took place at the end of the sophomore year, to describe to us their experiences with feelings of anxiety, depression, shame, and guilt. We gave the students a one-sentence definition of the affect. (See Appendix 2, Third Psychiatric Interview.) We then waited for an example, which was volunteered by more than 90 per cent. After the teen-ager gave the specific example, we explored his answer in detail. We wanted to know things like "How common is this feeling? How long does it last? How uncomfortable is it? What do you do, if anything, to overcome it?" We often asked for elaborations and more information, or possibly even attempted to help a subject understand a particularly distressing feeling.

ANXIETY

Students were likely to be *anxious* before a sports event, before an exam, before a class talk, or before giving a concert. Two also mentioned anxiety before the interview. The adolescents were anxious before performing in front of others—usually outsiders, not relatives. They were anxious about their own abilities; they were anxious about the evaluations others made of them; they were anxious about being part of a group for which they had been chosen. Would they live up to an expectation? Could they make the basket? Would we really find them normal?

What happened to the anxiety, the butterflies in the stomach, the palpitating hearts, the sweaty hands? Action usually overrode the anxiety, because the anxiety was not sufficient to paralyze them into inaction. Instead the anxiety was most often a prelude to performance. The students never characterized the anxiety as crippling. When the outcome of the anxiety-provoking experience was mentioned, we would hear: "I won first prize in the musical competition" or "I'm relaxed now, though." Almost uniformly our interview data indicated the type of anxiety that is facilitative rather than inhibitory in its impact on subsequent behavior.

DEPRESSION

Depression was usually seen as a reaction to a death of a grand-parent, a neighbor, a parent, a friend, or a pet. President Kennedy's death was also mentioned as a cause of depression. Sickness, too, of someone close to them could be the source of depression. Others attributed depression to a failure on their own part to react in a given manner: one boy was depressed because he had quarreled with his girl friend; others became depressed when they did not achieve a given mark on an exam or performed poorly in a team effort. A few times depression was associated with a feeling of rejection. "I felt depressed when my uncle didn't invite me to stay on the farm with him for the summer. He told me before that he would like to have me come."

The duration of the depression was longer than that of the anxiety. It came as a reaction to an event and generally lasted in proportion to the gravity of the event, from a few hours to a few weeks; then it was "forgotten." Obviously, it still was not totally dismissed, and the mention of it to the interviewer was sometimes sufficient to reawaken the affect. Yet it was not, again, a long-term affect that produced marked withdrawal patterns or other behavioral signs associated with severe clinical depressions.

It was interesting, though, that many subjects did dip back to a time when they were much younger for some of their affect examples—particularly depression. Again, this tendency showed the residue or the depth of the feeling despite the claim of having dismissed it. Also there were times when the same event, particularly an act of delinquency, would be mentioned several times, at different points in the different interviews. Perhaps the lessons learned were lessons that the boys felt they needed to remember.

Here is an example of a depression following a recent sickness in the family. The boy was trying to handle the depression without avoiding it. "My father had a heart attack a few weeks ago and he's still in the hospital right now. When he originally was admitted he was put in an oxygen tent. I got quite depressed when that happened but I had to learn to live with it. I think that when you're down it's important to get active and forget about your worries." (Subject was asked whether he worries about his father at present.) "Yes, right after my father's heart attack I didn't sleep for two nights. I was continually thinking about him. Also, I feel much closer to my father now than before he had the heart attack. I also saw it affected my mother very strongly and I think I can be of more help to both my father and my mother. I think that you have to take these kinds of problems straight and tell yourself that you can lick it. Also think about the real danger, for example, that my father may pass away." (At this point in the interview the boy was obviously depressed and would not talk any more about his father.) As an incidental note of interest, after the father recovered from the heart attack the parents were separated and later divorced, while the subject changed his plans for going to college and is at present in the Army.

SHAME

Shame can be cited in relation to peers or the home or even oneself. Generally, the shame was over school or sports issues. There was shame about having done something one should not have done. "I was late to school so had to ask my mother to drive me. I know my father does not like this, and I was ashamed." There was shame over being exposed in an unfortunate position. A good example of the latter was told to us by a subject who broke his leg in an accident during the freshman year. He had a cast up to his mid-thigh and he couldn't wash himself, so his mother had to give him a bath. He felt very ashamed in front of his mother because he was naked in front of her. Another subject stated that he was very upset and very ashamed when by mistake he walked into a women's toilet in a theater and all the girls giggled. The subjects in general had strong feelings about what is right and what is wrong, and they felt ashamed when for some reason they

didn't follow these feelings. Only rarely did we hear that the subjects were ashamed about being with a parent, or ashamed for
something the parents did. Many times, for both shame and guilt,
examples were given of having done something for which others
were blamed or punished. Also examples of having disappointed
someone were given. "I was ashamed when I was caught stealing.
I felt I had let my mother down." Some students cited incidents
where they bragged about something in front of other children.
They felt ashamed about their actions.

GUILT

Guilt is most frequently related to the home. "I argued with
my mother and should not have done it because she is a good
mother, and I shouldn't have opened my mouth to her." It is
amazing how many examples of guilt were associated with not
taking out the garbage. "I had told Mother I forgot to do it, but
that was not true." The dishes rated second in areas of domestic
guilt-raising issues between mother and son, or at least in those
issues mentioned. "Mother told me to wash the dishes, but I
wanted to watch TV; so the dishes stayed dirty and I felt guilty."
Guilt may be a reaction to being caught in a dishonest act. "I told
my parents I was going to a dance and later they found out I had
been out drinking." But often it is a reaction to an inner feeling
or something that is known about oneself and left unconfessed,
as in the garbage example or "I felt guilty when I didn't feed the
dog and knew Mother would do it instead of me." The mother is
mentioned in relation to the affect of guilt far more frequently than
in any other affect example. Among the teen-agers who had a
history of delinquency, more than 80 per cent stated that they had
felt guilty about their activities.

We found that the majority of the associations with guilt had to
do with the home. Probably it was here that the students felt most
obligated, and hence felt guilty when they did not fulfill their
obligations. None of the students seemed to feel guilty about

having missed an appointment with us. Our relationship with them was obviously not strong enough to arouse such feelings.

ANGER

We did not ask specifically about examples of anger but got many examples spontaneously. The students did not have difficulty in expressing anger when they felt it against their peers, girl friends, teachers, or parents. They would blow off steam and then they would get over their anger. As a group, they were not the kind of students who would nurse a grudge or feel anger inside and not express it. For example, if we were late for an appointment the students would not hesitate to ask us the reason or make a sarcastic comment. They would ask us how we would feel if they were late (and at times at the next appointment they tested us in turn).

We found that a large number of our subjects experienced the affect of anger directly, often without any reason that would satisfy them. The students were rarely overwhelmed by their angry feelings and even more rarely lost control of their impulses, i.e., acted on the basis of their angry feelings alone, even though they were worried about this alternative. One subject told us that at times he was afraid that his anger would get hold of him and make him join the wrong (delinquent) crowd. He specifically asked for advice from us. It is interesting to note that his father was a probation officer. Anger was often expressed toward us in the interview situation. A subject would come in and say: "In school there are some students who can't keep from being nosy. They always try to find out things about other people. They are busybodies." Obviously, as we pointed out to the student, he was talking about us, being angry about our inquiring into his private life. Hostility directed implicitly to the interviewers was so common in our project that it almost became second nature to us to discover it and point it out to the student. When a student said at the beginning of the project that "All psychiatrists are nuts but smart," we thanked him for the "smart" but questioned him about the "nuts." This brought out a smile on the subject's face and an elaboration of his feelings about the interview.

A different kind of subdued anger was exemplified by the student who came in for the first interview and when asked about his family responded: "I love everybody in my family. There are no favorites in our family and I am equally loved by everybody. I have no problems with my family and that is all!" The subject was tense. He also sounded angry. The interviewer responded with: "Relax, take it easy—it is well known that we all have problems. What is important is for us to identify them." The soothing effect was immediate. We would not like, however, to leave the reader with the impression that anger was always amenable to interpretations. In one example a subject came half an hour late. He did not apologize. He just answered our inquiries with monosyllables. We tried unsuccessfully to broach the subject of his feelings concerning the project. The subject never returned.

The Case of Jack

Here is an example of one boy's responses to our four affect questions. He used sports as the arena for much of his emotional life.

1. *Anxiety:* I usually feel anxious before a test. If I know the material I don't worry, but if I'm not prepared my hands get sweaty and I feel lousy. Before a basketball game I get butterflies in my stomach and my hands are shaky. I overcome it by facing it. [How?] The moment I get ahold of a ball I feel better. If, as sometimes happens, I don't get hold of a ball at the beginning I stay anxious for a long time, sometimes throughout the game. The best way for me to relax is to take shots; even if I don't score I usually feel more relaxed.

2. *Depression:* When I was with my girl friend I always got in a fight with her [he blushes]. I was cutting her off continuously and finally broke with her. I felt depressed, kind of blue. I took out other girls but thought a lot about "my girl." Then after a few

weeks I completely overcame it. [How?] By going back with her.

3. *Shame:* I have a lousy temper and sometimes lose control of myself during a game. For example, the other day the referee called a foul on a guy who elbowed me. Though this was nothing to be angry about I lost my temper and cursed the other guy. I gave him a real hard time. Later, when I went back to the stands, I felt ashamed. I thought I had made a fool of myself in front of the other guys.

4. *Guilt:* A few weeks ago we lost the game by only two points. I had the ball last, took a shot but didn't make it. I felt the whole game depended on me. I usually make it under similar circumstances. My friends tried to tell me that I should not feel bad, but I did feel bad because I thought that they felt I was trying to hog all the shooting. I felt kind of guilty until the next time we had a game one week later.

Stabilized and Pleasurable Affect

What do they like to do? This was the source easiest to tap. They brought their hobbies and their pastimes into the conversations unsolicited. In direct questions, the responses were there. Thus, on their favorite subject in school: "Math" or "Math and science— although I enjoy physical education the best." That nearly all were able to cite specific courses did indicate some enthusiasm over at least a part of their school work. Also, although most found studying to be a problem area, the majority (see Appendix 3) claimed that they did enjoy studying by themselves.

Hobbies such as building mechanical devices brought pleasure to several of the boys. A few enjoyed making model cars; others spent hours fixing cars. One boy told us both his mother and father had cars. He liked to take care of his mother's car, which, he added, was a pretty red. Sports were realms shared by father and son. Not all were team-oriented sports. In fact, the closest father-son relationships might be connected with hunting or fishing. "My father favors me over my two sisters because we can go hunting together."

What about girls? Some said that girls did not interest them, and frequently we heard in the freshman-year interviews: "I don't date." "But is there anything you like about girls?" The response would be a blush. Then, sometimes, "Their figures," or "They are pretty." We asked one student if his mother was pretty. His response: "I never thought about it, but yes, she is. She definitely is." This response was followed by a need for assurance that the interviews were strictly confidential.

They would eagerly await reporting an improvement in grades. Interviews might open with "I got an A in English," or "This year I raised my average."

The students not only manifested an ability to derive a sense of satisfaction from their work but also were eager to share their pleasures with others, whether peers or adults. They would bring a cherished item to the interview. One student who was particularly adept at mechanics brought a very complicated toy to the session. He wanted to show the interviewer exactly how it worked and took pride in setting it up in the room. Another boy, active in the school dramatics club, shared with us a set of pictures which were taken of a show he had helped direct. Students often came dressed in their football uniforms because they "didn't have enough time to change clothes between practice and the appointment." That may have been true, but obviously the students enjoyed coming dressed in their uniforms and telling us about football practice and their participation in various games.

It was, however, in the students' ability to laugh at themselves and others that they displayed their most striking ability to enjoy life. The range of humor was broad, although we rarely encountered a purely sexual joke. The students would often answer one of our questions with a joke. When one student was asked about his dating pattern, he acted as if he were going to go over to the telephone and said, "Wait until I call up my girl friend and ask her if it is all right for me to talk about her with you." On one occasion when Marcus came to the school for his scheduled six interviews, he saw that all of his subjects were sitting in the waiting room. Each of them told him that he had the first appointment (3:30 P.M.). Marcus thought that our secretary must have made a mistake and apologized profusely to the subjects. But Marcus noticed that they seemed to enjoy the incident rather than being perturbed. Finally one of the teen-agers said with a grin: "We all came together just to see how a psychiatrist acts under stress"—and they exploded with laughter.

The Symptom Rating Scale

In rating symptoms, our purpose has been to discover the extent to which we, as clinicians, observed the presence or absence of

TABLE 8–1

Frequency Distributions, Means, and Variances for the Symptom Rating Scales

SCALE	RATING					MEAN	VARIANCE
	1	2	3	4	5		
1. Depression	1	37	34	0	1	2.48	0.31
2. Anxiety	0	17	46	9	1	2.92	0.41
3. Shame	2	42	28	1	0	2.38	0.32
4. Guilt	1	51	21	0	0	2.27	0.23
5. Phobia	11	55	6	1	0	1.96	0.29
6. Dissociation	10	62	1	0	0	1.88	0.14
7. Distortion	8	62	3	0	0	1.93	0.15
8. Turmoil	1	68	4	0	0	2.04	0.07
9. Suspicion	9	53	10	1	0	2.06	0.31
10. Obsession	2	37	31	3	0	2.48	0.39
11. Compulsion	2	48	19	4	0	2.34	0.39
12. Acting out	2	35	29	7	0	2.56	0.50

NOTE: The ratings range from 1, no manifestation of symptom, to 5, extreme manifestation.

symptoms in our subjects. We are familiar with evaluating these symptoms in the group of disturbed teen-agers whom we have been diagnosing and treating in our clinical practice. We selected the twelve most common symptoms (or defenses) which we encountered in working with disturbed adolescent populations. The ratings were done by each of the psychiatrists after the fifth psychiatric interview, at the end of the junior year. They were to be all-inclusive, attempting to evaluate the presence of each of the symptoms as rated from all five interviews combined. We were looking for a subjective clinical evaluation of our subjects. In studying the results of the ratings, we immediately note that the vast majority of our subjects were rated within the average range for all the twelve symptoms. In spite of the clustering of the ratings between 1 and 4, we factor-analyzed the symptom rating scale in an attempt to discover the major dimensions underlying symptom variability in our sample.

The factor analysis was performed in the following way. Pearson

TABLE 8-2

Factor Analysis of the Symptom Rating Scale

SCALE	LOADING		I	II	III
		Factor I (Anxiety)			
6	.88	Dissociation		09	18
7	.83	Distortion		—03	16
5	.78	Phobia		14	11
9	.74	Suspicion		13	13
2	.59	Anxiety		37	45
		Factor II (Obsessive-compulsion)			
10	.88	Obsession	01		09
11	.88	Compulsion	04		06
1	.48	Depression	17		44
		Factor III (Turmoil)			
8	.76	Turmoil	—09	23	
4	.70	Guilt	26	01	
3	.61	Shame	31	21	
12	.38	Acting out	30	—04	

NOTE: Factor II differentiates hysterical and obsessive-compulsive characters; other factors do not.

product moment correlations were computed among the twelve symptom ratings made for the sample of the 73 subjects. The matrix of intercorrelations was then factor-analyzed by use of the principal-components method, with unities in the major diagonal. The factor-analytic procedure followed a sequence outlined by K. Howard (see Appendix I, p. 238). Factor extraction was halted

TABLE 8-3

Intercorrelation Matrix for Symptom Rating Scales

SCALE	1	2	3	4	5	6	7	8	9	10	11	12
1		42	42	28	30	16	16	25	13	33	36	19
2			55	44	51	54	48	35	48	34	31	20
3				32	37	36	31	36	25	22	17	18
4					37	35	25	35	26	11	10	24
5						67	52	01	48	10	17	17
6							72	05	58	02	−05	32
7								17	67	02	04	30
8									17	30	25	17
9										08	16	36
10											67	01
11												16

NOTE: Decimal points omitted. $N = 73$.

when two of the principal component factors had latent roots (eigenvalues) below 1.00. The extracted factors were then rotated by the use of Varimax and a search for specific factors was made. If a specific factor was found, the rotation was repeated with one less factor. This rotation procedure continued until there were no specific factors. Five factors accounting for 76.45 per cent of the total variance were extracted and rotated through the Varimax procedure. Both the five-factor and four-factor rotated solutions produced a specific factor (with only one symptom rating having its highest loading on this factor), so the first three factors were rotated and this solution retained.

The symptom rating scale was then scored for three summative factor scales, each consisting of those symptom ratings which had their highest rotated factor loading on that factor. Each symptom rating was given unit weight. In all cases these are salient loadings, exceeding .45.

The three factor scales obtained appear to be meaningful clinically. They include the following: Factor I: *Anxiety*, which can be interpreted as a generalized response to stress with severe anxiety, hence the relatively more serious symptoms of phobia, dissociation and distortion. Factor II: *Obsessive-compulsion* is

TABLE 8-4

Means, Variance, and t-Tests for the Symptom Rating Scales for the Modal Adolescents from the Two High Schools

| SYMPTOM | HIGH SCHOOL A | | HIGH SCHOOL B | | |
	Mean	Variance	Mean	Variance	t
Depression	2.50	0.35	2.45	0.26	0.39
Anxiety	2.91	0.50	2.93	0.28	−0.14
Shame	2.50	0.39	2.21	0.17	2.21*
Guilt	2.27	0.25	2.28	0.21	−0.03
Phobia	1.98	0.35	1.93	0.11	0.36
Dissociation	1.89	0.15	1.86	0.12	0.27
Distortion	1.95	0.14	1.90	0.17	0.63
Turmoil	2.02	0.07	2.07	0.07	−0.74
Suspicion	2.02	0.35	2.11	0.25	−0.63
Obsession	2.45	0.44	2.52	0.33	−0.42
Compulsion	2.36	0.47	2.31	0.29	0.35
Acting out	2.52	0.49	2.62	0.53	−0.58
Factor					
I. Anxiety	10.75	4.57	10.66	3.59	0.19
II. Obsession-compulsion	7.32	2.69	7.28	1.28	0.12
III. Turmoil	9.32	2.08	9.17	1.58	0.44

* $p \le .05$.

closely tied with depression. Factor III: *Turmoil* goes along mainly with guilt and shame. These three factors tell us then that our teen-agers, although not showing any serious affective disorders, can be differentiated from each other even on the basis of the *minimal* symptoms they have demonstrated.

We correlated the three factor scores with our other variables, and found that Factor I correlated with dating behavior in the freshman year ($r = -.29$; $p < .01$). In other words, the more anxiety a subject demonstrated, the less likely it was that he would go out on a date. By the junior year the anxiety factor drops out ($r = .02$) and the correlation between dating and Factor II becomes significant ($r = -.20$; $p < .01$). The obsessive-compulsive teen-agers were dating less by their junior year. When measuring the strength of the subjects' responsiveness in their relationship with us (see Chapter 10), we found that Factor I did not correlate

$(r = -.04)$ but both Factors II $(r = .23)$ and III $(r = .23)$ correlated significantly $(p < .01)$ with the ability to develop a relationship: the less obsessive-compulsive depression and turmoil, the better the relationship with us. But the presence of anxiety did not make it easier or more difficult to develop a relationship with our subjects (see Chapter 10). Some teen-agers came closer to us when experiencing anxiety and some withdrew from the relationship. The three factors did not correlate significantly with delinquent behavior, scholastic achievement, or teachers' ratings.

Conclusion

We have found that when examining the subjects' feelings, we did not note any marked fluctuation between the affects. Neither did we notice serious or debilitating forms of anxiety or depression among our subjects. The feelings of anxiety or depression were transient and were always coped with adequately. Anger was expressed when felt, and was not allowed to build up to the point where loss of controls was the only way out. We have described guilt and shame as experienced by many in our group. We were impressed by the relative attenuation of these affects and, over time, by the overwhelming number of adolescents who were not operating under great pressures of guilt and shame. Despite the relative lack of manifestation of symptoms, a factor analysis of the symptom rating scale generated three clinically meaningful factors, which we termed Anxiety, Obsessive-compulsive, and Turmoil.

The students were introspective and able to communicate with themselves and others. They were aware of many affective experiences and were able to describe them in detail. We believe that the majority of our subjects experienced these affects autoplastically, without necessarily resorting to the group to resolve their conflicts. Finally, they experienced pleasurable affects from the achievements and relationships with others.

9

Psychological Testing:
Thematic Apperception Test, Rorschach Test, and WAIS Vocabulary Scale
by Paul R. Singer

The application of psychological tests to normal populations presents special problems and special opportunities. The opportunities are readily apparent. To understand more fully the means with which normal people cope with everyday experiences and with their own unique problems is to understand in basic terms what makes for normality. Projective tests afford an evaluation of how their world looks to people, how they see themselves in relation to their world, and how they deal with their world. If a continuum of normality is definable in terms of such processes, then a definition of normality, though a complex one, arises from an examination of such testing of normal people.

Problematic issues, however, are quick to arise. For the most part, our everyday use of projective techniques is restricted to abnormal populations. The tests are used to understand the particulars and sources of pathology. It is largely within the range of psychopathology that our understanding and theorizing about projective techniques has taken place. The concepts with which we deal with projective test data are, then, concepts relevant to psychopathology. The application of projective tests to normal groups runs whatever risks may lie in applying concepts relevant to psychopathology to categories of normal functioning. For example, we must evaluate afresh the meaning of ordinarily pathological signs in a normal population. Poor form quality of percepts on the Rorschach of a person we know to have been defined as normal (and hence perceiving the world with reasonable accuracy) will present us with a very serious conceptual problem. To suggest that this normal person has a serious ego defect is to chase one's tail and to choose sides in a game that cannot be won. A much more cogent question has to be the meaning of this score in terms of his total integration into a state we have defined as normal. The issue is one that has important implications for psychological-test theory.

In our 73-subject sample, then, it is meaningless to comment on the normality or pathology of a particular Rorschach protocol. In effect, all the tests from these boys are normal (given our original selection of the sample), and it is our responsibility, at the very least, to ascertain what coping mechanisms are evident that allow normal functioning in the face even of levels of anxiety traditionally viewed as high and in the face of personality factors reflected as psychological test variables traditionally viewed as morbid or disturbed. Projective material of normal adolescents must indeed reflect their normality. It would seem most prudent to approach the test data freshly, attempting to discard our prejudicial expectations of what a normal Rorschach, for example, should look like in view of what we know about the Rorschachs of abnormal populations. The issues are to find ways to use the tests most constructively to enhance our understanding of the ways normal adolescents handle themselves and their environmental tasks.

Testing Procedure

The Rorschach, the Thematic Apperception Test (TAT), and the Vocabulary subtest of the Wechsler Adult Intelligence Scale (WAIS) were the instruments chosen for investigating with standard psychological procedures the personality functioning of this adolescent sample. This choice was determined by the generally wide use of the tests, allowing comparison with other groups now and in the future. It was felt, too, that this combination of tests yielded a rather full picture of a subject's personality functioning—his conflicts, his mode of coping and handling his situation, his fantasy, his psychological assets, his vulnerabilities, his concepts of himself and others.

Pressure of time made the use of additional tests formidable; it was thus felt that the Vocabulary subtest, since it correlates very well with total score on the WAIS, was a relatively quick way to approximate general level of intelligence, especially in view of the relative homogeneity of educational and social backgrounds in this sample.

It was decided, also, to restrict the number of TAT cards—to use those cards which were most likely to deal with conflict areas common to our sample. It was important, however, that the same cards be used with each of the subjects tested. Seven cards (1, 15, 3BM, 6BM, 4, 10, 7BM) were chosen as the battery of TAT stimuli for this sample. The pictures on these cards are described as follows (Murray, 1943):

   1. A young boy is contemplating a violin which rests on a table in front of him.
   15. A gaunt man with clenched hands is standing among gravestones.
3BM. On the floor against a couch is the huddled form of a boy with his head bowed on his right arm. Beside him on the floor is a revolver.

6BM. A short elderly woman stands with her back turned to a tall young man. The latter is looking downward with a perplexed expression.

4. A woman is clutching the shoulders of a man whose face and body are averted as if he were trying to pull away from her.

10. A young woman's head against a man's shoulder.

7BM. A gray-haired man is looking at a younger man who is sullenly staring into space.

All subjects were tested by the same person, a clinical psychologist with extensive training and experience in psychological testing. An attempt was made to test each subject as close to his sixteenth birthday as convenient to the schedule of the examiner. Because each subject was to be seen for only one testing session and because the subjects varied in the amount of time needed for each test, not all subjects were given all tests. In total, the Rorschach was administered to 74 subjects, the Thematic Apperception Test to 63, and the Vocabulary Scale of the WAIS to 54. All three tests were administered to 46 subjects, the Rorschach and TAT only to 17, the Rorschach and Vocabulary Scale only to 8, and the Rorschach alone to 3. The procedures involved in the testing are elaborated in Appendix 20.

Thematic Apperception Test

The kinds and styles of the stories given as responses to the Thematic Apperception Test displayed considerable homogeneity in this group. Although there is a great deal of variability in the nuances of the stories these boys tell, one is very impressed by the commonality of main themes. For each picture, a large percentage of the sample gives only few varieties of stories. Thus for Card 1, over and over again, the *mother* has just given the boy a violin, although he had wanted a different kind of gift; he decides either to practice in spite of his not wanting to because she will insist, or to do nothing and to say that he had practiced during that time; when his *parents* realize he is not interested, they regret having pushed this on their son and force the issue no longer. For Card 15, when the figure is seen as a male, something diabolical is involved (he is robbing graves, or rising out of a grave as a vampire, or hating the person buried there); when the figure is seen as a female, she is mourning the death of close kin (usually in a concentration camp). On Card 7BM, repeatedly, a young man is on trial for a crime he did not commit; he is defended by a wise and able lawyer, but on the basis of perjured testimony is found guilty. Another large group of stories given to this card involve a young man rising in business, sometimes ruthlessly, sometimes kindly, replacing his older superior. And so too for the other four cards used here.

Given this homogeneity of TAT records, it is possible to describe our group on the basis of this test. Although many of the individuals within the sample will vary on discrete issues from a composite portrait, the homogeneity allows such a composite some considerable predictive value. It is worthwhile then to describe this group on the basis of their TATs, if we keep in mind that each statement is not true for some members of the group.

An additional word of caution is necessary before this description is presented. There is a considerable literature about the effects of the test situation on the results of projective tests that indicates that the testing experience itself significantly modifies the subject's response to the test material: see Alden and Benton (1951), Baughman (1961), Bernstein (1956), Gibby, Miller, and Walker (1953), Holtzman (1952), Masling (1960), Schachtel (1966), van Krevelan (1954). A significant aspect of the test experience is in what goes on between the examiner and the subject, overtly and covertly. In this project, the examiner was an attractive adult woman, and it is not unlikely that this fact had some impact on the boys that would carry over to the test responses. Aspects of their feelings and orientation toward mothers, women, and girls may have been stimulated by the test situation, while other aspects of these feelings and orientation may have been suppressed. We cannot know the extent of this effect or what may have been colored; we must, however, consider that parts of our understanding are perhaps exaggerated or de-emphasized by this particular test situation.

The following, then, is a description of the more common personality attributes discernible in the TAT records. Included are typical stories that highlight some of the issues described.

For the most part, their mothers are seen by these boys as sources of solace, comfort, and instruction. They feel considerable warmth and closeness in their relationships with their mothers. Mothers are more understanding and interested than fathers, who are more pragmatic and practical and who are good models, but for the future. Mothers are concerned that their sons do the right and proper things for the immediate situation, while fathers are concerned in their investment for the future. Mothers are willing, even eager, to do for their sons; fathers might offer advice but want their sons to build for themselves. While respectful toward their fathers, even when they are mildly rebellious, these boys are quite ambivalent about their mothers. They cherish and deplore their dependency, and though eager to move out on their own they are reluctant to move away from their mothers' care. Thus:

> This man is this woman's son and he's telling her he's going away. And I think maybe he's lived with her up to this time and he won't be around. Maybe he's gone for a job in some other country or something and it seems like she loves him very much, maybe so much that she's babied him and is wondering if he can get along. . . . I think he goes away and probably proves himself, that he can get along. . . . I think he loves her very much and he wouldn't go away unless it was necessary.

> This fellow looks old enough to be married. This would be his mother. Looks like he's having problems with his wife. Ran away to Mama, I guess. He's consulting his mother, who would probably know more about how to handle a wife—make up to her, etc. She seems a little surprised. She'll probably give him information. He'll go out and make up with his wife. . . . She probably told him to go

out, make up as best he could—probably by not getting so mad at her when she does something wrong, give her a few gifts, take her out to dinner once in a while.

This group of boys has almost ambiguous sexual identifications, and though they can categorize masculine and feminine sexual roles well enough, they are not sure where they themselves fit ("Well, someone, is that a man or a woman?" "It doesn't seem to show enough to know whether it's a girl and boy or two boys or what it is."). When they experience feelings that they see as soft (and these feelings are frequent for them), they feel most unmasculine, that is, unlike their fathers. They communicate and identify more easily with their mothers, but they are certain that when they are older they will be men like their fathers.

Sexuality, though it can be seen as emerging, does not preoccupy these boys. They are certainly concerned about themselves sexually, doubtful of their sexual adequacy now, but hopeful—even confident—that in the future they will make the grade. They give little indication, however, of much investment in the sexual aspects of dating. Rather, girls are seen, like mothers, as potentially understanding and able to control boys so they don't do anything wrong. Girls are capable of good judgment and know better how people get along. ("Looks like a guy in trouble, and he's got a girl friend, and he's done something wrong evidently. She's trying to tell him to go, give himself up or something of that sort. He's not listening to her. He'll probably run, be caught. They'll have him anyway, so he should have listened to her.") Yet girls (again, alas, like mothers) are apt to be faithless. Their faithlessness is not exploitative, but rather more a feeling that any boy will do.

The lack of pressured investment in heterosexual relationships seems in part to result from their expectation that serious involvement with girls will take these boys away from their mothers' interest and care. Although their mothers do not discourage their interest in girls (from the viewpoint of these youngsters, their mothers often encourage it), these boys are again ambivalent about moving away from their mothers. ("Well, this guy is her son and he probably got married and he's ready to move out, out of the house now, and he's probably thinking about when he was a little boy. She's staring out the window. Probably thinking about how much she'll miss him and everything. He'll leave and they'll be sad at first. After a while they'll get over it. Probably still be close.")

There seems to be some concern over their somewhat confused child-adult status. ("Well, he looks rather like he's had a—well, something bad has happened to him, like his birthday party has been called off or he's broken something or else he's angry. Let's see—I'd say his birthday party was called off and—gee, he looks older than that, he looks about, oh, well—oh, gee, I don't know— he didn't get anything for Christmas—it's hard to figure out a story or something. I don't know. Looks like he might have been older than a person who'd be sorry about a birthday party being called off all of a sudden—he looks bigger or something.") On the one hand, independence and taking care of themselves is valued and is a source of pride; on the other hand, working and being on one's own is seen as frustrating and, apart from the pride, does not pay off. In addition, there is considerable self-consciousness about their lack of conviction about what their talents are and what they will be and do as adults. There is almost consistently a nostalgia about the pleasantness of childhood, but at the same time an understanding that they are selective in what they remember. The issue about independence and separation from their parents is compounded for some of these boys by their fear that separation from their parents and making decisions for themselves implies loneliness. It is not only that they look to their parents to do and decide for them, but often, too, to be with them.

Although there is frequently concern over impulses and a wish for controls outside themselves, this concern is not pressing. ("This is the story of a little boy who has just come home from school. He's taking violin lessons, he doesn't like them—wishes he was out playing with the rest of the children. He's thinking about taking the violin and smashing it so he can go out and play, and he's wishing he never would have started taking violin lessons. . . . I think he'll make up his mind to practice, and then go out and play.") Rather there is more frequently an expectation that they will not be understood and that damage can be done them through such misunderstanding. They themselves are aware of their resentments, their anger, and rebellious pushes to establish independence, and for the most part they have little trouble keeping these in check.

Often these boys are quite concerned about subtle questions of morality. Issues dealing with the difference between *good* and *legal* occupy them and they are sometimes concerned that their behavior, though within the law or even overtly justified, is in other terms reprehensible or bad. It seems that they are often willing to assume the responsibility for the fault of things, as though there is always a possibility that they are to blame for untoward events occurring about them. This does not seem to imply a burden of guilt they always carry about and are thus able to set down whenever the opportunity affords itself. Rather they are unable to understand fully the distinction between thoughts and deeds, not as causes of events but as sources of judgments about themselves.

Relationships with their fathers are very complicated. They are willing to settle for the respectful distance they experience with their fathers, but they are not aware that they would like something closer, warmer, and more affectionate. They are not surprised or displeased by their fathers but accept this frustration as minor, as part of reality. They see their fathers as models, and do indeed want to be like them but with enough differences of their own thrown in to make them something more than copies. Examples:

> This is a little boy sitting at a table with a violin. His mother has told him—it's new—the wrapping paper is on the table—his mother bought it for him and told him to practice because his father was a violinist. He's dead now. The boy doesn't know whether

to practice. He knows he should but he doesn't want to. He doesn't want to take up time practicing the *piano* or any musical instrument. He sort of wants to become a famous violinist and so he finally decides to do it. He practices and goes on to become a great violinist.

Johnny Stokes never liked to play the violin. Since his dad was one of the greatest violinists of his day, he expected Johnny to follow in his footsteps. But Johnny didn't exactly like to play the violin, mainly because he thought his fingers were too short to work the strings. Anyway it takes up too much of his time. He would rather do something constructive like playing baseball—or go to school and make better grades than the rest of the class. But there is that violin still there. One day there was a choice of going out with his friends to a party that had been planned for months—more a field trip that the teacher had planned. Johnny made a grave mistake by not practicing the violin before he left. Father wanted him to play the violin before he left. But Johnny didn't exactly have enough time. So his father made him stay home from the field trip and Johnny did his two hours' practice. . . . Johnny didn't know that he was going to be one of the greatest rock 'n' roll violinists of his time. Johnny quit his classical violin and started studying with a professional rock 'n' roll group to become a great rock 'n' roll virtuoso.

The boys readily accept their fathers' values, but even this acceptance has to be shaded into their own terms. These boys, in general, despite their conformity and ready assumption of parental values, want to be recognized as themselves, as unique individuals, rather than as shadows or extensions of anybody. ("A young man and his father, and the father's always trying to help him—never lets him do anything himself. So he went off and stole a car. He decided he'd run away. While driving the car, he hit another boy and killed him. He stopped the car and called the police and he was jailed and when his trial came up, his father got him off for involuntary manslaughter, under false pretenses, and the boy's pretty unhappy because he has to live with himself and he's proven to himself that his father has been wrong.")

Rebellious behavior is limited not only by their reluctance to jeopardize their dependence on their parents and by their routine incorporation of parental behavior, but also because, from their point of view, it's easiest. Parental authority is, after all, parental authority—and in the end, whatever issues one raises, however rebelliously and loudly one asserts one's position, parents have the last word. One must ultimately do what they want and say, so why make noise? They incorporate, too, the code that one must honor one's father and mother, and suggestions by these boys that might dishonor or compromise their parents are alien and uncomfortable and stimulate guilt. They develop a striking capacity for compromise in that they are willing to go along with demands and expectations but often with a twist that makes the behavior uniquely their own, or at least in part on their terms.

There appears to be a good deal of rivalry with their siblings, and the competition they feel is quite open. These boys are not reluctant to feel anger with their siblings and almost literally and overtly to wish them out of the way. It is very clear that in their competition with siblings for maternal affection and for achievement, they do not anticipate that they will come out ahead. ("Just came home, the man did. Found out his wife was seeing another man. The other man was his brother, so he's going to start out and get even with him. . . ." "Looks like maybe this guy could be maybe Lindbergh's brother, if he had a brother. Lindbergh just took off across the Atlantic. They're all—this is Lindbergh's mother, and they're all wondering if he's going to make it to Paris or not. He could be thinking of things that could happen to him while he's in flight. He's probably thinking now what if something goes wrong with the engine—not enough gas—he'd go plunging into the Atlantic. Anything to worry about, he's worrying about.") Although they are open about the competition and anger, it does make them feel somewhat uncomfortable and guilty, but the discomfort and guilt are easily borne.

Perhaps most significant about these protocols is how open these boys are in their stories. Certainly some of them demonstrate a very defensive approach to the task or to specific pictures. ("I might mention here that I never understand this type of art. These lines—I've read a book or two on them. Horizontal and perpendicular lines to draw a picture. I can't really see too much except that this is a graveyard maybe and that this man is rather old. Can't tell you anything.") In the main, however, the richness and openness of the stories would perhaps indicate that the boys in this sample are not unwilling to deal with conflict issues that are of importance to them. They do not close things off from themselves, but rather face straightforwardly the issues of living and cope with them. They are able to trust adults enough to be open with them, and it may be this trust in adults that enables them to be open with themselves. For the most part, these youngsters know themselves well; they know what they feel and what they need, and which of their feelings and needs give them trouble. They admit to themselves how they see their parents, and themselves in relation to them. This openness may, of course, be an artifact of the research alliance developed in this study. Even then, however, their capacity for self-awareness must be present to be elicited by an alliance.

The Rorschach Test

To describe the modal adolescent by elaborating how he "looks" on projective tests is ofttimes indeed a difficult task. We can present averages on a series of test scores, but must be clear what such measures of central tendency imply about all members of the group and how much prediction to individuals can be done on the basis of group norms. Since we have used projective test data to enhance our understanding of individuals, the question of how to use group data is an important one. Also implied is the question whether a composite description of a group based on the averages of their test scores has any meaning.

Table 9-1 is a Rorschach profile of our modal adolescent obtained by the use of median scores. (Medians are used because means would assume equality of units within Rorschach variables,

TABLE 9–1

Medians and Ranges for Rorschach Scores

		R 18 (2–60)		P 4 (1–
W 7 (1–27)	M 2 (0–14)	H + Hd 3 (0–14)		F % 61 (20–1
D 10 (0–41)	FC 0 (0–5)	A + Ad 8 (3–26)		F + % 75 (40–1
Dd 0 (0–13)	CF 1 (0–4)	Other 4 (0–19)		E.A. 5 (0–
S 1 (0– 9)	C 0 (0–4)			Aff. ratio: .305 (.10–
	Sum of C 2(0–17)			
	FY 1 (0–5)			
	Blends 1 (0–6)			

NOTE: A total of 74 subjects received the Rorschach administration; 5 of these 74 did not complete series of interviews and are not included in the analyses of Rorschach and interview data; 4 of the completing the other interviews did not complete the Rorschach.

All Rorschach variables used in this study are derived from Beck (1961). A very brief and perhaps n definition of each of the categories used in this chapter is warranted and may clarify some of the conc and relationships discussed later. These definitions have been put together from Beck.

R: total number of scorable responses.

Location Scores:

W: a response where *all* portions of the blot have been attended to.

D: a response using a portion of the figure that prominently attracts atter to itself—a portion that is commonly selected.

Dd: a response using a portion of the figure rarely selected in relation to o portions of the same figure.

S: a response in which the subject perceives a white space as something meaning, whether in connection with another detail or by itself.

DW: a response in which the subject associates to the entire figure in accord with a form suggested by one of the details.

(DdD similarly works up from a Dd to a D.)

Determinants:

F: a response in which the form alone determines the percept.

$F+$: a response using good form defined on the basis of normative tables.

$F-$: a response using poor form, again defined normatively.

M: a movement association, suggesting activity within the repertoire of hu beings.

C, CF, C: responses in which color is a more or less important determiner of the cept. (The presence and position of F in the score reflects the amount form contributes to the percept.)

Sum of C: the sum of color responses with each response weighted as follows: $C = C = 1.0, FC = 0.5$.

Y, YF, FT: responses in which the shading or grayness of the stimulus determines percept.

V, VF, FV: responses in which the variations of shading assign the percept a th dimensional effect.

T, TF, FT: responses reflecting an experience in which the skin feels directly, i.e textural quality.

Blends: responses in which the subject uses any two or more determinants (in a tion to or apart from F).

Contents:

H: a perception of a human figure.

Hd: a perception of some part of a human.

A: a perception of an animal.

Ad: a perception of some part of an animal.

P: a popular response; those responses most commonly given.

$F\%$: percentage of pure F responses.

$F+\%$: computed as $$\frac{\text{number of } F+}{(\text{number of } F+) + (\text{number of } F-)}$$

Experience balance: presented as a ratio of number of M responses divided by the sum o responses.

Experience actual: addition of the values making up the Experience Balance.

Affective ratio: the percentage of the total number of responses that occur on the las cards—the chromatic cards.

and clinical experience has demonstrated that this is not correct.) The numbers in parentheses are the ranges for each of the categories, i.e., the highest and lowest amounts or scores within our sample. Thus, the median number of whole responses (W) is 7, but the boys in this sample give anywhere from 1 to 27 whole responses.

It is well to compare our findings with previous investigators' normative work with the Rorschach.* Although some of her figures are presented differently from ours, Ames's data (1959) for sixteen-year-old boys are relevant. The Rorschach profile that follows is put together from general data she presents in a form that makes it easily comparable with our data.

TABLE 9–2

Medians for Rorschach Scores of 16-Year-Old Boys as Reported by Ames (1959)

			R 16				
W%	52	M	2	H%	15	P	6
D%	44	FC	0	A%	47	F%	64
Dd%	2	CF	0			F+%	93
		C	0				
		Sum of C	1				
		F(C)	0				

Comparison of the two Rorschach profiles reveals very few actual differences. The number of various determinants used by the boys in each sample is almost identical, as is the amount of attention paid to human- and animal-content categories. (Such similarities are found in studies by Hertz, 1951, and Suares, 1938, on adolescent Rorschachs.) The differences that are clear are in location areas stressed by boys in each sample (that is, in the Ames

* Studies in which data are presented as averages for groups within age ranges of two years or more, such as Hertzman and Margulies (1943) and Rabin and Beck (1950), would be of little comparable relevance here, since Ames's findings demonstrate appreciable Rorschach difference from year to year in adolescence. Studies on girls, such as that of Steiner (1951), or studies on younger children, such as Paulsen's (1943), are also limited in relevance.

TABLE 9-3

Intercorrelations of Rorschach Variables

	App	FC/CF/C	F%	F+%	H+Hd	A+Ad	Other cont.	Exp. bal.	Exp. act.	W/M	Rejections	P	Aff. ratio	H%	Sequence	S	Blends	W
R	.49	.04	.16	-.29	.71	.78	.83	-.02	.59	.28	-.40	.48	.03	-.05	.40	.73	.22	.25
App		.01	.28	-.02	.45	.39	.31	-.03	.07	.45	-.21	.24	.05	.13	.17	.33	-.08	-.28
FC/CF/C			.08	-.13	.02	.08	.03	-.06	.00	.13	.08	.11	-.10	.05	-.11	-.04	-.03	.05
F%				.17	.13	.27	-.02	.09	-.50	.02	.24	.14	.01	.06	-.07	-.03	-.49	-.50
F+%					-.12	-.20	-.35	-.04	-.26	.06	.16	.08	-.02	.09	-.27	-.32	-.32	-.33
H + Hd						.55	.40	-.36	.53	.51	-.27	.53	-.04	.60	.40	.53	.07	.23
A + Ad							.47	-.20	.33	.32	-.33	.56	.15	-.12	.29	.57	.09	.10
Other content								.25	.60	.06	-.38	.17	-.01	-.28	.32	.64	.30	.32
Experience balance									-.14	-.52	.11	.35	.06	-.42	-.02	-.07	-.00	-.13
Experience actual										.30	-.37	.21	.05	.06	.32	.61	.66	.69
W/M											-.22	.35	.00	.36	.06	.20	.08	-.24
Rejections												-.10	-.32	.07	-.33	-.34	-.21	-.14
P													.12	.24	.16	.26	-.08	-.04
Affective ratio														-.05	-.07	-.06	-.07	-.06
H%															.13	-.10	-.21	-.02
Sequence																.39	.38	.26
S																	.46	.41
Blends																		.61
W																		
D																		
Dd																		
M																		
FC																		
CF																		
C																		
DW																		
DdD																		
Sum of C																		
FY																		
YF																		
Y																		
FV																		
VF																		
FT																		
TF																		
A%																		

group there is more stress on whole responses, while in our sample the stress is on large details); in form quality (that is, in the Ames group, form quality expressed as $F + \%$ is much better than in our sample), and in number of popular responses. It would seem, however, that these apparent differences are to be explained as an artifact of the particular scoring system employed in each study. Ames comments that her study tends "to score W somewhat more

D	Dd	M	FC	CF	C	DW	DdD	Sum C	FY	YF	Y	FV	VF	FT	TF	A%	Sum C/R
.94	.77	.32	.30	.27	.51	.01	−.12	.58	.40	.45	.52	.00	.00	−.06	.16	−.31	−.13
.57	.58	.01	.04	.00	.08	−.11	−.09	.09	.01	.04	.15	−.10	−.10	.07	−.03	−.18	−.19
.05	.06	.04	−.15	−.26	.10	−.04	−.24	−.04	−.21	.04	.17	.01	.07	.00	.10	.06	−.15
.32	.31	−.43	−.11	−.23	−.29	−.12	.02	−.31	−.37	−.22	−.23	−.52	−.19	−.24	−.14	.27	.60
−.17	−.24	−.14	−.16	−.10	−.25	−.08	−.12	−.25	−.20	−.29	−.31	−.01	−.09	−.29	−.21	.23	−.13
.66	.51	.56	.27	−.03	.26	.02	−.16	.26	.29	.16	.38	−.12	−.15	.02	.05	−.34	−.28
.79	.55	.32	.36	.00	.13	.07	−.13	.19	.24	.13	.30	.12	.00	.05	.14	.24	−.34
.73	.70	.16	.23	.40	.70	−.02	−.02	.76	.37	.56	.58	.05	.00	.02	.21	−.51	.17
−.03	.21	−.64	.07	.41	.34	−.16	.00	.43	−.10	.14	.05	−.02	.00	.01	.02	−.11	.52
.38	.30	.76	.37	.30	.72	.11	−.05	.74	.44	.34	.63	.21	.06	.17	.37	−.43	.38
.39	.23	.56	−.01	−.06	−.08	.03	.04	−.09	.10	−.11	.08	−.11	−.17	−.07	−.05	−.10	−.27
−.37	−.26	−.26	−.25	−.17	−.24	.09	.07	−.29	−.26	−.24	−.25	−.18	−.01	−.28	−.13	.25	−.12
.52	.34	.29	.12	.05	−.03	.00	−.14	.03	.18	.06	.05	.16	.04	−.11	−.01	.06	−.37
.06	.04	.00	.13	.14	.01	−.11	.00	.09	−.20	−.13	−.09	−.03	−.12	.00	−.01	.06	.08
−.04	−.04	.32	−.02	−.34	−.13	−.08	−.11	−.23	−.07	−.16	−.09	−.23	−.22	−.16	−.08	−.24	−.28
.30	.34	.20	.33	.10	.23	.00	−.10	.29	.46	.28	.18	.13	.14	.07	.17	−.23	.00
.60	.58	.42	.21	.18	.48	−.04	−.01	.50	.39	.40	.52	.12	.06	.23	.22	−.24	.02
.02	.03	.50	.35	.19	.47	.21	−.01	.49	.48	.21	.47	.34	.50	.34	.46	−.27	.40
−.06	.12	.58	.31	.04	.51	.20	−.12	.47	.35	.33	.49	.25	.26	.35	.30	−.23	.29
	.74	.18	.22	.24	.30	−.01	−.08	.40	.33	.35	.36	−.05	−.09	−.04	.05	−.22	−.26
		−.03	.13	.27	.45	−.17	−.10	.50	.14	.34	.36	−.15	−.06	−.06	.14	−.27	−.07
			.25	−.09	.18	.22	−.01	.14	.03	.06	.34	.18	.02	.13	.27	−.15	−.06
				.02	.17	.06	−.08	.29	.16	−.08	.30	.10	.03	.15	.22	−.02	.12
					.21	−.06	.13	.55	.28	.22	.20	.05	.05	−.07	.01	−.30	.44
						−.04	−.10	.91	.25	.46	.59	.12	.05	.17	.30	−.48	.58
							.22	−.05	.07	−.06	.02	.24	.30	−.06	.02	.10	−.08
								−.04	.02	−.13	−.09	−.18	−.09	.00	−.06	−.02	.03
									.34	.44	.60	.12	.06	.11	.27	−.49	.63
										.31	.25	.32	.15	.12	.01	−.27	.10
											.23	.16	.18	.05	.10	−.38	.10
												.15	.05	.19	.26	−.35	.27
													.20	.09	.14	.10	.22
														.19	.22	−.04	.04
															.21	−.12	.12
																−.10	.15
																	−.33

liberally than do some American authors, notably Beck." Since
we used Beck's criteria (1961), it is understandable that our sample demonstrates fewer responses scored as wholes. Scoring of
$F + \%$ in the Ames study is determined primarily by Hertz's
tables (1951) which may be viewed as less stringent than Beck's
norms; thus in the Ames study there is to be expected a higher
$F + \%$ than in ours, irrespective of the form quality itself. With

regard to popular responses, there is little difference for standards of scoring in the two studies, and it may be that the sample Ames dealt with was simply somewhat more conforming or socially minded than ours.

To return to Table 9–1, the picture these median scores give us is that of a rather restricted person who, though not having fully integrated societal demands, is rather easy and stereotyped in his thinking, insensitive to both what goes on in him and to what others are like and want. His thinking is gross, missing not only nuances of situations but also very practical considerations. He has limited interests, probably resulting from the rather tight control and defensiveness he exerts. He has the capacity for ideational and planning activity and does this constructively. Feelings are communicated moderately, but their expression is likely to be without much thought about their effect.

The question arises as to how realistic it is to generalize from this description to most of the members of our sample. Inspection of Table 9–1 reveals how wide the ranges are for each category of responses. Thus, while the median affective ratio (i.e., the percentage of responses given on the last three cards—the completely colored cards) is .30, the percentage ranges in our sample from 10 per cent to 67 per cent. The spread throughout our list of Rorschach variables is similarly great, and elaboration of the meaning of our results on the basis of the median scores excludes a large number of subjects who score far from the median. Rather, the considerable range of scores must be taken into consideration in our understanding of the personality functioning of our sample. There is no typical Rorschach here, and we must stress the fact that whatever functions are reflected in Rorschach data are distributed in a very heterogeneous way among our sample of normal adolescents.

For descriptive purposes, we attempted to evaluate the inter-correlations of our Rorschach variables. The correlation matrices presented in Tables 9–3 and 9–4 demonstrate that in our sample few Rorschach variables correlate with others. Cronbach (1949)

TABLE 9-4

Intercorrelations of Rorschach Variables Presented as Percentage of Total Number of Responses

	S%	W%	D%	Dd%	M%	FC%	CF%	C%	FY+YF+Y/R	FV+VF/R	FT+TF/R	FC+CF+C/R	F%	F+%	Exp. actual	Numb. cont.	Affect. ratio	H%	A%	Sum C/R	Numb. reject.	P	Blends
R	.24	-.51	.48	.51	-.16	.02	-.22	-.06	.07	-.18	.00	-.15	.16	-.30	.60	.84	.03	-.05	-.32	-.13	-.40	.48	.22
S%		.04	-.05	.24	.15	.02	.09	.08	.30	.11	.24	.12	-.19	-.26	.27	.02	-.21	-.04	.12	-.32	.00	.44	
W%			-.80	-.54	.25	.13	.26	.26	.28	.25	.20	.38	-.46	.10	.02	-.34	-.10	-.10	.06	.37	.18	-.46	.18
D%				.30	-.24	-.09	-.16	-.50	-.29	-.27	-.24	-.45	.52	.11	-.05	.28	.15	-.01	.05	-.51	-.27	-.46	-.21
Dd%					-.30	-.05	-.18	-.07	-.12	-.26	.08	-.18	.39	-.26	.10	.45	.04	-.01	-.01	.15	-.24	.22	-.02
M%						-.04	-.53	.06	.15	.05	.02	.08	.00	-.09	-.01	.41	.10	-.41	.41	-.11	.03	-.10	.29
FC%							.04	.03	.07	.03	.06	.45	-.34	.00	.13	.05	.02	.14	-.07	.04	.20	-.21	.21
CF%								-.01	.18	.09	.04	.64	-.17	.06	.05	-.03	.15	-.35	.07	.53	.04	-.20	.11
C%									.07	.28	.26	.65	-.48	.18	.14	-.02	.07	-.11	.04	.83	-.13	-.32	.34
FY+YF+Y/R										.36	.17	.38	-.68	-.25	.36	.35	-.18	.24	.07	.42	-.13	-.17	.49
FV+VF/R											.21	.24	-.50	.00	.05	-.06	-.22	.02	-.30	.05	.27	-.08	.42
FT+TF/R												.24	-.29	.00	.22	.12	-.10	-.21	-.33	.26	-.26	-.17	.40
FC+CF+C/R													.24	-.26	.33	.12	.15	-.14	.05	.94	-.15	-.36	.39
F%														-.60	-.10	.17	-.50	.09	.06	-.28	-.33	.12	-.49
F+%															.17	-.50	.09	.06	.01	.05	-.28	.08	-.32
Experience actual																-.26	-.35	-.02	.09	.06	.23	.16	.66
Number of content categories																	.60	.01	.05	.06	-.43	.21	.31
Affective ratio																		.01	.05	-.28	-.51	.17	-.07
H%																			.05	.06	-.33	.12	-.27
A%																				-.24	-.28	.25	.40
Sum of C/R																					-.12	-.37	-.21
Number of cards rejected																						-.10	-.08
P																							-.08

has pointed out that some correlations of Rorschach data are expected, since those variables which are related to the total number of responses correlate somewhat, though even then not generously, with one another. In our sample, then, youngsters who give many of a certain kind of response are by no means likely to give many of a different kind of response. Thus it is clear that a single individual's Rorschach profile here tells us nothing about anybody else's Rorschach profile. We cannot predict from one person's patterning of Rorschach variables to anyone else's in our sample.

The significance of the large ranges here and the general lack of correlations among the Rorschach variables cannot be overlooked. What it indicates is that on whatever factors that are tested by the Rorschach, members of our group of normals are very different from one another. That our group is heterogeneous on such factors need not surprise us. Any theory of personality postulates that people develop a spectrum of methods of dealing with conflicts, of seeing and dealing with other people. We would, therefore, expect in examining the orientations of and mechanisms used by a group of people, whatever their level of adjustment, a reflection of a whole spectrum of combinations of personality attributes.

It is important to see how specific Rorschach data correlate with some significant life variables and with ratings of our sample by psychiatrists and by teachers in this study. In order to remove some of the variable influence of R, the number of responses or productivity, each of the location scores (W, D, Dd, S), determinants (M, FC, CF, C, Y, V, T, F), and content scores (H, A) was expressed as a percentage of R. Each of these percentage scores was then dichotomized at the median into a high and low group. This dichotomized ratio score was deemed the most appropriate to use in associative analysis because of the descriptive emphasis of this report. These scores were chosen despite the more general questions such as those raised by Cronbach (1949), Murstein (1960), and Fiske and Baughman (1953) about such scores, since no more acceptable alternative was available. The other scores (P, number of cards rejected, number of blends, number of content categories, affective ratio, experience actual, and sum of C/R) were also dichotomized at the median into high and low groups.

TABLE 9–5

Rorschach Percentages Dichotomized at Median for 69 Subjects with Interview Data Available

Variable	Above	At or Below
R	34	35
S	36	33
W	34	35
D	35	34
*Dd	36	33
M	33	36
*FC	24	45
*CF	46	23
*C	34	35
FY + YF + Y	35	34
*FV + VF	30	39
*FT + TF	16	53
FC + CF + C	35	34
F%	35	34
F+%	33	36
Experience actual	36	33
Number of content categories	33	36
Affective ratio	36	33
H%	31	38
A%	34	35
C/R	36	33
*Number of cards rejected	21	48
P	33	36
*Blends	38	31

* Zero equals modal category; split as present versus absent rather than at median.

Inspection of Table 9–6 indicates that few single Rorschach variables show any significant degree of correlation with other information we have about our sample, and that even when correlations are significant, the relationship is small and contributes

TABLE 9-6

Biserial Correlations of Rorschach Categories with Background and Interview Variables

	R	S%	W%	D%	Dd%	M%	FC%	CF%	C%	$\frac{FY+YF+Y}{R}$
Class standing	−.06	−.14	.16	.04	−.02	.18	.06	.30**	.16	.07
Dating pattern:										
freshman	.03	.20	−.23*	.34**	.23*	−.16	.13	.08	−.13	−.17
junior	.05	−.06	−.19	.22	.18	−.11	.09	.24	.12	.03
Delinquency	−.04	.00	.13	−.13	−.05	.09	.06	−.06	.18	.31**
Teacher rating, senior:										
Leadership	−.03	.03	−.05	−.03	.02	.11	.12	.16	−.03	.01
Creativity	.11	−.18	−.11	.14	.10	−.07	.26*	.10	.11	−.01
Social sensitivity	−.12	−.02	−.08	.12	.10	.00	.12	−.08	−.04	−.12
Responsibility	−.22	−.07	.08	.17	−.10	.11	.07	.03	.07	−.08
Industry	.06	−.15	.01	.16	−.12	−.02	.25*	.09	.16	−.08
Interview ratings of affect:										
Experience	.08	−.02	−.09	.22	.06	.06	.20	.16	.00	−.12
Expressiveness	.10	−.09	.00	.14	.01	.22	.13	.01	.03	−.16
Relationship	−.05	−.02	.02	.13	−.10	.17	.00	−.08	−.16	−.10
Father's education	.16	−.09	−.20	.05	.02	−.14	.05	−.16	.00	−.14
Father's occupation	.02	.08	−.06	.08	.19	.11	.00	.24	.16	.06
Likability	.18	.02	−.13	.13	.07	.10	.30**	.15	.00	.04
Cooperation	.14	.01	−.33**	.33**	.09	.03	.12	.29*	−.17	−.02

very little of the variance. This will not surprise any experienced users of the Rorschach. Clinically we do not evaluate our patients or make predictions about them on the basis of single Rorschach variables. Rather it is the nuances of the interrelationships of these variables that are our clinical data.

Apart from the routine scoring of the tests, there emerges, in their manner of relating to the examiner and to the test materials, evidence for consistent coping mechanisms that these youngsters use constructively. Perhaps foremost of these mechanisms is an attitude of humor. There is frequently an attitude of lighthearted humor in the response itself (for example, in describing an animal, the subject comments that he "looks a little crosseyed" and laughs); sometimes the humor shows up in the subject's reaction to what he sees as peculiarity in his response (e.g., subject says "looks kind of like a bear with horns," and laughs; after seeing

$\dfrac{FV+VF}{R}$	$\dfrac{FT+TF}{R}$	$\dfrac{FC+CF+C}{R}$	F%	F+%	Exp. actual	Numb. cont.	Affect. ratio	H%	A%	$\dfrac{Sum\ C}{R}$	Numb. reject.	P	Blends
.13	.05	.23*	−.06	.01	.18	.28*	.08	−.21	−.04	.21	−.14	.02	.12
−.08	.12	.03	.30	.04	−.21	.17	.03	−.21	−.03	−.08	−.06	.04	.01
−.04	.18	.24	.03	.06	.00	.34**	.03	−.24*	−.08	.15	−.25*	−.18	.04
.05	.18	.13	−.31**	−.22	.13	−.04	−.13	.14	−.09	.13	−.03	−.04	.13
−.11	−.02	.02	.01	.10	.21	.19	−.14	.04	−.08	.02	−.08	−.10	.11
−.05	.22	.02	.14	.05	−.13	.35**	−.13	−.20	−.15	.05	−.15	−.10	.08
−.06	.10	.06	.00	.14	.02	.12	−.10	.02	.06	−.04	.08	−.02	−.14
−.04	.01	.19	−.04	.17	.04	.22	.01	−.14	.02	.10	.09	−.04	−.10
.05	.25*	.11	.02	.16	.04	.35**	.04	−.16	−.14	.06	−.09	−.04	.02
−.02	.25*	.01	.09	−.19	.06	.32**	.06	−.13	−.13	.02	−.06	−.10	.00
.04	.20	−.06	−.03	−.08	.14	.12	.08	.04	−.10	−.06	−.06	.09	−.08
−.03	.13	−.17	−.13	−.05	−.10	−.05	.01	.22	.02	−.21	.09	−.05	−.11
.08	−.09	−.12	.07	.11	.00	−.04	−.01	.11	−.05	−.09	−.02	.19	−.05
.09	.22	.29*	−.02	−.03	.06	.27*	−.09	−.26*	.00	.30**	−.19	−.13	.14
.09	.12	.04	−.14	−.16	.03	.15	.12	.08	−.17	.03	−.18	−.12	.10
.16	.04	−.14	.13	−.01	.01	.30**	.17	−.20	.02	−.14**	−.16	.22	−.12

* Significant at .05 level. ** Significant at .01 level.

an animal in a red area on a blot, subject says, "I don't know how the animal got red. Maybe he's sunburned"). Most of the humor is in the subject's relating to the examiner (e.g., "You ought to send some of these to an art fair"; ". . . a beetle. I don't mean guys singing—I mean a bug"; "Sort of has the shape of a butterfly and it looks like it's been folded—like to make a double image. Both sides are the same. The line looks like it bisects it. It also looks like it dissects it," and he laughs). There is thus, for the most part, an active and constant engagement between these boys and what they are dealing with—they relate to the examiner, being aware of or alert to their effect on the examiner, whatever the task. This shows up not only in the humor but also in the overtly self-critical statements described above.

Another aspect of their coping shows up in their rationalizing the distance or formal difference between the stimulus itself and their response. When they are aware that the blot is not a very accurate representation of their response, they handle the situation not only by joking or by being critical but also by explaining intellectually why the blot lacks accuracy (e.g., "Maybe it's like a photo and part of it didn't make an impression there"). The ability to rationalize in terms of the stimulus itself demonstrates considerable flexibility and creativity in the sense that they are aware of the task and the stimulus on two levels; that is, they can play games with the environment and even approach it somewhat loosely, but they do not lose sight of what the reality of the situation is.

Many of the Rorschach protocols reflect a very impressive capacity on the part of these boys to incorporate easily, with awareness and humor, what goes on about them as part of their own experience. For example, there is an almost curious abundance of elephant responses in the records of those several boys who were tested during the 1964 Republican National Convention. Likewise, Christmas trees and other symbols of Christmas abound in the records of those tested around that season. Frequently, these responses are made self-consciously, with humorous comments connecting up the response with the environmental event. On occasion, too, the event is used in the response as an arena onto which apparently conflictual or driving feelings can be projected so that the personal issue is dealt with, though perhaps not mastered, in the context of an acceptable ideology or an intellectualized position (for example, "Well, this is a little far out. Looks like two of the GOP elephants clashing, two of the candidates. A little blood flying between the two. They're still trying to get together on one idea, but still not seeing eye to eye"). Usually, however, there is simply an easy incorporation of cultural issues or environmental events, and this sometimes allows an acceptable expression of what might otherwise have been unpleasant feelings. (Example: "It could look like the Fourth of July—the firecrackers and all that stuff exploding in the air.") Here destructive or chaotic feelings get bound into order and even pleasantries without a reduction in the drive or the feelings.

The tests are replete with comments that reflect a constructive self-criticality on the part of the subjects and a constant, cautious evaluation of their thinking and feeling. What is important here is that the caution does not result in a pulling in or in a limitation of experience and spontaneity (here expressed in number and kind of responses) but rather in directness and openness that is constantly reevaluated. Rather than narrow their range of responses, they express the criticality in such remarks as "Boy, is that farfetched!"; "I'm getting too many animals in here, but this one looks like a bat somehow"; "I don't want to say that it looks like an insect again because that would be the same thing over again"; ". . . I don't think it really looks like it, though"; "I'll go far out on this one just to be different. . . ." There is a feeling throughout that while they reserve their right to be different, the difference they sense makes them uncomfortable and they have to apologize for it. They want to be creative, original, and interesting, but are not sure where to set the limits for this position. Sometimes, perhaps, the lack of sureness and the criticality become excessive and the subject gives few responses or couches his responses, even when they are normatively frequent responses, in apologies and explanations to the point that it is apparent that he simply does not trust his judgment. ("The only thing that it might look like would be this top part here—this is pretty factual —it might look like the head of a Siamese cat. The whiskers. I don't think it really looks like it, though.") The boundary between what appears to be a constructive criticality outlined above and this doubt and lack of self-trust is an uneasy one; it does seem, however, that most of our sample, though not always sure of themselves and their judgment, are willing to give themselves the benefit of the doubt.

Although a substantial number of these boys demonstrates an overall level of form quality ($F + \%$) that would be considered low by clinical standards (see Table 9–7), it is rare in this group to find a record in which there is a consistently poor form quality over several cards. What we find instead are frequent shifts; to borrow clinical phraseology, the lengthy or complex records are characterized by repeated regressions and recoveries. It would seem, then, that when the functioning of these boys becomes loose or based on unshared personal considerations rather than on what is relevant to or appropriate in the situation, the maladaptive behavior, the poor judgment, and the disruptions are short-lived; the boys are able to muster up their strengths quickly and move away from what might be called short-lived pathological positions with smoothness and aplomb.

TABLE 9–7

Distribution of F+% Through 74
Adolescent Rorschachs

F+%	Frequency
35 to 40	1
41 to 45	1
46 to 50	6
51 to 55	2
56 to 60	6
61 to 65	2
66 to 70	7
71 to 75	12
76 to 80	8
81 to 85	7
86 to 90	6
91 to 95	3
96 to 100	13

A similar but more regular shifting of gears occurs when the subject follows up a sad, unpleasant, or frightening response with a percept in which the content is similar but the affect has been reversed to be gratifying, pleasant, and pretty. (Thus, from Card 2: "Here I see two people arguing . . . not even wanting to acknowledge the other person, much less argue with them. They're both putting out all their force against each other—straining themselves." This is followed on Card 3 with "Here are two people playing with each other. They are happy—they are not arguing—they're pleased with each other.") This seems not to be so much a mechanism of denial but rather an ability to master situations by attending to their less threatening aspects without disavowing the threat. This latter ability shows up too when a pleasant response is followed by a negative expression of affect. (Example: On Card 10 one subject gives the abstract response "Happiness" and follows this immediately with "Fear.") It seems that these youngsters allow themselves an awareness of their ambivalence and refuse to assume a Pollyanna attitude. Their world is both welcoming and uneasy; they see both these aspects and attempt to function within that context.

Similarly, essentially frightening percepts are often handled by minimizing or ridiculing the frightening aspect of the percept or by stressing the subject's freedom and mastery of the situation. ("I think it looks like the front of a dog, or maybe a wolf's face. *Floppy ears hanging down.* Looks like it may be growling—the mouth's open and it looks like it's ready to attack—*it looks a little crosseyed.*" "Oh, man! This looks like at nighttime. This one right here looks like a bomb that's just exploded on the water and this one—*they just cut off the film before it got big.* In the background, it's got mountains and flashes from other bombs. That's about it. *That one hit me good.*") Again, the world is seen as supplying fearsome situations; and although these boys insist on meeting these situations, it is with a feeling that they can and will master them. There is frequently a counterphobic or grandiose quality to this feeling, but the reality of the threat to them is not lost to or ignored by these youngsters.

References to movies and comic strips are frequent; these seem to be mechanisms to minimize threat, to rationalize inaccuracies or peculiarities, and at the same time express humor and maintain an ease in the subject's relating to the examiner. (Example: "And then again it looks like a rat standing, looks like a real tough thug of a rat standing with his hands on his knees." To the inquiry on this response, the subject continues: "I don't know, it just looked like one in sort of a way and then again it didn't. Like one of the rats you see in cartoons. A stupid sort of thing. Looks tough. Usually you don't see a rat standing on his hind legs with his hands on his knees.") In this example we see most of the coping mechanisms outlined above, and it is clear, despite the oddness of the response, that the subject never believes that rats behave this way. He copes with the ambiguity and firms up what may have begun as looseness in his own thinking with the rational use of a cultural device—the cartoon. This enables him not only to use the peculiarity of his percept but also to minimize the threat of this perhaps vicious rat.

Vocabulary Scale

Among these adolescent boys, scaled scores on the Vocabulary subtest of the WAIS range from 5 to 15 and the distribution approaches normality. The mean score is 10.33, with little difference between the two schools (10.68 and 10.05). What we see then is a group of boys, average in intelligence though not remarkably homogeneous in it. Some of these boys demonstrate (on this test) considerable intellectual potential while others show significantly limited intellectual ability. Most of our sample groups itself around the average level.

TABLE 9–8

Distribution of Vocabulary-Scale Scores

Score	Number of subjects
5	1
6	1
7	2
8	3
9	10
10	16
11	7
12	7
13	1
14	1
15	4

An important question is, how important a role does their intelligence play in the important variables from the interview and background data in this study? Correlations were computed, relating vocabulary scores with the significant variables of this study. The results are given in Table 9–9.

TABLE 9–9

Correlations of Vocabulary-Scale Scores with Background and Interview Variables

Variables	Correlation coefficient
Class standing	—.44**
Dating pattern—freshman	—.19
Dating pattern—junior	—.28*
Delinquency	.05
Feelings about self	—.26
Teacher rating—senior year	
Leadership	—.06
Creativity	—.30*
Social sensitivity	—.09
Responsibility	—.39**
Industry	—.34*
Interview ratings of affect	
Experience	—.28*
Expressiveness	—.25
Relationship	.04
Father's education	.21
Father's occupation	—.35*
Likability	.02
Cooperation	—.29

NOTE: Unequal point biserial coefficients, $N = 49$.
* Significant at .05 level. ** Significant at .01 level.

It is, of course, difficult to know whether intelligence is a factor (and perhaps a confounding one) in the ratings of those variables in which the relationship is significant or whether those variables are a significant factor in the subject's test behavior. For example, it may well be that those boys who are rated high on experience of affect are able, because of how they handle feelings, to score higher on a vocabulary test than other boys. We do not know, however, whether teachers are biased by students' intelligence in rating their responsibility or whether brighter students are more responsible in school than duller students or even whether boys who function more responsibly than others in their senior year of high school will score high on a vocabulary test. However the correlations may be understood, despite significance, none is above .44; thus at best only a small amount of the variance in the ratings among these variables can be accounted for by the boys' intelligence.

Similar issues arise in correlating vocabulary scores with our Rorschach variables. The Rorschach variables have been dichotomized as described above.

We see in Table 9–10 that percentages of both M and CF are related to performance on the vocabulary test and that understandably Experience Actual approaches a significant relationship

TABLE 9–10

Correlations of Vocabulary-Scale Scores with Rorschach Variables

Rorschach variables	Point biserial R
R	—.10
S%	.18
W%	.05
D%	—.20
Dd%	—.02
M%	—.29*
FC%	—.20
CF%	—.29*
C%	—.05
Number Y responses/R	.14
Number V responses/R	—.23
Number T responses/R	.11
F%	.04
F+%	—.25
E.A.	—.27
N of content categories	—.27
(Number R on 8–10)/R	—.08
H%	.11
A%	.08
C/R	—.19
Number of cards rejected	.12
Number P	—.06
Number blends	.10

* Significant at .05 level.

with Vocabulary, since it amounts to the sum of movement and color responses. The fact that the number of content categories approaches a significant relationship raises the question of whether brighter boys are interested in a wider range of areas or whether those boys who are interested in a wide range of areas, in part as a result of this interest, score high on a vocabulary test. Here again the correlations, even when significant, are so small that only a very limited amount of the Rorschach variable variance can be accounted for by intelligence.

Whatever the sequence, our expectations are confirmed that intelligence is related to class standing, to how teachers evaluate students in a number of areas of functioning (not including their leadership qualities and their social sensitivity), and to what their fathers do for a living (though not significantly to their father's education). That intelligence is related to how much these boys date as juniors is interesting but difficult to explain. It is interesting too that intelligence relates to ratings of cooperation but not of likability. Predictably, intelligence here relates to M on the Rorschach. It is interesting, however, that the total number of responses shows no significant relationship with intelligence, while the number of CF responses does. Again, the complexity of all these variables is a factor we must stress, and it is only in terms of that complexity (as evidenced by the smallness of our most significant correlations) that we can begin to understand the presence and lack of relationships throughout. Thus, while likability may be thought to be a factor in ratings of cooperation it is likely a small one; and while we may possibly be biased toward rating brighter boys as cooperative, we have been careful to leave such biases behind in our ratings of likability. On the other hand, if brightness is a factor, however small, in determining cooperation, it does not enter into those qualities which are involved when we speak of likability. Similarly on the Rorschach, intelligence seems to be of no importance at all here in determining how many responses a subject gives. At the same time, both number of responses and intelligence relate to such variables as M; one can begin, then, to see how complex, at least in this sample, such variables as Rorschach movement responses are, especially when it becomes clear that both these correlations leave much of the variance unaccounted for.

Summary

One of the most significant findings we have in this study of normal adolescent tests is the striking difference between the group's homogeneous Thematic Apperception Tests and their heterogeneous Rorschachs. There are a number of ready explanations for this difference. First there is the issue of stimulus pull. The figures in the pictures on the Thematic Apperception Test do indeed suggest something and provide the limits of a structure (Eron, 1950). A picture of a boy and a violin will of necessity suggest a theme somehow relating this boy to the violin. This definition and structure then limit the content of the responses: the story the subject gives is limited to a theme about a boy and a violin, reducing considerably the number of available responses. Rorschach stimuli are much less structured and therefore permit a wider range of responses (see Fiske, 1959). Of course a wide range of possible responses increases the probability of heterogeneity of responses in a particular group.

In addition, it is reasonable to conjecture that in a group that is homogeneous for age, sex, culture, and, within limits, social class, similar problems and issues are being dealt with. We would maintain that the specific manners in which the problems are being coped with are unique for each individual, but also that, very generally, psychological issues, conflicts, and orientations within the group—i.e., content aspects of personality—are shared. For the most part, it is with this content area that the TAT deals, while the Rorschach allows more the evaluation of structural aspects of personality.

The fact that there is no typical Rorschach for this group would indicate that personality functioning among these boys is quite diverse, and it is clear that normality is not a unitary function. What we find instead is that these youngsters, using widely varying techniques, hold their own. They commonly employ humor; they stick to the issues of their day and use those issues to act out or solve problems they experience; they relate to people with whom they find themselves, frequently with charm and almost never carelessly; they are aware of themselves and of their awkwardness and take steps to make up for their limitations; they come to grips with what they experience. But they do all these things in ways that are unique to each of them, even though in general their conflicts, their experience of the world and themselves in relation to the world, are common to most of them.

In addition, we find that discrete personality attributes that are reflected as single Rorschach variables are of little help to us in making predictions about specific aspects of these boys' lives. Correlations of Rorschach variables with certain significant life variables or with how they are seen and rated by teachers and psychiatrists are at best low. Nor can we predict from the very similar Thematic Apperception Tests to the very diverse Rorschachs. This lack of covariation reinforces our clinical impression that we can understand little about a person from looking only at discrete aspects of particular tests. It is our impression, rather, that the usefulness of psychological tests is dependent on the complex interaction of many variables. This conclusion, however, presents us with very serious research problems in view of the heterogeneous Rorschach patterns and low intervariable correlations in such a sample as this. The diversity and lack of commonality themselves make prediction difficult.

The ranges of scores in a number of the Rorschach categories that we investigated demonstrate that some normal adolescents function on the Rorschach at levels that are described as pathological in other populations. For example, Table 9–7 indicates that in more than 10 per cent of our sample, when percepts are solely determined by form, the form quality is "bad"—i.e., quite personal and different from how others see it—at least 50 per cent of the time. The whole issue of the meaning of an apparently "abnormal" Rorschach protocol from a subject we know to be "normal," in view of our definition of normality and the checks involved in that definition, is a very important one. The most important question to emerge is what mechanisms of coping, of dealing with oneself and the world, enable a person with certain personality problems or liabilities to function at a level that we define as normal. These assets and mechanisms become readily apparent in a sample such as ours where our procedures are designed to detect them. Since we have called these boys "normal," we seek out evidence of their normality at least in qualitative aspects of their Rorschach protocols. The plea implicit in our findings is that such evidence of coping mechanisms, of normality, not be ignored in clinical Rorschach work.

Many of the problems that arise in our attempt to understand normal functioning in adolescents by examining these tests would be reduced in an important way if we were able to compare the test performance of this sample of boys and the interrelationships of test variables with those of a similar group of adolescents who have been diagnosed as abnormal. Of course new issues would be presented with such a paradigm, since abnormality, in terms of diagnostic categories and symptom complexes, is not a unitary concept. If abnormality is not unitary, then we would predict considerable heterogeneity on the tests of a sample of abnormal adolescents. Comparing heterogeneous data from one sample with heterogeneous data from a second sample (since we have shown that the Rorschachs of our normal sample are heterogeneous indeed) limits the probability of significant difference between the two groups. Qualitative evaluation of the tests of these two samples may allow some elaboration of difference. Thus such factors as response style or quality and consistency of relationship with the examiner may be significant variables.

In addition, it may be that the abnormal group will demonstrate more internal consistency than we were able to find in our group of normals; for example, we may be able to demonstrate that more

Rorschach variables correlate with one another than was true of our sample, establishing perhaps that in abnormal groups difficulties, problems of control and coping, etc., are consistent features of functioning rather than limited to discrete areas. At any rate, we are limited in our freedom to make statements about normality in general on the basis of our data because we lack important reference points. Thus, it may be sixteen-year-old maleness that determines our test findings and not their normality. It is only by comparing our data with a sample from another population— one that does not meet the criteria we set up in defining normality—that we can parcel out which aspects of our findings do indeed relate to normality and which relate to other variables or factors whimsically present.

PART III

Discussion

10

The Nature of the Relationship: The "Research Alliance"

How reliable are our data? Why should the students tell us the truth? Will they distort their true feelings in order to try to hide from us or will they, perhaps, distort in an effort to please us with the type of information they might think we would want? In other words, did the teen-agers attempt to conceal psychopathology from us because they knew that we were interested in normal behavior?

How might we, the interviewers, have changed the data? Did we err on the opposite side of our colleagues so that we failed to see rampant psychopathology present in our subjects? Or did we tamper with the data by doing some form of therapy, unknowingly entering into a psychotherapist-patient type of relationship with these students?

To be able to best attain our goal of research-interview situation, we have developed the concept of a *research alliance*. It is our belief that the research alliance enabled us to view the adolescents with the least amount of distortion. The longitudinal planning of interviews gave us time to build up a working relationship with the teen-agers and time to see the students in a way that might not have been possible after one, two, or even three interviews.

Why use the interview at all? As psychiatrists, we were convinced that a series of interviews and the one-to-one involvement of interviewer with interviewee could not be replaced by psychological testing or by one-shot interview sessions. In a series of interviews, we could take time to encourage the subject to cooperate and give him time to learn to trust us. The variety of topics discussed with marked affect emphasized the extent of the psychological world of the students. The repetition of a theme or of a particular event allowed us to learn which areas were of most significance to the teen-agers. As we gained their confidence, we could ask more personal questions without encountering as much resistance as we might otherwise have observed. By watching them over a period of time, we could ascertain the intensity of their feelings, while comparisons of interviews revealed their patterns of responses. Comparisons of responses also led to a more accurate assessment of the subject's self-awareness. Finally, we could decipher general psychological patterns of behavior from observing and interpreting attitudes toward the interviewer and the project.

It is our impression that our interviews with normal adolescents compare more closely with sequence in psychiatric therapy than with the single diagnostic interview, even though the purpose is closer to that of the diagnostic evaluation than to psychotherapy. By developing a relationship with a number of teen-agers, we are able to study their individual patterns of behavior. As a result we are not forced to rely solely on conscious reporting, as in large-scale questionnaire studies, or on generalizing from a few cases studied in depth.

In this chapter we shall present our formulation of the research alliance and examine the responses which we received from the teen-agers. It is meant to demonstrate the way in which we tried to minimize data distortion.

Definition of "Alliance"

In recent years psychiatrists, psychoanalysts, and psychologists have become more interested in the concept of "therapeutic alliance." The origin of the concept can be traced to Freud (1937), who stated: "We know that the essence of the analytic situation is that the analyst enters into an *alliance* [italics ours] with the ego of the patient to subdue certain uncontrolled parts of the id." This concept of entering into an "alliance" with the observing ego of a patient has been described by Zetzel (1956) as depending essentially on the real object relationship between the patient and the psychoanalyst. Other psychoanalysts have described the phenomenon in a similar fashion; cf. Sterba (1934), Greenson (1965), and Gitelson (1962).

The development of the concept of "therapeutic alliance" has had a strong influence in other areas of psychiatry. For example, in a recent article entitled "The Teaching Alliance," Muslin *et al.* (1965) described their concept as

> a state in which communication of the teacher can be optimally apprehended by the student as a function of the problem-solving behavior in which both teacher and student are intellectually and emotionally joined during the learning activities.

The term "alliance" is also used when authors describe the supervisory relationship ("supervisory alliance" or "learning alliance," Fleming and Benedek, 1966). We too have found the term "alliance" useful in describing the kind of relationship we have developed with our research sample.

The term "research alliance" has not, as far as we know, been used in the psychiatric or the behavioral-science literature. Many psychiatric researchers, however, have implicitly commented upon the subject in previous years. The fact that the experimenter cannot be viewed solely as an objective observer whose emotional neutrality can be depended upon has been emphasized by a number of investigators: Linn (1958), Malmo *et al.* (1957), DiMascio *et al.* (1957). Kubie (1953) warned of the effect that the unconscious mental processes and conflicts may have upon the design of a specific experiment. Direct observations related to the importance of the experimental situation and its influence on the results obtained had been done by Fisher (1953 and 1956), and Reiser (1955). Reiser (1955) states:

> It is clear that manipulation of the psychological context of the same basic procedure was associated with important differences in the physiological findings. . . . Small variation in technique, personnel, mannerisms, etc., which may seem unimportant and irrelevant may lead to surprisingly large changes in what actually transpires during an experiment.

As can be seen, researchers have been cognizant of the strong effect that seemingly "small" variations have on the results. Rosenthal (1966) has organized much of the literature and experiments on the subject of the experimenter's influence on behavioral-science research. Rosenthal considers experimental situations in which significant results have been obtained as related significantly to covert communication between the experimenter and the subject. In these situations the goal of the experiment has unwittingly been communicated to the subject, who becomes eager to please the experimenter and give him the results he is seeking. Rosenthal clearly demonstrates that one needs to take the relationship between subject and experimenter into consideration and establish controls for it.

It is of interest to note that in the vast majority of the psychosocial studies on normal populations, the investigators do not even take into consideration the possibility that their studies have affected the subjects. See, for example, Gesell *et al.* (1956), Kagan and Moss (1962), Symonds *et al.* (1961), Hendin *et al.* (1965). The interaction between the subject and his interviewer, the kind of relationship they developed, and its impact on the *type* of data collected were not taken into consideration, nor was an attempt made to study them. This missing link is especially noticed in a study such as White's (1966). White followed the progress of the lives of a selected group of men and women over many years with detailed interviews, exploring and uncovering many feelings and conflicts. Surely these interviews must have had *some* effect. But the meaning of the relationship is left to the imagination of the reader. At no point in the book does White discuss the kind of relationship he developed with his subjects.

The Research Alliance

The concept of "research alliance" is introduced to describe the optimal form of ". . . transaction or relationship between the psychiatric researcher and his subject, where the aim is to obtain valid psychological data in a limited number of interviews" (Offer and Sabshin, 1967). The thesis is that through an active and open interview posture in a series of well spread-out and clearly structured research interviews, an alliance based on mutual trust and respect and the congruence of goals will be developed which will enable the interviewer to obtain more reliable and "deeper" material. In order to obtain as reliable data as possible, one has to be cognizant of the interaction between subject and interviewer and attempt to regulate the effect that the interviewer and the interview situation have on the subject.

In our opinion, one of the central methodological problems that confront researchers working with "normal" populations concerns the number of interviews necessary to gather significant psychological data. We usually needed at least three successive interviews before the typical teen-ager developed a meaningful research alliance with us. It was only then that we could begin to be confident of our clinical assessment.

We experimented with our interview technique, proceeding first as our psychiatric experience directed us and, later, from the lessons we learned while the project progressed. As interviewers, our purpose was to avoid extremes of involvement, detachment, seduc-

tion, and rejection. We could form two continuums and informally assess our own stance in relation to each of the subjects we
were interviewing and in relation to the subject population as a
whole. In order to evaluate the research alliance, we needed to be
aware of not only our own part of the interaction but also the
students' reactions. We wanted them to comply, without opening
themselves completely to manipulation by us and without defend-
ing themselves totally against our attempts to learn about them.
Hence the subject's level of resistance was another important area
for us to understand. Awareness of the complicated transactions
between interviewer and interviewee would enable us to lead the
relationship more skillfully into an optimal one for sound data
collection. The areas we discuss are those which our experience
has taught us are important. They are, of course, only a part of a
highly complicated field of interactions. Finally, these areas are
dynamically interrelated and can be separated only artificially for
purposes of explanation.

1. DETACHMENT-INVOLVEMENT

In the name of scientific objectivity, the interviewer might refuse to enter into a relationship with the teen-agers. In the same
vein, the "overobjective" interviewer might deny that the subject
might learn something from the interview experience and insist that
he would not answer any questions since his answer might "con-
taminate" the interview. In a significant number of cases, the result would be a lack of trust and a failure to engage the adolescent
in the project. In interviews for the purpose of research, the psy-
chiatrist-investigator must be more active than he would be in
most kinds of psychotherapy. This is especially true in research
with adolescents, where even in psychotherapy the therapist has to
engage the teen-agers actively in the relationship (see, for example,
Holmes, 1964).

Being aware of the danger of detachment, we attempted to
develop an appropriate and occasionally a lively exchange with our

research subjects. They were curious about the research, the results, our own work, and at times our personal lives. Our approach consisted in answering as many questions as possible without coloring the data. We always answered personal questions about our work, such as: What does a psychiatrist do? Do you treat disturbed adolescents? How many papers have you published? You have a funny accent—where are you from? Many subjects asked questions about the career of medicine; what is it like and how long does it take to become an M.D.* When the adolescents asked us about the general attitudes of teen-agers toward dating we responded in general terms, after they had answered the question themselves. Later we would tell them, in percentages, how many adolescents go out with girls and that most feel anxious during the first few times. If the teen-ager posed questions about his own behavior, we usually talked about some of his own problems. In most cases general discussions sufficed. Our response communicated to the teen-ager that we were interested in him as a person and took him seriously.

We welcomed the opportunities given to us for a certain degree of involvement. For example, when one subject was asked about his dating pattern he told us that he was going steady with a particular girl. The answer would have been adequate, but this subject proceeded to tell us more about the relationship. He was dating a girl three years his senior. Both sets of parents were against the relationship, although they did not forbid it. The subject asked for our opinion. We did not give him any direct answer but asked for his thoughts and feelings concerning this matter. The subject was able to explore his own ambivalent feelings concerning the relationship. He told of his needs to be dependent and stated that he hopes he will grow out of the need to have a "motherlike person be my girl friend." He admitted enjoying his mother's apparent annoyance over his relationship with his girl friend, and what seemed to him the envy of his peers. We were

* At the time of writing, five out of 73 are planning a career in medicine; and of these five, two say they want to be psychiatrists.

impressed with the frankness and openness with which he was able to discuss his relationship with his girl friend.

Overinvolvement with our subjects would have posed problems, since it is very likely that we would then have lost our perspective as investigator-scientists. We might have become zealous reformers, attempting to change various situations in the schools and possibly calling a few parents and talking to them about their children, simply because "we were concerned." We believe that overinvolvement would have lost the research alliance not only with the specific subjects with whom it happened but with the group as a whole. To show appropriate sympathy and understanding, however, was crucial in our project. When a teen-ager lost his father suddenly, we believed it was fitting to devote a whole hour to discussing the subject's feelings about his crisis. But we always had to remind ourselves that we were there as observers and not as therapists.

2. SEDUCTION-REJECTION

We must be able to induce the subject to cooperate in giving us meaningful psychological data without the bait of the psychiatric contract. To what depth can we go without deceiving our subjects or skewing our data by causing transference responses and the subsequent distortions? How can we seduce the subject into talking to us while rejecting pleas for help that such a seduction could easily arouse? Will we give the subject reason to trust us? Our attitudes of seduction and rejection need constant regulation. We must not slip into the role of therapist or, in an exuberance of pure research motivations, imitate recording machines that have no concern other than the accuracy of the recordings. We must play it by ear, and for this we are, we hope, well trained.

In psychotherapy, the patient feels that *we* can help *him* although he has to lead us to the areas that present emotional conflicts for him. The patient begins by a conscious realization that he needs and wants psychiatric help. The patient seeks out an accredited psychotherapist and consults him, feeling, "This man can help me." The therapist, on the other hand, believes, "I can help this patient." This feeling of mutuality begins a process of interaction between patient and therapist, optimally one that continues throughout treatment. The patient develops a basic trust toward the therapist, which is enhanced, of course, by the ability of the therapist to be empathic and understanding. The therapist learns to respect the patient's individuality and continues to be curious about the patient's emotional life and understanding of his difficulties. Although the "therapeutic alliance" is usually strengthened over time, its ebb and flow depends to a large extent on the specific interactions between patient and therapist at particular points in time. Even during a phase of negative transference, the therapeutic alliance provides a reliable vehicle for continuity of treatment. Over a period of time the therapeutic alliance is cemented by the therapist's actions, the most important of which are the therapist's communications to the patient that he does understand him and wants to help him.

When a psychiatrist undertakes a research project that is separate from his usual clinical role, one of the crucial differences between psychotherapy and research is immediately apparent. In the research, it is the psychiatrist who goes to the subject asking for his cooperation and help. He may offer the subject money or other types of rewards, such as increased self-knowledge or the feeling of being of help to others.* There is no question, however, that the purpose of the research interview is to help the investigator, not to aid the subject therapeutically.

What motivations did we offer the students in our project? We told them the goals of our project and asked them to help us to

---

* Friedenberg (1965) felt strongly that offering teen-agers money for their participation in his project meant that he recognized and accepted their dignity as individuals. He admitted that the teen-agers might have strained themselves harder to give him his money's worth and what they perceived he wanted, i.e., a more mature and adult attitude. (See the discussion of Rosenthal, 1966, p. 150.) What is perplexing to us is that according to Friedenberg, paying adolescent subjects money is the *only* way of showing them respect.

help others. "By learning about you, we can learn to understand the abnormal adolescents better." Several students accepted this motivation. We also offered a means of helping teen-agers in general by providing information from the adolescents to the adult world which would help narrow the generation gap. Surprisingly, but in accordance with our other data, few were impressed by this. Although we had fed them this motivation in our introduction to the project, only one boy responded: "Adolescents are misunderstood, so it is a good idea to find out what they really think about." As we shall see later, we seduced them most successfully by arousing their own interest in learning about themselves. For those who enjoyed introspection, we had something to offer.

Was this sufficient to cause them to "tell all"? The patient comes to the psychotherapist with the expectation that in the course of the interview or interviews he will reveal much that is personal and private. The psychiatrist has the "right" to know everything about the emotional life of the patient. As with the patient, the subject in the research project did feel the obligation to be honest. Our culture has been sufficiently invaded by this concept of trust in the psychiatrist that those whom we could motivate to cooperate seemed almost to take this axiom for granted. There were resistances, but we did not probe deep into areas where the subject displayed resistance, not wanting to endanger the subject's equilibrium or to stimulate undue antagonism toward ourselves or the project. We had to maintain a balance between gaining information and maintaining the subject's cooperation. We did interpret to the subject his resistance to the project itself.

Although in doing this type of research we consciously disavow the title of therapist, the question can be legitimately raised whether we can validate the disavowal. The subject may, after all, strive for therapeutic benefits and put us in the role of the healer, without our being aware. There is no question that some subjects do gain therapeutically from participating in a research project.

However, if we gratify the possible needs of our subject in the sense that we turn the research into therapy, the research value of the transaction will be considerably reduced; there will be a basic change in the transaction. In psychotherapy, regression takes place and the therapist usually becomes a transference object for the patient. This kind of relationship, although desirable from a psychotherapeutic point of view, is conducive to the bringing forth of a variety of distortions into the relationship. Furthermore, when the investigator promises the subject more than he can fulfill (as in, "I can help you with your problems"), there is apt to be disappointment and bitterness, with a resultant discontinuation in the project. If the interviewer indicated that he could help solve problems, the subject would inevitably be disappointed.

Regression is intensified in the unstructured interview which allows unconscious conflicts to come out somewhat more easily. The careful structuring of the interviews for the purpose of research helps keep the relationship in the here and now and attempts to minimize regression or transference reactions related to a regressive position assumed by the subject.* But we have to be aware that in research such as ours *some* regression and transference will take place. The relatively long intervals between interviews (three to four months) helped minimize the therapeutic wish on the part of the teen-agers. It also helped minimize the potential therapeutic effect.

When the subject develops a positive relationship with the researcher and continues to cooperate in the project in a realistic fashion, we would say that a research alliance has begun. The degree and intensity of the alliance vary from individual to individual. As we have stated above, the research alliance includes mutual trust and respect. The intellectual process is stimulated

---

* The fact that the interviews were held in the high school rather than in our offices in the Psychiatric Institute helped again to minimize the regression. For some people the psychiatrist's office with its special decor (the couch, etc.) is enough to bring out certain fantasies and feelings which they might not divulge in an "ordinary" office.

and the subject must be allowed to satisfy his curiosity about himself to some extent. Although few psychodynamic interpretations are made, it is crucial for the development of a research alliance that areas which are of interest to the subject be explored. Although we cannot gratify longings for understanding and help in our subjects, we believe that we must develop a mutually meaningful interaction with them. Not to have listened to what the subject had to say when he shared his private conflicts would have amounted to a flat rejection. It also would have minimized the research alliance which we had with the subject. An example of the seduction-rejection problem occurred when a subject told us that he had impregnated his girl friend. He proceeded to tell us the whole story, adding that he had never told it to anyone. He told us how upset he was and how guilty he felt about it. He promised the girl he would pay for an abortion. He worked hard to earn the money, and without his parents' knowledge was able to save the necessary amount. He made all the arrangements and was present when the girl friend was aborted. In this situation we were careful not to pry deeper or interpret anything to the subject. To make him feel that we could help him with this very complex problem would have amounted to seduction by a false promissory note. On the other hand, a failure to listen to his concerns sympathetically would have amounted to a rejection.

Did the fact that we offered some of our adolescent subjects what Rogers (1961) calls a "helping relation" alter significantly their adjustment in high school? To be sure, at times we have performed "miniature psychotherapy"* with our subjects. Is it reasonable to assume that our relationship with our subjects altered the teen-agers so much that without it they would have grown differently? In spite of the apparent difficulty in answering these questions, we believe that each individual has many helping relationships that he will seek out in case of need. A few of our subjects have unquestionably tried to utilize us in such a capacity.

---

* This term was suggested by Dr. M. Basch in discussion of one of our papers.

Whether even they were successful in utilizing us specifically in a psychotherapeutic fashion is doubtful. The "contract" that is an essential part of any psychotherapeutic encounter was not present. What the students might have obtained instead was a "helping relationship." We liked our subjects as people, and the recognition of this may have been helpful to some of them. We hope that in limiting our seduction, we never flatly rejected.

3. LEVEL OF RESISTANCE

We wanted the subject to come, to answer our questions in a way that best reflected his own awareness of his psychological life, and to lead us to the areas of importance to him. His level of resistance should, optimally, be such as to keep the project from seriously disturbing him. We wanted to lower his level of anxiety about coming but we wanted to do this by encouraging him in the process of self-examination.

Psychotherapists have their own individual styles of working with patients, but they all consider the first encounter with the patient highly significant. The transaction begins with the telephone call, the making of the appointment, the handshake at the beginning of the first hour. It continues with the more complex questions: Did the psychotherapist and the patient like each other? Even more importantly, did they think they could work with each other? When we originally conceived the project, foremost in our minds was whether the teen-agers would participate in such a project. Would a "normal" teen-age boy agree to talk about himself to a psychiatrist for an hour every three months throughout the high-school years? Might not such acquiescence in itself be a sign that there was something wrong with him? It was, therefore, with apprehension that we first made contact with a board of education in order to ask permission to conduct the study in their school. We had four rejections. It took us a year to find the two courageous suburbs whose boards of education agreed to participate and let us study their students in depth. We

needed the cooperation and support of the high-school adminis-
trations, the teachers, and the parents before we ever approached
our first adolescent subject. Once the teen-ager came to the office,
however, the major question was: Will he cooperate to reveal his
internal thoughts and feelings, including the socially unacceptable
ones? Obviously, not all teen-agers can be motivated to cooperate.
Eight per cent refused originally to participate in the project and
another 8 per cent dropped from the project after three interviews,
but it is of significance that we lost very few subjects after four or
more interviews.* One subject was dropped after we had talked
to him on the phone and he voiced no objections to the project,
but still persisted in not showing up. When a subject missed three
appointments in a row, an attempt was also made to talk to his
teacher and/or peers to find out what his objections were, if any.
Only 4 subjects (out of the total of 16 eventually dropped)
contacted us personally and told us they wanted no part of the
project. The other 12 had to be dropped by us, after they had
dropped out passively. In one case the father of a subject called
us to say that his son was being asked too deep and personal
questions and that he, the father, objected to it. When we asked
the father whether his son objected, the father replied, "No, he
doesn't but I do." The father seemed to be irritated by his son's
interest in some of our questions!

The great majority of the subjects were able to develop a
research alliance with us and to continue in the project for four
years. Once the subject came, the first interview was especially
important in establishing the nature of the relationship. The first
encounter may create special problems for the subject as well as
the investigator, especially when the encounter is a negative one.
For example, an initial negative attitude of the subject toward
the project and the interviewer may in turn produce a cool and
angry response from the interviewer. This in turn would
strengthen the negative feelings on the part of the subject, etc.,

* With the exception, of course, of those students whose families moved
away from the communities.

etc. It has been our experience that these difficulties may make it impossible to develop a research alliance. In addition, the lack of the subject's motivation in the classical psychiatric sense (that is, absence of therapeutic contract) makes it imperative for the researcher to build a congenial atmosphere for the project. It is important to understand negative feelings toward the project early and actively explore their sources. The latter task turned out to be a matter of importance for the project.

When the relationship causes resistance, in most cases the resistance must be interpreted so that the subject will remain active in the project. For example, during the second interview a subject told us he was discontinuing in the project because he had heard that we offered cigarettes. He was against smoking on principle. When we told him that we did not offer cigarettes, we observed a trace of disappointment in him. With further encouragement he was able to discuss the anxiety concerning his participation in the project, and resolve to continue as a research subject. The opposite problem of overt compliance is more subtle and difficult to recognize, since it often pleases the investigator and puts him at ease. It has been our experience, however, that eventually (generally after four interviews) the subtle hostility that usually underlies this form of overtly compliant behavior creeps out and turns into just another form of resistance.

To what extent did we unconsciously communicate to our subjects our own expectations from the research? There is no doubt that some teen-agers tried very hard to please us. But was not this, in a sense, just what we were seeking? Our job was to transform their compliance into a proffer of just what we wanted —their true feelings or their honest, free cooperation. We wanted them to help us understand them. We stressed that to be normal was not to be conflict-free, and that we did want to know about their conflicts. Their antagonism would serve the purpose of causing them to cover up or to protect themselves from what they might see as our prying. Their wish to please could be utilized to gain a more honest picture of their internal lives. This is why their

TABLE 10-1

Frequency Distributions and Reliability Coefficients for the Ratings of Subjects' Responsiveness

Variable	Excellent	Good	Fair	Poor	Total	Reliability*
Emotional experience	7 (9.6%)	38 (52.1%)	26 (35.6%)	2 (2.7%)	73	.73
Expressiveness (or ability to communicate)	21 (28.8%)	19 (26 %)	31 (42.5%)	2 (2.7%)	73	.84
Relationship with interviewer	26 (35.6%)	30 (41.1%)	16 (21.9%)	1 (1.4%)	73	.73

* Pearson-product moment correlations between two raters of a randomly selected subsample of 20 cases.

antagonisms needed to be uncovered and, whenever possible, overcome. We did this in part by the phrasing of our questions, asking for problem areas as well as those which gave pleasure. The subjects' wish to please allowed us also to ask more direct questions than might otherwise have been possible. Their responses did not always have to be of a type from which we could learn from their projections about, say, their friends' sex lives; we could ask them to share with us their own self-appraisals. Finally, their wish to please would lead them to present problems or psychologically meaningful events about which we had not directly inquired.

Thus, our aim was to obtain the subjects' cooperation, but we had to do this without the psychiatric contract of promising aid to them and, further, without giving any form of watered-down therapy. What was important was to be continuously cognizant of the nature of the relationship. As psychiatrists, our own self-awareness of message communications needed to be constantly reappraised.

Subjects' Responsiveness

How successful were we in gaining the subjects' cooperation? We used our half of the interaction as a tool, hoping it would be the best one to gain the alliance of the students. On the basis of the first five psychiatric interviews, the subjects' responsiveness was rated according to three variables: Emotional Experience, Expressiveness, and Relationship with Interviewer. The ratings were done by two raters who studied the records of the teen-agers independently. Each variable was on a four-point scale ranging from excellent to poor. The definitions for the two extreme points on each of the three variables were:

1. *Emotional experience*, or depth of emotions revealed. Excellent indicated revelation of rich inner life, deep emotions, and extensive range of experience with feelings. Poor indicated meager evidence of inner life or experience with affect.

2. *Expressiveness*, or ability to communicate. Excellent rating when subject gave elaborate answers and introduced new material of his own. Poor rating if answers were in monosyllables or indirect.

3. *Relationship with interviewer*. Excellent meant that as the relationship grew, the defenses changed and there was a sense of attachment to the interviewer. Poor connoted no noticed change in defense and a high level of anxiety present throughout.

The ratings reflect a combination of the effectiveness of the alliance and the verbal or introspective ability of the adolescent we were interviewing. It is important to stress that the above ratings are *not* construed as representing a measurement of health or illness, disturbance or adjustment. Our 7 subjects who were clinically disturbed were distributed among all three groups. This did not come as a surprise to us, since as psychotherapists we are well aware that the patient's ability to develop a "therapeutic alliance" is not necessarily related to the severity of his illness or to its phenomenology.

The three ratings together are seen as representing subject responsiveness which would be a partial index of the strength of the research alliance. The ratings do not show the full nature of the alliance, since we did not rate amount of therapy given or sought. Nor did we measure the indications of transference reactions or regression that might have been concealed within a high responsiveness rating. The responsiveness could be excellent while the research nature of the interview might be distorted.

The analysis of the rating shows that we have three distinctly different groups. First, the largest group, were the 35 subjects who were rated Good or Excellent on all three items. These students were able to describe their feelings well, their verbal ability was high, and they developed a meaningful relationship with us. Second was a group of 12 subjects who were rated Fair or Poor on all three items. These subjects did not develop a close alliance with us. They volunteered little or no information spontaneously and answered simply, often without revealing their deeper feelings.

Third, there was an in-between group of 26 teen-agers whose ratings were mixed, high in some answers and low in others. Since the intercorrelations between the three items were highly significant, we felt secure in adding them together to obtain a single index of subject responsiveness.

Within the high and low group ratings, it is difficult to know whether one variable, like Relationship with Interviewer, might not be the dominant influence affecting the rating of the other two variables. Did the low group represent our inability to engage all the teen-agers in the project? Our interviewing technique might not have been skillful enough to aid us in reaching beyond the inhibitions and antagonisms of certain adolescents. Nevertheless, we did feel that this group was also composed of those students who were most reluctant to examine themselves and those who had most difficulty in verbalizing their feelings in other than the interview situation.

In Table 10-2, the three variables (Emotional Experience, Expressiveness, Relationship with Interviewer) and their sum, which is taken to represent the strength of the subject responsiveness, are correlated with Likability, Cooperation, and Teachers' Rating (junior year). Likability was rated by the psychiatrist at the end of the seventh interview on a purely subjective basis. The subject's cooperation in the project was measured by scaling the number of missed appointments. Those with highest cooperation missed only once in three years; those subjects who missed two or three times were rated average in cooperation; and those who missed more than three interviews were rated as being less than average. These correlations suggest that there is a common element underlying subjects' Responsiveness, Likability, and Cooperation in the project. Those students who liked us came to the interview consistently and in turn were liked by us. The reciprocating factor of Likability might have increased the students' investment in us which resulted in a higher Responsiveness rating.

We correlated our Subjects' Responsiveness rating with the

TABLE 10–2

Intercorrelation of the Psychiatrist's Ratings, Teachers' Ratings, and Ratings of Interview Behavior

Variable	1	2	3	4	5	6	7	8	9	10	11
1. Emotional experience		.65	.40	.79	.23	.27	.07	.23	.40	.30	.41
2. Expressiveness			.64	.92	.23	.04	—.01	.12	.15	.27	.46
3. Relationship with interviewer				.82	.25	—.01	—.02	.04	.00	.24	.57
4. Subjects' responsiveness					.28	.10	.01	.15	.20	.31	.57
5. Leadership						.28	.38	.28	.27	.02	.10
6. Initiative							.33	.47	.68	.13	.00
7. Social sensitivity								.65	.45	.02	—.07
8. Responsibility									.66	.10	—.10
9. Industry										.17	.01
10. Cooperativeness											.23
11. Likability											

NOTE: Any value greater than .28 has $p \leq .01$. $N = 68$ for the correlation with Teachers' Ratings (Variables 5 to 9); $N = 73$ for the remaining variables.

Teachers' Ratings (see Chapter 3) because the teachers had rated variables similar to ours. In most areas our Subjects' Responsiveness ratings correlated significantly with the Teachers' Ratings. Leadership was the only Teachers' Rating that correlated significantly with all the responsiveness ratings. We did find it of interest that neither Social Sensitivity nor Responsibility correlated with the Responsiveness Ratings. Possibly this is because our three ratings represent responsiveness rather than maturity. Some of those who were responsive were also those who had regressed and were using us for therapeutic purposes.

We were also interested in exploring whether the type and depth of psychological information received from the adolescents depended on the development and maintenance of Subjects' Responsiveness. Out of the 12 major variables that we correlated with Subjects' Responsiveness, only two correlations were significant. Delinquency and Acting Out (see Chapters 5 and 8 respectively) correlated negatively. The better the student responsiveness, the *less* potential for acting out or delinquency. Because we found no other correlations, we cannot really say that subject responsiveness per se made a difference in our group as to the type of data collected.

We do believe, however, that more research is needed in this area before we can make a definite statement in this regard. We would also like to be able to test changes in our data induced by our "helping relationship." In the majority of cases, we felt that this change was very small but we have no controlled analyses.

Attitudes Toward the Project

Individual reactions to our project illustrate both the material from which our Subjects' Responsiveness ratings came and the nuances of the research vs. helping relationships. Many of the interesting and significant clinical data in the modal adolescent project resulted from the nature of the relationship we were able to build with the teen-agers over the four years. Many questions were directed toward reaching the students' feelings about our project. Within the context of every interview, we asked the subjects what they thought of the interview and of the project as a whole. From individual responses, we can evaluate the research alliances in operation. We can see, too, how the boys formed their alliance in accordance with their own psychological patterns.

Why, for example, were some students who impressed us as immature resistant to the project while others were almost too cooperative? Bob, for example, was worried about losing his parents and seemed afraid of what we might "force" him to reveal, so he talked little to us. He was the one who most often refused to answer our questions. He did not, for instance, want to tell us what he felt were the problems of adolescents, what his wishes were, or what he would do with a million dollars. Whom would he like to be with on a desert island? "I'd like to have my parents with me because then it would be safe and secure." Was he aware of his immaturity and afraid to join in a research alliance with us because of what his direct answers might reveal? He did frequently volunteer the subject of his mother's working for a particular firm. He liked neither the firm nor the idea of his mother's working. Bob himself was worried about not being able to succeed in carrying out his wishes. This fear he showed us in other ways throughout the interviews and also, perhaps, by his refusal to mention the wishes. We can make this interpretation of his refusal to cooperate on the basis of a series of other responses. He wanted to go to a particular university with high admission standards, but he did not think he could be accepted because, as he regretfully reported, he had only a C average. If rejected by the university, maybe he would become a pilot. He felt shame when he had bragged. He could not really achieve what he had claimed to have done. Bob's guilt was aroused when he did not study enough and then did poorly on an exam. We can gain insight into Bob's problems by the answers he did give and also into at least one of his ways of handling them—by camouflage, by his refusal to answer several questions. Bob formed a beginning of a research alliance by attending, but by refusing full cooperation he was protecting himself.

There was one other boy, Gerry, who came but refused to discuss several issues with us. He had difficulty forming the research alliance in the beginning. He seemed to have problems with forming most meaningful relationships. He refused to tell us his wishes. "What would you do with a million dollars?" "That is part of wishes, so I won't discuss it. Besides, I can't think of anything." "Whom would you like to have with you on a desert island?" "I'd like to be alone because alone, under pressure, I think better." By the Third Psychiatric Interview, we were able to involve this boy. He said he was glad to see the interviewer and he was answering all the questions. He closed the Fourth Psychiatric Interview with: "I'd like to see you more often." Was this a mood shift, a heightened self-confidence, or a development of an alliance? Although the former two may also be true, his plea for more sessions tended to support the theory of a growth of the alliance.

Phil read in a magazine that it is dangerous to poke around people's feelings, and especially their heads. He added very quickly after he made this critical statement, "I didn't mean any offense, mind you. People who don't know much about psychology should not go around asking people questions. Psychology is really very similar to philosophy and isn't a science at all." In a later interview, Phil was quite cooperative and said he had enjoyed the interview. He wanted to know how many had dropped out and why. After much probing, he admitted that he had considered dropping out but that because the interviewer had become personable and because he was curious each time before he came to see us, he was staying on.

Tom gives us an example of a form of alliance that failed, not in the sense of its strength to provide cooperation, but in that it became more of a therapeutic alliance than a research alliance. Tom caused us to feel slightly uneasy about our explicit intention not to do psychotherapy. This subject, who had been particularly uncooperative during the first two sessions, settled down and developed a meaningful research alliance with us. There was a seven-month interval between the Fourth and Fifth Psychiatric Interviews. When the subject came to the Fifth Psychiatric Interview, in the spring of 1966, he told us that during the preceding fall he had developed a strong urge to scream out in church. He had the urge almost every Sunday. At times he had it in school too. He also felt like running away from home. He had done neither of the two things. But the urges continued to bother him. During Christmas vacation he received a letter from us, as did every subject, thanking him for his past cooperation, stating that we would see him in the spring, and wishing him a merry Christmas and a happy New Year. The subject told us that he was very pleased to receive the letter and planned to tell us about his special feeling; but amazingly the urge had disappeared since his receipt of the letter.

Naturally, there were degrees in which we were used as therapists. Some subjects had difficulty in breaking away from their families. In forming outside relationships, they reacted not by fear of us but by leaning upon us and the alliance. Some of these subjects who we felt were immature, to judge by a series of responses, formed such a strong relationship with us that they had difficulty leaving at the end of an interview. One such boy, Ken, who was having problems of control, came to see us on a day when he had cut classes in order to go to the movies with a couple of girls from a different town. He told us that he enjoyed coming to see us. "I get a lot of things off my chest when I come here."

Frank, too, wanted to talk and talk with us. He had trouble leaving. His mother had been away in California for extended periods, and he seemed to be transferring his problem with separation to our "research" interview.

Gene began to develop his research alliance or trust in us at the First Psychiatric Interview. After answering many questions, he remarked just before leaving: "I thought you might want to know that my parents have been separated for the past two years." He must have felt defensive about this, because he had not mentioned it when asked questions about his family. Can we credit the alliance we formed with having made him comfortable enough to add this "afterthought"?

Paul, who had formed a strong alliance, coped with his needs for us by joking about them. "I don't know if I'll let my psychiatrist see my parents. Doesn't the psychiatrist have to ask his patient first?" In a later interview Paul told us: "Some people still think that the project is a joke but they also feel left out if they weren't taken for the project. But I really don't know what other people feel."

Still another boy, a sports star well accepted by his classmates, said he valued the opportunity to talk with us because he could really say what was on his mind.

Not all were anywhere nearly so cooperative; more usually they would cooperate with hesitation. "Your questions are probably important," was a not infrequent commentary on the project. These subjects were not too sure. Jack wondered if people were really telling us what they felt. He felt that he was but he wondered if the others would.

Mike thought that by now (the junior year) we had lost at least one-half of our subjects. He said he came out of curiosity. When told that few had dropped out, he was surprised but said, "I guess they have nothing better to do. I will probably drop later." This boy continued. The above conversation came after he had said that his father scared him. He seemed a little afraid that we would repeat this to his parents. In the opening interview, Mike had said that he was bigger than both his parents, but two years later he still felt that his father could beat him. As with so many of the subjects, his resistance to the project was a part of his general pattern of functioning. He proceeded with fear but he proceeded nonetheless and responded to our questions.

Tim said he objected to the project only when it took him away from athletic practice. When we pointed out that the interviews had never conflicted with his sports activities, he responded: "Oh, yeah. I guess, then, I like it." Another subject said: "I think other people might be sensitive about this interview, but I didn't mind it. I think maybe I can learn something from the interviews."

The nonchalant attitude was best epitomized by John. "Would you like to participate, John?" "Not emphatically." "Drop out?" "Not exactly." "Continue?" "Probably." This boy proved to be open and talkative. His commitment to the project, despite the unconcerned surface, was sufficient to motivate him to continue even after he later changed high schools. Here again, this boy's verbalized attitude toward the project was indicative of his attitudes toward many things. There was a combination of an "I don't care" attitude with a "But I really do." He thought school and vacations are boring *but* he liked hunting and fishing and wanted to be a better student.

Several of the examples presented are illustrative of only the individuals cited. At the least each example shows part of an individual pattern, and also indicates just why we enjoyed seeing the teen-agers. Although psychological patterns or statistical clusters might make the "normal students" sound uninteresting, the individual was not. As may sometimes be forgotten, the statistically "typical" student is not to be found. One of our subjects who had serious delinquent problems could be understood on the basis of a psychoanalytic model of adolescence. We wanted to do a profile of him, contrasting him with a boy who might illustrate the "normal" of our data. After searching through the files we found Bill, who really seemed to typify our subjects' responses. But Bill in his three wishes had wished for a change in physical size. He was the only one to wish for a change in size, and one of the few to indulge in a wish which was not also a goal toward which he could strive. Another subject looked good for the profile example, but he was one of the minority who felt different from his parents and by his senior year was not yet dating. So, obviously, he was not the boy to represent the majority. And then there was Kevin, a well-rounded sports enthusiast; but Kevin was getting high grades and was dissatisfied with his school perform-ance. Most of his classmates, in contrast, had C averages and told us they got good grades. It is this diversity which now makes sitting and reading through nine times 73 interviews with suburban boys so fascinating. It was this diversity (plus the suspense of not knowing whether or not they would "remember" their appoint-ments) that made the afternoons of interviewing the boys so rewarding.

We interviewed 73 students. We planned the program of the interviews in order to gain the maximum of information with the minimum of distortion. As we proceeded, we worked on engaging the students in a research alliance with us. We watched ourselves in order to maintain a middle position on the detachment-involve-ment and rejection-seduction continuums. We interpreted resist-ance to the project, unless it was too great in proportion to be easily interpreted. We wanted the students to join with us in our project of understanding psychological and behavioral processes of the adolescent. We rated the Subjects' Responsiveness and, finally, glimpsed at the types of responses we elicited about the project itself. These were our ways of involving the subjects. This was our own and the students' informal technique of interaction within the interview situation. Our data must be assessed for depth and accuracy within the knowledge of our technique, which limited us in some ways while also opening avenues into the study of normals that are not often followed.

11

Adolescent Turmoil

Definition of "Adolescent Turmoil"

The term "adolescent turmoil" has been utilized freely by psychiatrists and psychoanalysts when describing disturbed adolescents, as well as when discussing the developmental process of normal adolescence. The concept can be traced to G. Stanley Hall (1904), who in his two-volume treatise *Adolescence* introduced the phrase *"Sturm und Drang"** ("storm and stress") to characterize the psychology of adolescents. Hall stated that it is typical for adolescents to oscillate between the various extremes of psychological functioning. The adolescent will feel gay and altruistic one day and on the next day will feel nothing but hopelessness and depression. Apathy and enthusiasm are present almost concurrently, so that "Promethean enthusiasm" and deep romantic *"Weltschmerz"* represent the basic psychological characteristics of adolescents. Hall's biogenetic theory assumed that each individual

---

* "Sturm und Drang" comes directly from a German literary movement that stressed idealism, romanticism, rebellion against the old, and the expression of deep passions. Representative of this movement are Goethe's *The Sufferings of Young Werther* and Schiller's *Don Carlos*.

recapitulates the evolutionary developments of the human race in his own development (ontogeny recapitulates phylogeny). The past psychological experiences of the human race have become part of the genetic structure of humans, which unfolds as the individual child grows up. Adolescence was seen by Hall as the last of four stages of development. It is the final transitional stage between childhood and adulthood and as such it is full of turbulence and prepares the youth for "higher and more completely human traits" (Hall, 1904, p. xiii).

Turmoil is defined by Webster (1956) as "tumult, disturbance, confusion and uproar." It is not surprising, therefore, that the term "adolescent turmoil" has been utilized in descriptions of disturbed adolescents, or, if Hall's description is correct, of normal adolescents. However, consensually validated statements of typical or normal behavior are particularly difficult to formulate. Emotional conflicts seen as "normal" adolescent turmoil by one investigator often are regarded as psychopathological processes by another. The problem is compounded in the area of the teen-ager because it has been customary for psychiatrists to think of the teen-age period as one in which great turmoil exists in the process of the final crystallization of the adult personality. The theory of turmoil postulates a lowering of ego strength together with the upsurge of aggressive and sexual impulses leading to disruption of the psychic structure.

According to psychoanalytic theory, the teen-ager has a "second chance" during adolescence to undo the effects of his previous personality and to restructure his character (A. Freud, 1946, p. 82). Eissler (1958, p. 250) puts it even more dramatically—psychic structure "dissolves" during adolescence. That such a drastic occurrence would cause utter psychological chaos in the individual adolescent is understandable. The adolescent is left a slave to his impulses, unable to control them with ordinary psychological means, and is subject to a large number of symptoms and problems: antisocial behavior, anxiety, depression, looseness of thinking, "as if" personality, poor reality testing, intensity and volatility of feelings, and a continuous search for "kicks" and immediate gratifications. "Adolescent turmoil" is not considered, however, to be a psychiatric diagnosis since it is too vague and unclear a concept to enable psychiatrists to use it constructively (Masterson, 1967), especially when it is considered to be ubiquitous.

Clinical Conceptions of Adolescent Turmoil

While our data in this volume may lack the depth of psychoanalytic data, it has the attribute of being collected from the population whom we want to understand. Clinicians make statements about the normal developmental process of adolescence without having systematically studied any groups of normal adolescents. They extrapolate from the deviant or the disturbed to the normal, constructing a theoretical system based primarily on extensive and intensive study of patients. The examples we give below are taken from investigators who have (as they themselves state) studied mostly adolescents who were undergoing a great disruption of their lives, who were utterly confused and ridden with anxiety. These adolescents, primarily patients seen in clinical practice, have been the population from which the investigators felt it was legitimate and scientifically valid to build hypotheses concerning the normal adolescent processes.

Gardner (1959) assumes that the characteristics of the normal can be clearly seen by looking at the patient: "By way of illustration . . . I shall present and discuss our intake interview with a sixteen-year-old girl and the subsequent intake interview with the mother. In my opinion, these two interviews highlight most of the problems and anxieties (and defenses against anxieties) that one will meet in an *essentially normal adolescent*" (our italics). The same use of clinical evidence can also be found in Blos (1967); Josselyn (1952); A. Freud (1958); and Fountain (1961).

Erikson (1959) stated that the study of psychopathology may be the best route to normal psychology. In the same vein, Blos

(1961) stated (p. 215): "It is an accepted fact that we learn about the normal progression of development through developmental disturbances and their disruptive influence on the homeostatic controls of the personality." We raise the question whether this is the only way or even the best way to learn about the normal. It is possible that the differences in theoretical formulations concerning adolescent psychology are due not only to basic differences in psychological understanding (for example, depth psychology contrasted with phenomenology and behavior) but also to the differences in the populations being observed. (See also our book *Normality* [Offer and Sabshin, 1966], where these issues are discussed in greater detail.) Our study of normal adolescents should be seen in the context of an overall attempt to assess from a different perspective those concepts that were derived from psychopathology.

In most of her psychoanalytic writings, A. Freud (1936, p. 188) emphasizes the changes that take place within adolescence and their totally disruptive nature: "We have seen when the basis of comparison between puberty and the beginning of one of the periodic advances in psychotic disease is the effect which we attribute to the quantitative changes in cathexis. In each case the heightened libidinal cathexis of id adds to the instinctual danger, causes the ego to redouble its efforts to defend itself in every possible way." In other words, the weakening of the ego, together with increased id forces, makes it almost impossible for the adolescent to function in a balanced and harmonious way. Earlier A. Freud (1936, p. 158) had stated: "The relation established between the forces of the ego and the id is destroyed, the painfully achieved psychic balance is upset, with the result that the inner conflicts between the two institutions blaze afresh." Adolescents remind her of the patients described by Helene Deutsch as being "as if" because they really do not have the capacity to have truly consistent and stable object relationships.

Blos (1961) has presented a cogent psychoanalytical theory of adolescence. Although he emphasizes the constructive nature of the ego mechanisms in handling the overwhelming problems of adolescence, Blos does not question the force of these problems for the adolescent. He believes in the strength of the ego but feels that, nevertheless, aggressive sexual impulses will bedevil the ego. Blos (1961, p. 98) states: "In the body sphere it is the exertion, pain, and excessive motility; in the experiencing ego it is the overwhelming affective charge and its explosive release; in the self-observing ego it is the keen perception of inner life which characterizes an adolescent condition not wholly relegatable to the mechanisms of defense. In fact these ego states are important for shaping the specific and egosyntonic individual variant of adult drive organization . . . he does oscillate between both positions; his *turmoil* [our italics] abates with a gradual strengthening of controlling, inhibiting, guiding, and evaluative principles which render desires, actions, thoughts, and values egosyntonic and reality-oriented."

In the clinical literature the usage of dramatic terms such as "turmoil," "turbulence," "tremendous changes," and "chaos" is frequent. Typically, Blos (1961, p. 73) states: "A profound reorganization of the emotional life takes place during early adolescence and adolescence proper, with attendant and well-recognized states of chaos." For other examples, see Jacobson (1961); Josselyn (1952 and 1967); Laufer (1966); Pearson (1958); Geleerd (1961); and Deutsch (1967).

Blos avoids behavioral examples that can have multitudinous explanations. Josselyn (1952), however, does cite some that are similar to those exhibited during the high-school years by a small minority of our normal subjects. As behavioral manifestations of the chaos, turmoil, and strong mood swings of the adolescent, she cites smoking against parents' wishes, coming home late at night, or driving at high speed. As we have seen in our data and will discuss (see below), this *type* of disruptive behavior occurred most frequently in the early adolescence of our subjects. In general, our high-school students had left the acting out of impulses behind them. Few parents or students reported difficulties in these areas. The conflicts did remain in the area of fantasy and of problems to be solved; the subjects were still unsure of their control and asking for aid.

The Questionable Validity of the Clinical Concept of Adolescent Turmoil

Adolescent turmoil represents a significant disruption in the psychic organization of the adolescent that leads to psychological disequilibrium and tumult, resulting in fluctuant and unpredictable behavior. Given this definition, we have not found turmoil to be prevalent in our normal adolescent population. Behavioral and emotional indices gained through interviews of the adolescents and parents, teacher ratings, and analyses of psychological testing all deny the existence of turmoil on a grand scale in our adolescent subjects. The concept of adolescent turmoil should be seen as only one route for passing through adolescence, one that the majority of our subjects did not utilize. Rebellion was seen in the early adolescence of our subjects; in all but a few cases the rebellious behavior was not a part of a total picture of turmoil but was coped with before it grew to chaotic proportions for the individuals involved.

If we could only have delved a little deeper, would we have found uncontrollable tumult? Or would we know a manifestation of turmoil when we saw it? Behavior and verbalizations can be interpreted in an almost unlimited manner. The question of the strength of turmoil is not, though, the problem of tying one particular behavior to one particular psychic aberration but, rather, that of regarding the whole pattern of the behavior plus the meaning of the pattern to the individual. If turmoil is strong, we should not have to probe deeper than our study did. Surely a state of internal chaos should be recognizable to the trained eye over a period of time, to the raters who reviewed the interviews, to the psychologists from their testing, or to other adults who knew the adolescents. The nature of turmoil is not such as to be able to keep itself hidden from the world, while presenting a picture of flexibility and good control over reality. We did find that seven of our subjects exhibited clinical syndromes that could be considered as indications of states of turmoil. For the rest of our subjects, the more suitable hypothesis is that the amount of turmoil experienced during their high-school years was slight. If we delved deeper without causing transference, regression, and the other manifestations of an analysis, we postulate that we would have found emotional crises similar to those of other transition periods when major decisions must be made and identity consolidated rather than the unique chaos of adolescent turmoil.

We are trying to bridge a gap between depth psychology and the type of information we were able to obtain through our interviews and testing. A relationship that is possible to evaluate must exist. "Theoretically, we cannot fracture mentation and behavior. They are both part of the total field, and behavior is the final pathway of the various internal dynamics plus the availabilities of the external environment" (Grinker, 1968). If extreme turmoil is conceptualized as an internal process, it is inconceivable that it will have only minute behavioral consequences. From our observations of our high-school students, they have not demonstrated any strongly deviant behavior. In home and school, they have presented an overall pattern of consistency. This being the case, we challenge the concept of great inner turmoil being a necessary part of adolescence. The turmoil experienced by the majority of our subjects is quantitatively different from the turmoil experienced by patient or delinquent populations. The rebellion we see in our subjects, the emotional conflicts and crises that are both seen and postulated, point toward theoretical conceptualizations of at least one type of normal adolescent with a lower level of turmoil than indicated in much of accepted psychiatric theory. We have studied our subjects for six years now, and have found no evidence to suggest that they are withdrawn, underdeveloped, or inhibited adolescents.

Investigators who have spent most of their professional lives studying disturbed adolescents stress the importance of a period of turmoil through which all teen-agers must pass in order to grow up into mature adults. On the other hand, investigators who, like us, have studied normal adolescent populations tend to minimize the extent of the turmoil.*

Many investigators in the social and behavioral sciences have previously questioned the universality of the turmoil theory of adolescence. Hollingworth (1928, p. 1) says: "The child grows by imperceptible degrees into the adult." M. Mead's (1928) study on adolescents in Samoa pointed to the lack of turmoil in the children and adolescents she studied. Most of the standard texts in the field of adolescent psychology have questioned the universality of the "Storm and Stress" theory of adolescence (see, for example, Ausubel, 1954; Hurlock, 1955; and Stone and Church, 1957). The question remained, however, whether the "Storm and Stress" theory was applicable to adolescents growing up in the Western culture. More recent psychosocial studies of Davis (1944), Hsu (1961), Keniston (1962), Friedenberg (1960), Elkin and Westley (1955), and Douvan and Adelson (1966) who have studied middle-class adolescents in the Western culture have all stated that they have not found emotional turmoil among their subjects. Similarly, Gesell (1956) described his teen-age subjects as not turbulent, erratic, or troublesome, but pleasant, easy to get along with, and living in harmony with themselves and their environment. Gesell sees the adolescent process as a ripening process, though not without irregularities. In the psychiatric literature, Grinker (1962, 1963) and Masterson (1967) have made similar observations.

Spranger (1955), a German psychiatrist, theorizes that basically there are three different patterns of developmental rhythms. First is the *"Sturm und Drang"* theory of adolescence, which would correspond to Hall's theory as well as to much of the

---

* An exception is Kiell (1964), who in his book *The Universal Experience of Adolescence* favors the turmoil theory. Example after example, carefully selected by the editor, seems to confirm his original hypothesis. It is true enough that Werther, Felix Kroll, or Stephen Dedalus will confirm the turmoil theory. However, are we not overzealous in our search for proofs, if we use the poets' creations as the *only basis* for our scientific theory?

psychoanalytic theory. Second is growth in spurts, which is often seen in adolescents who have much self-control and discipline and are power-hungry. In this pattern the adolescent participates actively in molding his career and future. Third, there is the group of adolescents in which no turmoil is observed; development is continuous and undisturbed, and there are no basic personality changes. This division of the adolescents into three groups is consistent with our contention that a high level of turmoil is characteristic of only one route from adolescence to maturity. While Spranger's theory leads him to make this three-way division which corresponds so well with our way of thinking, he believes in inborn and instinctual tendencies, which unfold in later developments. We would emphasize environmental and psychological conditioning. It would seem that the antecedent of a nonturmoil path through adolescence is a nonstressful childhood (one in which not very many developmental and accidental "crises" have occurred prior to reaching adolescence).

The Normative Crises of Adolescence

What manifestations of inner turmoil do we see? Anyone who reads the chapters in Part II, "Results," is surely aware that our subjects are not free from emotional conflicts or problems. It seems to us that Erikson's concept of *normative crisis* (1959) is more applicable to our subjects than the concept of turmoil. "Crisis" is defined by *Webster New Twentieth Century Dictionary* (1956) as "decisive or crucial time; a turning point." In other words, "normative crisis" does not imply chaos but typifies the kind of problems one sees in any of the major transitional periods in life.

Erikson (1959, p. 116) says:

> The final assembly of all the converging identity elements at the end of childhood (and the abandonment of the divergent ones) appears to be a formidable task: How can a stage as "abnormal"

as adolescence be trusted to accomplish it? Here it is not unnecessary to call to mind again that in spite of the similarity of adolescent "symptoms" and episodes to neurotic and psychotic symptoms and episodes, adolescence is not an affliction but a *normative crisis,* i.e., a normal phase of increased conflict characterized by a seeming fluctuation in ego strength and yet also by a high growth potential. Neurotic and psychotic crises are defined by a certain self-perpetuating propensity, by increasing waste of defensive energy, and by a deepened psychosocial isolation; while normative crises are relatively more reversible or, better, transversible, and are characterized by an abundance of available energy which, to be sure, revives dormant anxiety and arouses new conflict, but also supports new and expanded ego functions in the searching and playful engagement of new opportunities and associations. What under prejudiced scrutiny may appear to be the onset of a neurosis is often but an aggravated crisis which might prove to be self-liquidating and, in fact, contributive to the process of identity formation.

The normative crisis is a concept which is applicable to our data. Our only divergence is in the area of the appearance of similarities between the neurotic and the adolescent. Erikson says that although states of neurosis and the process of adolescence appear similar, they are really different. In our population we do not see evidence of them even appearing similar. (See also Masterson, 1967.) It is also of interest to note that where Erikson gives examples of eight problems or crises of the adolescent, he illustrates each by an example of psychopathology taken from the negative end of a continuum. Why are there no examples of healthy or adaptive responses to adolescence? Where are the examples of true "normative crisis"? It seems that for Erikson, too, it is easier to give clinical examples.

If adolescence includes normative crises, and we believe that it does, does it have the same characteristics that *all transitional periods* have? Again, we believe that it does. Our present state of knowledge does not allow us to make the statement Blos (1967) has made: "Adolescence is the only period in human life during which ego repression and drive regression constitute an obligatory component of normal development." No one has attempted to compare adjustment of the same individuals across different transitional stages. Only after such longitudinal studies are carried out convincingly shall we be able either to accept Blos's theory or need to revise it.

The transitional period of adolescence does present the adolescent with a special burden, a challenge, and an opportunity. He has to individualize, build up confidence in himself and his abilities, make important decisions concerning his future, and free himself of his earlier attachments to his parents. Our observations have led us to conclude that the majority of the teen-agers in our sample cope with these tasks successfully. They lack the turmoil of the disturbed adolescent precisely because their ego is strong enough to withstand the pressures. In their task they are greatly helped by their parents. If other subjects are found to have exaggerated turmoil and be just as well adjusted, or normal, as our students, they will have chosen a separate route to maturity.

Yet our subjects were not devoid of problems. They did not go through life sheltered and unscathed. It seems to us that someone might eventually raise an objection concerning our subjects that, because of their low level of turmoil, they are cases of arrested development. Certain investigators who have also observed the low level of turmoil in a large number of adolescents have interpreted their findings somewhat differently than we have. Friedenberg (1960), Adelson (1964), Douvan and Adelson (1966), and Keniston (1962) are concerned about the lack of turmoil and rebellion in their subjects. Implicitly these investigators have adopted the position that lack of turmoil is a bad prognostic sign and must necessarily prevent the adolescent from developing into a mature adult. All our data, including the psychological testing, point in the opposite direction. The adolescents not only adjusted well; they were also in touch with their feelings and developed meaningful relationships with significant others.

The adolescent must neutralize his ties with his parents in order to become a mature and independent adult. Our subjects go through the process gradually so that the change is not dramatic. In *Adolescence* (1958, p. 269), A. Freud mentions for the first and only time that the difference between normal development and psychopathology depends in part on whether the cathectic shifts in adolescence are gradual or sudden and precipitous. When gradual detachment from the parents is allowed to take place, the defenses are transitory, are less intense, and do not have an all-or-none quality. When the change is sudden, the sequence of events assumes more of a defensive and pathological quality rather than that of normal growth. This state of affairs, rather than her far more often quoted "the upholding of a steady equilibrium during the adolescent process is in itself abnormal," characterizes our adolescent subjects.

*Adolescent Rebellion**

Our subjects manifested the greatest amount of turmoil in early adolescence (ages twelve to fourteen). Both parents and adolescents agreed that the most difficulties in everyday relationships had occurred in the pre-high-school years.

According to Webster (1956), "rebellion" is defined as "open resistance to, or defiance of, any authority." The most important authority to the adolescent, of course, is his parents, though other authority figures are included.

The concept of rebellion has to be distinguished from the concept of emancipation from the parents. In tracing the relationship between the two, we believe that the main function of rebellion in the modal adolescent is to achieve an initial step in the process of emancipation from the parents. However, not all adolescent rebellion is in the service of emancipation. The concept of emancipation is not inherent in rebellion, although it is often associated with it. Clarification will be served if the definition of rebellion is kept strictly to the phenomena of *open resistance and defiance of any authority*. With the establishment of this definition of rebel-

---

* The section on rebellion is based to a large extent on a collaborative study done with Brahm Baittle (Baittle and Offer, 1969).

lion, some clarity may be brought to the literature. Questions such as the relative frequency of rebellion in different generations of adolescents, and the "healthiness" or "pathology" of rebellion, may be more easily and accurately answered when the definition is not complicated with the questions of values and emancipation.

Rebellion in our normal subjects is characterized by chronic infighting (lasting one to two years) with parents and school-teachers in the pre-high-school years. This infighting is over issues that seem small or undramatic. The rebellion does not involve serious or repeated delinquencies, nor does it involve the plunging and rising of great emotional states. "Bickering" is the word most characteristic of these disturbances. Our findings in this respect agree with some of the reports in the recent social-psychological literature (Keniston, 1962; Douvan and Adelson, 1966) which state that adolescents of this generation do not rebel against the entrenched important values of the parents' generation. These investigators say therefore the rebellion is insignificant. It is true that the rebellion we observe is microscopic in size as to the content of the issues; and it may easily seem to the adult outsider, especially if he happens to be a reformer as well as an observer, that the whole phenomenon is trivial and has no importance; that it connotes a complacency, conformity, and loss of autonomy or identity in the adolescent, terms that are more or less vaguely defined. In contrast, we emphasize that the rebellion has vital and important meaning to the adolescent in this stage of his development. Even though violent emotions are not involved, the same emancipation is at stake as for the adolescent who proceeds in a more tumultuous manner. At this stage the parents of our adolescent subjects did not regard their sons' behavior as trivial. For instance, the great majority of the parents say that the early adolescent years (twelve to fourteen) are the most difficult time they have in raising their children. A similar finding has been described by Gesell *et al.* (1956).

If the adolescent rebellion that we have observed is essentially independent of acceptance or rejection of parental values, then what is its main function? We see the main function of adolescent rebellion for our subjects as serving to initiate or reinforce a process that leads to emancipation from the parental objects (Pearson, 1958; Blos, 1961, pp. 73, 91, and 208). They accomplish this emancipation without having completely to decathect parents and parental imagos. They retain much of the parents' value system while establishing their independence in other areas.* Thus moderate rebellion contributes to the growth of the adolescent in one of his most crucial tasks. The adolescent becomes a general irritant to his parents, although, as we have seen, he respects his parents' opinion at the same time. Our adolescent subjects' rebelliousness is in the service of disengagement from the major influence of parental authority, and usually disappears when the adolescents become involved in the new world of the high-school years, with sports, school work, and girls becoming greater contenders for their interests.

When the adolescent rebels, he often expresses his intentions in a manner resembling negation (Freud, 1925). He defines what he does in terms of what his parents do not want him to do. If his parents want him to turn off the radio and study, this is the precise time he keeps the radio on and claims he cannot study. If they want him to buy new clothes, the old ones are good enough. In periods like this, it becomes obvious that the adolescents' decisions are in reality based on the negative of the parents' wishes rather than on their own positive desires. What they do and the judgments they make are, in fact, dependent on the parents' opinions and suggestions, but in a negative way. This period may be termed a stage of "negative dependence." Thus, while the oppositional behavior and protest against the parents are indeed a

---

* Conversely, Rabin (1965), Neubauer (1965), and Eisenberg and Neubauer (1965) found no rebellion in their studies of youth in collective settlements (kibbutzim) in Israel. However, these investigators point to a discrepancy between the attitudes of the parents and the children toward intellectual pursuits. Perhaps the rebellion of the kibbutz adolescents is accomplished in the area of academic values, though it is only one aspect of the parental value system.

manifestation of rebellion and in the service of emancipation from the parents, the behavior reveals at the same time that the passive dependent longings are still in force. The adolescent is in conflict over his desires to be emancipated, and the rebellious behavior is a compromise formation that supports his efforts to give up the parent and at the same time gratifies his dependent longings for them. That the adolescent is not confident of his emancipation—has not completed the process of emancipation—might imply an underlying persistence of unacceptable dependency wishes.

This negative behavior diminishes within the high-school years, when the "psycho-social" moratorium is established. The *psycho-social moratorium*, according to Erikson (1968, p. 157), is "a period that is characterized by a selective permissiveness on the part of society and of provocative playfulness on the part of youth." This period may be responsible for absorbing later rebellion. In the pre-high-school years, parents and adolescents are fearful of the outbreaks that come as setting precedents for the teen years; minor infractions may be taken more seriously than later when they are "supposed" to occur. In the high-school years, the psycho-social moratorium allows the student to some extent to test his environment without causing external traumata that might then intensify his inner turmoil.

To be differentiated from the "psycho-social moratorium" (Erikson, 1968) is a state of affairs in society which seems to encourage rebellion. One of the most subtle, in our opinion, is within the scientific literature on adolescence itself. In some articles, adolescent rebellion is romanticized. For instance, Gustin (1961) writes as follows:

> Rebellion, too, is an essential dimension of life. Life without the protest against serfdom, the search for new directions, would indeed be gruesome—if conceivable. The dream of overthrow, the promise of change, the discovery of the unusual, the joy of creation is the hope that continues to pump the blood in our veins and makes life worth struggling for.

The press, too, has romanticized the deviant adolescent. For the hippies' culture, LSD consumption, or just plain delinquency, the press finds a place among its most worthy news. We in the social sciences likewise glamorize the rebellions that offer us a possibility of change. Whether the young people of today, a sample of which we have studied, will change the world and make it a better place is a sociological question. Social engineers like P. Goodman (1962) feel that youth *ought* to change the world. It is our impression that, for better or for worse, the sample investigated by us is growing up to become very much a part of the culture into which they were born.

Affective Responses

With the diminishing of the mild rebellion of early adolescence, will we see other manifestations of turmoil? Swings of mood and unreliability were observed, but again, they were not characteristic of the adolescent population. Many writers have stressed the fluctuating behavior of the adolescent as one of the most obvious manifestations of his turmoil; see especially Blos (1961), A. Freud (1936), Josselyn (1952), Pearson (1958), Jacobson (1961), and Laufer (1966). These authors have said in essence that an adolescent can be showering love one day and be on a hateful rampage the next; be depressed, lonely, and hopeless one day, and be optimistic, altruistic, and overexhilarated the next. The mood swings in adolescence are presented as much greater than those in any other stage of life. Yet we have not observed any dramatic mood swings or affective lability in our subjects. On the whole, they were not weighted down by gross affective problems. When a teen-ager felt depressed or anxious (the two most common affects in our group), he recognized the feeling, used very little immediate denial, and usually coped with the feeling either by action or by change in focus. There was little brooding or rumination. Most of the affect was dealt with by adaptive utilization of denial, isolation, direct action, and rationalization.

Our subjects were not free of *any kind* of mood swings. For example, on the phone they would sound enthusiastic about the interview for the next afternoon. They would tell us that they had a lot that they wanted to tell us and that they were looking forward to seeing us again. Then they would not show up. When we would call them to ask whether anything had happened to them, they would answer in a detached and uninterested way: "No, nothing happened, Doctor. I just forgot." Thus we did observe mood swings in our subjects, but they were less extreme and less frequent than those described in the literature.

As in rebellion, the affective response may look minor while representing an emotional discharge of significance. Displacement would be accomplished without the awareness of the adolescent. In examining our interview data, we find that we cannot evaluate what individual responses meant to the subject himself. What is the meaning of his depression after the death of a pet? His exhilaration after shooting a basket? These responses represent emotional reactions to inner conflicts of great importance for the consolidation of his identity. But to say the emotional discharge is displaced is not to say that the inner turmoil need be poignant. As long as this displacement remains one that is manageable and the boy's reaction is a coping one, the original emotion could not have been chaotic. Had it been, the displacement or a whole chain of displacements would not have been effective.

In the majority of our students, ego mechanisms sufficed to handle aggressive or sexual impulses (see Chapter 13). The behavioral manifestations do imply inner processes that remain hidden from us in our type of study, but they give no support to theories of inner violence. Our students remained flexible, stable, and relatively consistent. If their inner psychic state was in constant unbalance, we would see the same manifestations of rigid emotional states or aggressive outbursts that we see in the behavior of our psychiatric patients.

We are talking in degrees, using terms such as "less," "strong," "low level of turmoil," and "exaggerated turmoil." There is a quantitative difference between the level of turmoil exhibited in the observed behavior of our adolescent subjects and in the normal adolescent process as conceived in much of the literature. Repeated inconsistencies in their actions, prolonged or swiftly changing affective states, and states of extreme altruism or egotism or of idealism or conservatism were rarely seen. (On a continuum from normal to psychotic, our data suggest that for our population, the normal adolescent process is closer to the normal end of the continuum than is often conceptualized.) Just how much of a change in our thinking is justified is more difficult to measure. Our symptom rating scale is suggested as one means of measuring affects; the scale (see Chapter 8) systematizes our evaluations of the subjects in the interviews and compares these to analogous patient data.

Our symptom rating scale shows that the symptoms that had the largest mean rating (that is, more of them were observed in our subjects) were anxiety, acting out, and depression, in that order. The second group of symptoms included shame, obsession, compulsion, and guilt. The group with the lowest ratings were suspicion, turmoil, phobia, distortion, and dissociation. From the factor analysis, we found that the two main factors were (1) Anxiety and (2) Obsessive-compulsion (plus depression). The third factor, Turmoil, was the least important. All the symptom ratings were done in comparison to those of patients. In general, our modal group is rated low on the scale of each of the 12 symptoms. The symptom with the lowest variance was Turmoil. Thus, when we implicitly compare our students with our patients, we note a difference between the occurrence of symptoms in the two groups. The low rating of turmoil compared to the relatively high rating of anxiety, acting out, and depression also serves to demonstrate that signs of turmoil were less often present in our group.

The symptoms were rated from the perspective of psychopathology. The clustering of symptoms in the factor analysis demonstrates that, if we use the 12 symptoms as a base line, our subjects utilize basically three different responses to potentially traumatic situations: (1) Anxiety, (2) Obsessive-compulsion and depression, and (3) Turmoil associated with acting out. Our data suggest that although the three factors overlap somewhat, the subjects who tend to use one pattern will not utilize the other two.

The symptoms that we observed were mild. They were easily handled by the adolescent, and only on rare occasions reached clinical proportions. The fact that the students could describe the different affective states to us meant that affective experiences were present and for the most part were ego-syntonic.

Conclusion

Studies of normal populations that exhibit little behavioral disequilibrium might eventually lead to the concept that adolescence as a period of growth can be undergone without serious disruptions between the generations or between the adolescent and his former identity. The transition to adulthood may be accomplished gradually, but accomplished all the same. Our findings emphatically suggest that a state of inner turmoil need not be the password of adolescence.

12

The Adolescent and His Parents: The Bridge Between the Generations

The teen-agers we have studied were by and large an integral part of the culture within which they lived. They were proud of their schools, their communities, and the achievements of their parents. The adolescents lived in the present although they had definite plans for their future life. It seemed to us that because the adolescents were so much a part of their times, their attitude toward psychiatry was sympathetic. The teen-agers reflected the increasingly positive attitudes of the general population toward psychiatry. We believe that the parents would not have supported the project if there had not been a generally favorable atmosphere for psychiatric studies in the community. Much publicity has been given to the various causes of mental illness, and community psychiatry has undertaken a vigorous campaign to "re-educate" the public concerning mental health and mental illness. Only one subject was not allowed to participate in the study because his mother was against psychiatry "in principle." And only two other subjects were not allowed to continue in the project because their fathers felt that we were asking their sons questions which were private and "the business of no one." The great majority of the parents were enthusiastic about the project and encouraged their children to participate. There is no question that the teen-agers would not have cooperated as fully as they did without their parents' explicit and especially implicit support. Both the adolescent and his parents expected us to be "sympathetic listeners" and positive forces in their lives, just like the psychiatrist who was so often depicted in the magazines or on the TV screens (as in the program "The Eleventh Hour").

The adolescent was not only an integral part of the community in which he lived but also a proud and contributing member to his own family. He was able to discuss most of his problems and concerns openly with his parents; the exception was his sexual feelings and impulses. Both the teen-ager and his parents believed that they had a relatively good relationship and they were proud of the relationship. The adolescent saw his mother as warm and understanding; although his feelings toward her were often ambivalent, he always felt that they understood each other. Communication was flowing and open. On the other hand, the relationship with the father, although comparatively stultified and less warm, was one of respect and distant admiration. The adolescent's communication with the father did not concern emotion-laden aspects of his life, but it did concern all his vocational and educational interests.

Because of these observations of "family harmony" for our group of students, we were perplexed as to the causes for the tremendous generalizations appearing in the professional literature concerning normal parent-adolescent conflicts. (For example, see Pearson, 1958; Josselyn, 1952; Ackerman, 1958; K. Davis, 1940; Coleman, 1961.) Among our modal adolescent sample only very few were members of deviant groups where parental values would be seriously challenged. In adolescent groups such as the delinquent gangs, the drug users, the emotionally disturbed, or the beatniks and the hippies, one can expect and does find conflicts over behavior as well as tremendous gaps between the generations. Even in the latter examples, there are often more shared values and/or psychopathology than is apparent on the first inspection. It seemed to us that the main reasons for the overgeneralization are that the deviant groups are more visible, are studied more often, and possibly excite the fantasy of the public more.

Many psychiatric writings have stressed the breakdown of communication in the modern family. For example, Ackerman (1958) writes about the psychological implications of the economic and industrial revolution and its effects on the family's adaptive response. Ackerman cites Burgess, who says change in the family is seen (among others) in the following items: relative decrease in the authority of the father, parental uncertainty, irresponsibility of children. Ackerman writes: "In our era, parents are notorious doubters. They feel chronically uncertain. They try desperately to be independent, to make responsible decisions on their own. But the striving for independence and self-sufficiency is often spurious, exaggerated, and defensive in nature. It is pseudo adequacy, not real strength or genuine autonomy. . . . The family is emotionally isolated. There is disparity between what the family believes it is or ought to be compared with what it actually is. Emotional sharing and identification are thinned, and effective communication is reduced." Ackerman's conclusions are based on his studies of disturbed families. (A similar view has also been expressed by Gardner, 1957.) We wonder why Ackerman feels impelled to generalize from his own direct observations on a select population to the culture at large. Our findings presented earlier in this volume are in direct contradiction to Ackerman's speculations (1966) that stem from studies and treatment of disturbed families.

Similarly, Keniston (1962) discusses the lack of "deep" commitment on the part of adolescents to adult values and roles. The adult world seems cold and mechanical to adolescents so, according to Keniston, they "play it cool." But the adolescents wish that there were "better" values and goals which they would be willing to join and better models for them to follow. Keniston has studied alienated youth at Harvard University for many years. His book *The Uncommitted* (1965) is a description of this population. We would speculate that he, like Ackerman before him, over-generalized from his own studies and observations to society at large.

Margaret Mead has also been critical of the "failure to adopt our educational and social system . . . [which] may be held responsible for some of the sense of self-alienation, search for negative identities, and so forth, characteristic of this present group of young people" (1961, p. 49). She feels that the pressure on the young people of today is so strong that it leaves the young person little room for experimentation. According to Mead, today's adolescents are too "success-oriented." The adolescents are accused by Mead of not being idealistic and romantic enough and are told that this is bad for their identity. Similar statements are made by Adelson (1964), who writes: "American adolescents are on the whole not deeply involved in ideology, nor are they prepared to do much individual thinking on value issues of any generality." Adelson concludes with the following statement: "These modes of dealing with inner and outer experience join to produce a pseudo-adaptive solution of the adolescent crisis, marked by cognitive stereotype, value stasis, and interpersonal conformity." (Similar views are also expressed by Friedenberg, 1960; Coleman, 1961; Goodman, 1962.)

These statements are selected to point to a dilemma confronting the present-day researchers in the area of youth studies. The American adolescent is one of the most frequently studied individuals in the world. More studies are performed on youth than on any other group. The large outflow of reports has increased our sophistication in understanding young people, but we are forced to examine the validity of the conclusions drawn by the investigators quoted above concerning their (1) methodology, (2) subgroups sampled, and (3) theoretical frames of reference that influence data collected and analyzed. In order to assess change, one needs to have comparative data. The studies on various populations reported do not have a base line. Those of us who are studying groups of normal adolescents are exploring populations that *have never before been studied.* There are no comparable studies on normal teen-agers in the eighteenth or nineteenth centuries. Even anthropological studies of adolescents in other cultures cannot serve as a model, since their data were collected for different purposes and are not directly comparable.* The available literature deals with the *visible* adolescents of former times. Similar idealistic and ascetic young men and women can be found today among our adolescent population. It is our thesis, then, that had Adelson, Mead, Keniston, Ackerman, and the others intensely studied normal adolescents of previous generations, their findings would very likely have been the same. Only the external factors would have differed. The studies of today utilizing the clinical interview will, we hope, enable the researchers of the future to compare their data meaningfully with ours.

The Adolescent Subculture: Myth or Reality?

An adolescent subculture is often thought to be the breeder of its own value system. According to this theory, the adolescent becoming a part of such a subculture would have the support of others in his rejection of his parents and their values. (See, for example, Coleman, 1961, who supports the thesis of a subculture; and Elkin and Westley, 1955, and Petersen, 1961, who question it.) Our findings do not support the suggestion that there is a subculture influencing or creating special value systems for adoles-

---

* Anthropological data have usually focused on observable behavior as means of gathering data on cultural norms. They have not concentrated on studying individual coping styles and internal feeling states.

cents. We have found a direct continuum between the adolescent and his parents, a continuum based on sharing the same basic values. This was confirmed by both the teen-agers and their parents.

Coleman has examined the question of the subculture in *The Adolescent Society* (1961), a study of 10 Midwestern high schools from a sociological point of view. One of the high schools he describes, Executive Heights, is very similar to our High School B. It too was in an upper middle-class suburb. Coleman concludes from his data that yes, adolescents definitely live in their own subculture. Athletics is the dominant factor in the subculture. In every question, in every preference scale, in every school, the image of the athlete dwarfs all else. Coleman believes that this dominance comes about because athletics is both action- and group-oriented while scholarship, for example, is individual-oriented. Coleman believes the parents of the teen-agers have a different scale of values than their children, but he found a sharp divergence between the professed values of the parents and the interpretation of the parents' values by the teen-agers. Coleman interprets the divergence thus (p. 34):

> Why this discrepancy? Is someone not being honest? Are the parents' professed values and expressed values as greatly at variance as they seem—or do boys and girls see their parents' values as they want to see them? Perhaps neither is the case. It may be that most parents hold academic achievement as an ideal for their children in school, as their responses indicate. But parents also want their children to be successful in the things that "count" in the school, that is, the things that count in the eyes of the other adolescents. And parents know what things count. Being a biology assistant counts far less in the adolescent culture than does making the basketball team for boys, or making the cheerleading squad for girls. Thus, even the rewards a child gains from his parents may help reinforce the values of the adolescent culture—not because his parents hold those same values, but because parents want their children to be successful and esteemed by their peers.

Thus parents were said to encourage something which they felt would make their child happy, yet something to which they would otherwise have been indifferent. Coleman is supplying an interpretation for his present data. Perhaps the adolescent data need a similar interpretation because of a discrepancy found there too —between individual values and the values of the adolescent culture. Must not the two have a close relationship if the existence of the latter is postulated at all? Coleman says (1961, p. 305):

> The average boy, as an individual, appears to be more oriented to scholarship than is the social system of the high school. The norms of the system constitute more than an aggregate of individual attitudes; they actually pull these attitudes away from scholarship. The implication is striking: the adolescents themselves are not to be held accountable for the norms of their adolescent culture. As individuals, they are less oriented away from scholarship than they are as a social system.

The reader of Coleman's book is left perplexed. He has found that the adolescents would answer the same question differently when asked individually and as a projected norm. Why does Coleman stress the "social system values" more than individual value systems? Do the former really influence the behavior of the person more than his individual beliefs? Even assuming that Coleman's data are completely valid, we would have to conclude that he found a conflict in the adolescent mind of what to value more—in his example, athletics or scholarship. We find that the adult society has not solved this dilemma either. If Coleman were to ask, for example, both the adolescents and their parents to choose between going to a football game and listening to a lecture by a famous scientist, we predict that the same percentage *in both generations* would elect each event. By examining the actual behavior (e.g., "How many times have you gone to a sports event in the past year? vs. What do you do to pursue your adult education?") of the parents, he might have found, as we did, that the "adolescent subculture" is a reflection of the adult culture. His view, though, is quite different (1961, p. 3):

> In our modern world of mass communication and rapid diffusion of ideas and knowledge, it is hard to realize that separate subcultures can exist right under the noses of adults—subcultures with

languages all their own, with special symbols, and, most importantly, with value systems that may differ from adults'. Any parent who has tried to talk to his adolescent son or daughter recently knows this, as does anyone who has recently visited a high school for the first time since his own adolescence. To put it simply, these young people speak a different language. What is more relevant to the present point, the language they speak is becoming more and more different.

Do the adolescents really speak a different language? At times they do—and certain specific adolescent groups do (for example, the hippies). However, in our experience the teen-agers talk our language, and vice versa. Our whole work, it seems to us, can serve as a recommendation for this point. In our studies of individuals we have found great congruence between the values of the adolescent and his parent. True, we did not observe at firsthand the peer culture, but we believe that our findings on individual psychology raise many questions about separate subcultures. Our findings are in agreement with Westley (1958), who stated that mentally healthy adolescents are well integrated into the value system of their culture (see also Elkin and Westley, 1955; Epstein and Westley, 1960; and Hollingshead, 1949).

The Integrity of the Family

The fact that most children follow easily in the footsteps of their parents is, however, nothing new. Elkin and Westley (1955), in a study of a suburb of Montreal, observed that "family ties are close and the degree of basic family consensus is high. The parents are interested in all the activities of their children. . . . In independent discussions by parents and adolescents of the latter's marriage and occupational goals, there was a remarkable level of agreement." In a different context, Solomon and Fishman (1964) have shown that the majority of adolescent participants in a civil-rights march had come from essentially liberal families where their actions were fully approved.

Coles (1967) has studied the effect of the recent social changes on children in the South. In his study, he describes his population with special emphasis on integration, segregation, and desegregation. In a particular example, Coles vividly describes the interaction between one of the first Negro students to integrate one of the high schools and his parents on the eve of their decision to allow him to go through with the ordeal. It is an excellent example, in our opinion, of a situation where *basically* there is understanding rather than misunderstanding between the generations. Coles (1967, p. 108) summarizes the situation thus:

> In a sense the week of struggle for his parents' signatures became a real time of intimacy and discussion between the three of them. It was also a confrontation of the generations, the past incredulous at what the present seemed to expect as its due. John heard from his parents stories of experiences which they themselves had long since "forgotten": accounts of terror, humiliation and repudiation which had formerly been handed down from parent to child as an inheritance, to be told and later relived. John was particularly moved by his mother's insistence that his generation was the first to be spared the worst of it—the constant possibility of lynching, the near-total lack of hope, the daily scorn that permitted no reply; no leeway. To be free of that, to be safe from night riders, to have steady work, to be left mostly alone, all that seemed enough. "They wanted me to be glad I could walk on the sidewalk," John summarized their conversations, "because they used to have to move into the gutter in their town when a white man approached them. But I told them that once you walk on a sidewalk, you look in the windows of the stores and restaurants, and you want to go there too. They said, maybe my children, and I said me, so that my children will be the first really free Negroes. They always told me that they would try to spare me what they went through; so I told them I wanted to spare my children going through any mobs. If there were mobs for us to face, we should do it right now. And besides, I told them they were contradicting themselves. My mother always brags about how wonderful the farm life was, and my daddy says he thought the city would save him, and it drove him to drink, so it's too bad he ever left South Carolina. Suddenly, though, all the truth was coming out.

John's parents signed the petition that allowed him to experiment in a new and challenging, possibly dangerous, situation. John was able to communicate with his parents and share with them the conviction that he "had to go through with it." He told them in essence that his values for his children were really only a continuation into present times of what their values had been for their children. Because of the basically good relationship between John and his parents, they were able to change with their son and adopt a relatively new position.

We have been impressed with the capacity of the parents to change with their children. They went through their sons' adolescence together with them and seemed to show a relatively high degree of tolerance and understanding. Disagreements between parents and children occurred frequently but were usually discussed openly. The only exception to this statement is the early adolescent years, when, as we described in Chapters 5 and 11, there was openly rebellious behavior by the teen-agers. It is very possible that once that hurdle was negotiated by both parents and children, there was an ushering in of the "psycho-social moratorium," when the parents began to consider seriously that their children were no longer to be treated as children. Once this was recognized and accepted, the relationship could again be a close one.

CHANGING RELATIONSHIP TO MOTHER

The majority of the subjects described the ideal father in terms of discipline and strictness and the ideal mother in terms of affection and being "nice." This response might give us a clue as to the adolescents' feelings about their parents. Basically the students felt closer emotionally to the mothers. They shared their emotional experiences with the mothers and were disappointed when the mothers did not reciprocate. Although at times the relationship was ambivalent, the ambivalence did not detract from its intensity. On the contrary, it gave a spark to it. In the beginning of high school the students had not begun to separate from their mothers, and girl friends had not begun to occupy an important place in their lives. The relationship with the mother changed slowly over the four years of high school, so that by the senior year part of the separation process had taken place. The boys were still emotionally attached to the mother, but they did not admit it as readily and gave the impression that in the future they would have to choose between the mother and the girl friend. In earlier years students would openly be proud of the close relationships with their mothers. One fourteen-year-old boy answered the question how it felt to have a one-year-old sister in the home in the following way: "It feels like she is my own child." Another subject said, "I had an older sister but I lost her last Sunday." "What happened?" asked the somewhat anxious interviewer. Subject: "She got married!" This open admission of oedipal feelings toward the women in the family was present in the freshman year. In the latter years there was more concern about how the mother would get along with the girl friend, with at times a secret hope that they would not get along. This would enable the boy to side with his girl (and by implication against the father's girl).

FATHER CAST AS DISCIPLINARIAN

The fathers, though not the disciplinarians of the family, were put into that role by their sons when asked to describe the ideal father. The question remains whether the boys felt that the father would have disciplined them more had he only known their true feelings, or whether this depiction suggested that the boys were afraid of closeness with their fathers. The fact that the boys were not so concerned with breaking the emotional ties with their fathers might also suggest that the boys had already begun the separation process and as a result had a more realistic, i.e., mature relationship with their fathers.

W. Lederer (1964) has pointed to the need of the adolescent

boy for a strong father in reality who not only loves and provides for the adolescent, but also inspires fear and respect for authority and his values. This gives the adolescent not only a worthy adversary but one who can set limits to his strengths. The strict father enables the boy to take responsibility for his own rebellion when he does rebel. It has been observed that good detached street workers never condone a boy's delinquency and further let him know they do not approve of it. They will have nothing to do with delinquent acts, and if the boys engage in them, they do so on their own responsibility. When Erikson (1956, p. 15) was discussing mass media in a Children's Bureau Seminar on Delinquency, he stated: "I do not like to fool around with such questions as to whether certain movies, T.V. shows, or comic books are good or bad for children. As a citizen and as a father I would insist that they are ugly and worthless, and I, for one, would tell my children so and would try to restrict their opportunities to see them. If they want to see them anyway, that is up to them. It is better for them to rebel than to have parents with totally compromised values."

The importance of the fact that both our high schools were in the suburbs should not be underestimated. The intensity of the relationship (in both its positive and negative aspects) is never so strong with the fathers as it is with the mothers. If the latter interpretation is correct, it will be of interest to observe what effects, if any, these environmental factors will have on the personality development of suburban children.

Shared Values

Our data strongly indicate that for the majority of the teen-agers we have studied there is no major gap of understanding and communication between the generations. In a similar vein, our findings from a different project (Marcus, Offer, Blatt, and Gratch, 1966), in which we studied normal as well as disturbed adolescents and their families, showed that members of families with normal adolescents were in better communication with one another than members of disturbed families. Specifically, we stated: "When the families were studied in terms of understanding and meeting social norms, it was clear that all members of the normal families understood what society expected of them, and generally they tried to live up to this expectation. When they didn't, they were well aware of the degree of this deviation. In the disturbed families a significant finding was that the mothers of disturbed children knew very well what society expected, and, at least in the areas studied, were not "out of it," as is frequently described. In fact, they were surprisingly "very much in it." However, this awareness was not so consistent as was that seen in normal families, and was considerably decreased in stressful situations. It was as if these mothers had memorized "the correct answer" but could not keep to this line of reasoning for consistent periods. Our modal suburban families are very similar in their patterns of responses to the ones described in this project.

We have shown above that parents and their teen-agers have a basic understanding concerning what is important. Our evidence indicates that both generations *share the same basic values.* Basic values should contain, in our opinion, those aspects of an individual's life which he believes are of utmost importance to him. This scale of values would include the religious, moral, ethical, and political standards of the individual. Further, it would include the individual's goals and aspirations in life. In terms of our teenagers it would embrace their attitudes toward education, work (or vocation), and social and familial relations. In our opinion it would not include such superficial preferences as the kind of clothes one wears and how one wears them, the kind of music one listens to, or the kind of food one likes.

A more careful analysis of the basic values in line with what we have said above showed that most of our subjects believed that the existing social order, with its laws and regulations, was just and good. This attitude probably was a direct result from their own individual experiences, where the majority of the teen-agers found their parents to be just, good, and consistent to them. They argued that certain things should be changed (example: "The Negro man should definitely have the same rights as the white man"), but in general they were satisfied. They were middle-of-the-roaders with very few dissenters. They used to like President Kennedy and now they liked President Johnson. If they or their families were Republicans, they would mention the current Republican leader. The vast majority of the subjects liked their communities and were proud of them. They agreed with their parents that the open-space suburban life was good and felt sorry for anyone living in the city. They were interested in family life, found it pleasant and gratifying, and when grown up wanted to have a family similar to the one in which they grew up, in a suburb "within a two-hundred-mile radius" of their parents' home. As we have stated in other parts of this book, the subjects valued money as an end in itself, not just as a means to an end. The majority of the teen-agers were interested in pursuing their education further in order to be able to get better jobs. Few were interested in education for its own sake, to obtain further knowledge. There was some difference in the religious beliefs between the generations in the sense that the children were not as ardent churchgoers as their parents. Finally, none of our subjects were vocal nonconformists.

The question might legitimately be raised: How do we know that these were also the parents' values? True, our studies of the parents did not include these facets in depth. However, we have been told by both children and their parents that on the whole no arguments occurred over crucial or significant issues. Even more significantly, both generations voiced satisfaction with each other. Had there been any great issue over values there would not have been such satisfaction.

The parents were nostalgic about the 1930's and the Depression; they felt very strongly that the economic pressure which forced them to go to work, sometimes before they were "ready for it," made them stronger human beings and better ones, and also allowed them to cope with life in a more meaningful and successful way. When later we asked the parents to discuss their children's school, they clearly stated that the scholastic pressure was not good for their children and possibly might "break" them. It is interesting to note the discrepancy between these two statements. On the one hand, economic pressure in the 1930's made the parents "better human beings"; on the other hand, scholastic pressure on their children would "break" them rather than possibly make them better scholars or human beings. The only conclusion we can draw is that for these parents economics and financial success were more important than scholarship, or learning for learning's sake. This value orientation would support Coleman's (1961) notion that scholarship is not highly esteemed by the teen-agers. But it would strongly suggest that the source of these values is the parents themselves.

Concluding Remarks

We have emphasized that the sample studied in this investigation is different from the ordinary groups seen by the mental-health clinicians in psychotherapeutic work. It must also be stated that the sample would be different for teen-agers who are visible in a variety of other contexts. Much of the popular and professional literature on teen-agers has emphasized the struggle between the generations, the rebellion against parental and societal values, and the general tumult in this particular age group. It is not surprising that the turbulent qualities of adolescents are more visible, since in general we pay much more attention to conflicts and difficulties than to an underlying structure which is much less tumultuous. In fact, we believe that we are describing a population that is larger in numbers and has greater influence than the sample described either in the psychiatric, psychoanalytic, or social-science literature. In other words, we have come upon a sample that, in our judgment, is representative of many adolescents in suburban America. They are less visible because they share the values of their parents and society. They are less visible because they are able to communicate effectively with adults. They are less visible because, in general, they have fewer problems and move into normative social roles with relative ease and comfort.

We can, therefore, conclude that though there are many gaps between the generations, in a sample such as the one we have studied the gaps are small and there are always bridges over them. The bridges are made of open and flowing communication, a willingness to empathize with each other's emotional position, and a potential for growth through learning. Emotional security is vital in maintaining and developing the bridges from both sides.

13

Coping Behavior of the Modal Adolescent

Definition of Coping Behavior

What is the coping behavior of one population of modal adolescents? With Hamburg and Adams (1967), we ask why our adolescent subjects did not break down. In this chapter we speak again of the paths of the majority. Individuals vary, and we generalize for the purposes of discussion. Our capsule generalization resulting from our data is that this adolescent population remains satisfied with itself in an environment that it does not find to be alien.

The interest of behavioral scientists in studies of coping and adaptation has increased rapidly in the past two decades. A variety of definitions of coping has been offered in the literature. Webster (1956) defines "to cope" as "to strive or contend with successfully." Hamburg and Adams (1967) define coping as "seeking and utilizing of information under stressful conditions." Heath (1965, p. 31) defines adaptation as "to so regulate behavior as to optimize simultaneously both the stability of the self

structures and their accommodation to environmental requirements." All the above definitions see coping as part of the ego
apparatus. The definition of coping behavior that comes closest
to our own is the one used by Kroeber (1963): "Coping is how
effective people deal with demands, often conflicting, of a biological, psychological or social nature." If individuals can cope internally, their competence in the external sphere will be the parallel
phenomenon. Competence, according to White (1960), means
"fitness or ability. The competence of an organism means its
fitness or ability to carry on those transactions with the environment which result in its maintaining itself, growing or flourishing."

Assessing Coping Behavior

Originally, when behavioral scientists began to study the adaptation, coping behavior, or competence of nonpatient populations,
they began by studying the way people adapted to or coped with
extreme situations. Investigations were conducted on the adaptation of individuals to wars (Grinker and Spiegel, 1945), serious
illnesses, and injuries and traumas of childhood and adulthood
(Richmond and Waisman, 1955; Hamburg et al., 1953; Visotsky
et al., 1961; Hilgard et al., 1960; Bowlby, 1960; and Rochlin,
1965). In the last two decades investigators have been studying
the coping behavior of individuals to the ordinary stresses of
everyday life—to such situations as (1) displacement by siblings
(Koch, 1955 and 1960); (2) adjustment to growth in childhood
(Murphy, 1962); (3) transition from high school to college
(Silber et al., 1961: a and b; Coelho et al., 1963; Nixon, 1962);
(4) adjustment to college life (Grinker, 1962 and 1963; Sanford,
1962; White, 1966; Heath, 1965); (5) marriage (Goodrich et al.,
1966); and (6) pregnancy (Bibring, 1961: a and b). In addition,
methods of systematically assessing coping abilities have been
formulated by, for example, Barron, the Barron ego-strength
scale (Barron, 1963), and by Cooper et al. (1966) in their scale
on coping within the psychotherapeutic relationship.

Our methodology, though similar to that utilized in some of the longitudinal developmental studies, is different in an essential characteristic. (See Kagan, 1964, for an excellent review of the major longitudinal studies of psychological development.) We did not ask identical questions at the yearly or twice-yearly intervals (see our interview schedule, Appendix 2). Hence, as has been pointed out in Chapter 1, we cannot trace the specific changes in coping behavior in our subjects over the high-school years. Our perspective was psychiatric and our major focus was on the nature of the relationship that our subjects developed with us rather than developmental comparisons (see Chapter 10 for details).

The studies that are probably most like ours in methodology and approach have all dealt with college populations, perhaps because college students are the most available, the easiest to approach, and the most conscientious participants. (See studies by White, 1966; Nixon, 1962; Silber *et al.*, 1961: a and b; and Grinker *et al.*, 1962.) But a direct comparison of their results with our findings would not be relevant because of the significant age and situational differences. The basic psychological mechanisms may be very similar, but the conflict areas, developmental levels, and coping behavior are distinctly different. Nevertheless, their theoretical frameworks have proved translatable to our population. For example, our subjects' ways of coping can be discussed in terms of Nixon's (1962) theory. Nixon states that the college students he studied underwent three different stages in their development: (1) discovery, (2) experimentation, and (3) mastery. Nixon discussed his data specifically concerning the transition from high school to college. His concepts can also be applied to our subjects. In the transition from grammar school to high school our modal adolescents discovered themselves psychologically at puberty (age twelve). They experimented with rebellious behavior between twelve and fourteen, and when they entered high school they were in a position to begin the mastery of many of their feelings and impulses.

There have been very few studies on the adaptation and coping behavior of normal adolescents within the high-school years. Gesell *et al.* (1956) stop at sixteen, Kagan and Moss (1962) stop at fourteen, and Symonds (1949) does not concern himself specifically with coping, dealing primarily with the fantasy life of the adolescents and their actual behavior. Peck and Havighurst (1960) emphasize character development and its relation to psychopathology. The study by Coles (1967), *Children of Crisis*, resembles ours in its theoretical conceptualizations as well as its methodology (especially the use of the interview as the major information-gathering device). In Chapter 12, we cited some of Coles's data that paralleled ours. However, Coles worked with a different socioeconomic as well as cultural group, which makes it hard to compare the two populations.

Manifestations of Coping

In the previous two chapters we have discussed the subjects' inner turmoil, behavioral manifestations of unrest, and relationships with significant adults in their lives. In the remainder of this chapter we shall discuss the methods by which the subjects have combated distressing feelings, averted crises, or mastered situations with ease rather than emotional upheaval. With the developing sophistication of ego psychology, it has become increasingly obvious that there is a direct correlation between the behavior and coping ability of subjects and their overall psychological health and normality. It is with this connection in mind that we feel competent to generalize about conditions of health in our population.

COPING WITH AGGRESSION

Our subjects have often told us that controlling their aggression was one of the most difficult tasks for them. Coping with aggressive and hostile impulses seemed much more difficult for them than handling their sexual impulses. As we have stated in Chapter 5, our subjects lost control of their impulses only on rare occasions. What, then, did the subjects do with their aggression? Most often the aggressive impulse was sublimated into competitive sports. This sublimation was supported by the students' total milieu, from teachers and parents to peers. Open aggression in athletics in the high-school setting was fostered. The student who did well in sports was handsomely rewarded. He became the hero of the school.

The students used sports as their route for aggressive discharge far more than intellectual pursuits. Yet they participated in our project, which demanded a kind of passive behavior (talking as contrasted to doing). The gratification they received was twofold. First, they had the opportunity to talk to an "objective" adult. Second, they obtained intellectual gratification from participating in this project: they expanded their knowledge about themselves and learned more about other teen-agers.

We described the students' controlled use of anger and hostility in Chapter 8. Direct angry outbursts were one other way of ventilating aggressive impulses, but these were either kept within socially controlled limits or indulged in briefly and then later smoothed over. The anger was most often directed toward siblings who formed handy targets. For some students, aggression could be sublimated into school work, but we saw few who attacked a political theory or a mathematical problem with fervor. The family car was a likelier recipient of this extra-enthusiastic attention.

COPING WITH SEXUALITY

The subjects had the most difficulty with controlling their aggressive impulses during early adolescence, possibly because they were driven by the onset of puberty and the increase of biological drives. The students were, however, inactive on the whole in expressing their sexual impulses. Dating started on a low key and although the students were not distressed by the "increase of libido," they seemed to cope with sexuality by ignoring it in general. As we have detailed in Chapter 6, the sexual behavior of our subjects is not what it is reported to be in the popular press. The public myths of the "appalling increase" of sexuality among high-school students may apply to some teen-agers, but it is not applicable to our group. The sexual feelings and impulses were recognized slowly and seemed to parallel, in a negative reciprocal way, the attachment that the adolescents felt to their mothers. In the beginning of the high-school years the majority of the students tended to deny the existence of strong sexual feelings. They coped with the energizing sexuality by becoming active in sports, studying, or "going out with the boys." Toward the end of the high-school years the attitude changed. They were now interested in being with the opposite sex and wanted some experimentation in order to understand their own feelings and those of the girls. Did the fact that sexuality was essentially repressed during the first three years of high school harm the students? We have not found any evidence to support the theory that our students suffered either from arrested development or inhibited development; they are, however, developing slowly.

Our findings in the area of sexuality are similar to those reported by H. Deutsch (1967, p. 24): "My own opinion is that, specifically in adolescence, the sublimation of genital sexuality plays an extremely important role and may often be the decisive element in the whole development." According to Deutsch, it is not harmful to repress sexuality, possibly even to deny it and seek other outlets for the increase in drive tensions that result from the increase in biological drives at the onset of puberty and afterward.

We have not attempted to relate any of our data to biological factors. We started our project when all but four subjects had undergone puberty (as defined by voice change and appearance of pubic hair). Many of the writers cited in this chapter correlate the turmoil of adolescents with the onset of puberty, and our data seem to concur. The specific forms of rebellion and defiance might be considered the modal adolescent "rites of passage." In our

American suburban culture, as we have observed, certain forms of adolescent rebellion are accepted and even institutionalized. Such institutionalized rebellious acts may make it easier for the young adolescent to move into adolescence proper. In high school, he quickly assumes responsibilities in some areas similar to those of an adult. He is constantly told that he is on his own. At age sixteen he can drive a car (which to him symbolizes independence). Soon afterward he starts dating much more seriously.

Deutsch tells us of a seminar in which Freud suggested the value of delayed sexual activities (H. Deutsch, 1967, p. 24): "Years ago, Freud, in a meeting that was limited to a small number of participants, expressed his opposition to Wilhelm Reich's insistence that sexual activity should begin in adolescence—that is, as soon as the biological readiness is manifested. Freud regarded the *postponement of gratification* [author's italics] as an important element in the process of sublimation and thereby essential to development."

We have found that in heterosexuality our subjects were afraid of settling down too soon, of making an inexperienced decision. Here they would tread lightly, "not get in over our heads" before they thought they were ready. In fact, they never seemed anxious to set their sights above what they felt they could handle. Yet what they could handle was generally not underestimated.

SOCIAL ACTION

Our adolescents were able to incorporate environmental variables selectively and make them part of their life experience (see Chapter 9). They were perceptive and were able to utilize their cognitive apparatae well. No significant distortions were created as a result of an inner need to change the outside world. In a few cases we saw idealism and charity-orientation that seemed to be a result of control problems. But though we looked for these examples, they remained few in number.

If some teen-agers are an active part of the various protest movements of our times, they do not come from groups like our modal sample. Only one student has ever taken part in a "peace march," and that was when he joined his parents in going to Washington for the 1963 civil-rights march. Were our students idealistic? No. Were they, therefore, conservative or even reactionary? Again, no. In politics, as in self-description, they trod the well-worn middle of the road, veering but little from side to side.

GOAL-DIRECTED BEHAVIOR

The students were optimistic about the future. No doubt this attitude was related to the low incidence of actual economic or social frustration in their lives. The relative affluence within which they grew up and which surrounded their communities also had a tendency to protect them from the uglier part of life. The students seemed surprised when asked what they would do if their plans could not be fulfilled; their immediate responses contained a certain naïve attitude like "How could that happen to me?" But they soon recovered and began to explore various other possibilities that might be open to them. This characteristic is similar to what Hamburg and Adams (1967) describe as information seeking about (1) new situations, (2) new roles, and (3) potential future difficulties. We observed the first two activities in our subjects, while the third item was not so apparent, possibly because of the basic trust and confidence which they possessed (Benedek, 1967); Erikson (1968). The basic trust and confidence no doubt gave rise to the positive, realistic self-image we observed. To paraphrase Benedek (1967), it served as a feedback regulator and allowed the students to gain satisfaction from a job well done, which in turn pushed them forward in the developmental processes.

Grinker (1963) has observed that "One attribute of mental health is flexibility depending on the number of environments into which the personality type fits comfortably." We observed that our subjects fitted well within their particular social and cultural environment. Whether this "fit or adjustment" will persist as they move to new environments and take on new roles will be important to observe in the follow-up study.

As has been stated, the students had relatively little difficulty in coping realistically with their immediate environment. Whether the ability to be alone during adolescence is essential for stimulating creativity among our adolescents (Arieti, 1966) is an interesting question. They are gregarious doers. Their life style has not affected their ability to cope successfully with their environment. Will it affect their potential creative ability adversely? These adolescents' fantasy life is necessarily limited since they are a group of doers.

The modal adolescents' inclination toward action has also been described by Korchin and Ruff (1962) in their work with the Mercury Astronauts. It has been explained by Blos (1961) as depending on the fundamental antithesis of this period, namely activity and passivity. The adolescents often associate passivity with femininity and action and self-assertion with the negation of femininity, hence with masculinity. Sports supplied the teenagers an active outlet; whether it was playing on the high-school team, going hunting and fishing with their fathers, or just going for a ride with their friends.

The belief that they might be of help to others in the long run was important to our subjects. This might seem to contradict our earlier statement about the students (Chapter 4) that we did not find them altruistic or idealistic. The difference was that in their cooperation with us they found satisfaction and could sense the fact that they were being of help. Pure lofty idealism was too far removed for them to appreciate it. It has often been described in literature that the most idealistic and prophetic men are at times cruel and distant toward the people who actually know them. An example is Gandhi, so admired by millions, whom Koestler (1960) describes as hateful and sadistic toward his own family.

In attempting to differentiate between a normal and an abnormal person, Shakow (1967) has discussed the observation that a normal person has an ability to rationalize his distance and formalize the difference between the stimulus and the response, hence the "generalized perception of input." The majority of the modal adolescents showed a capacity to respond to appropriate stimuli in their environment. They had a range of affectual experience that they could utilize. The subjects felt gratified when a task they had undertaken was successfully completed. This feeling of pleasure served as a feedback reinforcer for seeking and obtaining new gratifications. (See, for example, White, 1960, effectance motivation; Hendricks, 1943, "Instinct to Master"; and Howard and Diesenhaus, 1965, change-seeking behavior.) We have found that our subjects were curious about themselves and their environment. They were, so to speak, constantly in search of new stimuli, a search that probably served as a motivating factor in their continued participation in our project.

The students gained satisfaction in giving as well as in taking. Their enjoyment of the interview situation, which was a prototype of the phenomena, can be explained on the basis of two factors. First was the more "pure" pleasure involved in competence. They felt anxious about the interviews, but rather than discontinue in the project, they came to face the challenge (i.e., the interviewer and his questions). Once they coped with the situation, they felt proud of themselves, thus reinforcing their positive self-image. Second, they enjoyed the fact that a psychiatrist was paying attention to them, their verbal behavior and their psychological problems. The fact that the enjoyment was mutual helped increase the pleasure gained from the relationship.

CAPACITY FOR SELF-OBSERVATION

The students whom we saw had the capacity to assess their own strengths and weaknesses. Their sense of reality was strikingly accurate, and they could describe themselves with a certain degree of detachment. Their wishes or problems reflected the next step on the developmental ladder that they knew they had to take. Their vocational choices were related to their actual abilities. Their self-images were surprisingly in accord with our interview observations and other data we had concerning their performances in home and school. The progression of the interviews undoubtedly gave the students as well as the interviewer a clearer insight into their own patterns of functioning. Throughout the years, they spoke warmly of their friends. They chose the kind of friends who rarely disappointed them. The teen-agers were both satisfied in their academic performance and worried about working hard enough in school to meet future requirements. Although they were concerned about the transition from high school to college, we did not observe the ambitiousness or concern over performance that Silber *et al.* (1961:b) described in their study of superior students.

The adolescents were critical of themselves and used external as well as internal (self-) criticism. They were able to change as a result of self-criticism without feeling ashamed or losing self-esteem in the process. In general, the teen-agers were willing to deal openly with conflict areas. This openness of self-disclosure and willingness to face "inner realities" (Jourard, 1964) typical of our subjects. They searched for interpretations of their behavior and thus felt less need for a wall of privacy. This effort implied that they did not view their veneer of behavior as essential; their behavior reflected their emotional needs and they were not afraid of their needs as they saw them. Here, of course, a limitation is entailed, in that we are speaking only of needs readily available to consciousness. The students did not wish to concentrate upon themselves and their motivations long enough to cause them more distress than they could work off in a football game or in tinkering with a car. Their search for interpretation was more a search for reassurance about themselves or comfort; they wanted no arousal of disequilibrium, as they demonstrated in their irritation at being asked to explain their rationalizations concerning the avoidance of sexual intimacy.

Within the context of this necessarily limited self-observation, the majority of the students were in remarkably close touch with their feelings. Similar to Gesell *et al.* (1956, p. 178), we found that the fourteen-year-old is an "amateur psychologist" and has an intuitive grasp of his own psychological being. This state of awareness is also reminiscent of Rogers's description (1961) of the fully functioning person. This self-awareness remains acute throughout the high-school years. It enables the student to perceive problem areas that might otherwise be closed to him, and with this ability he is better prepared to deal with his mixed emotions. For example, the many statements made by our subjects concerning sibling rivalry and the awareness of the jealousy and the competition have encouraged less denial and more comprehension of a complex state of feelings.

The adolescent had a keen sense of humor (see also Gesell *et al.*, 1956). He appreciated other people's sense of humor and could laugh even at his own expense. The humor was utilized often, as when the subject was anxious, late for an appointment, or under pressure. It was not limited to an ability to appreciate jokes and laugh, but contained a refined ability to look at the more humorous aspects of existence. Humor was also used as a vehicle for self-criticism.

AFFECT

When the adolescent experienced anxiety, depression, shame, guilt, and anger he generally coped with them, first, by admitting to himself that they existed and, second, by allowing himself to continue to experience these feelings. This state of open communication with the self allowed the teen-ager to handle the feeling directly without resorting to an elaborate erection of defense mechanisms. When the teen-ager felt anxious, he experienced it physiologically. When he was depressed, he preferred to be by himself. Our observations have been that our adolescent subjects do go through periods of feeling lonely, being isolated from their peers, having difficulties with their parents and their teachers, and questioning their existence in general—what they are doing here and where they are going. But these periods do not persist for any significant length of time.

SPECIAL CRISES

Finally, our subjects' ability to master special crises was impressive (see Chapter 7). It was not that they had no anxiety. On the contrary, they experienced a considerable degree of anxiety. They coped with the situations by attending to manageable details first, concentrating on them and thereby minimizing the threat (or even repressing it altogether). They were able to keep shifting gears and to concentrate on different aspects of the same problem. They could also leave one topic of conversation and follow to another, even though they still felt that there was unfinished business to take up. The subjects adapted to traumatic situations, such as a death of a parent, with initial overconcern about the reality of the situation. (Examples: Will Mother have enough money to support me? Should I still plan to go to the college of my choice?) The subjects tended initially to deny the emotional loss, isolate it, and handle it intellectually. At the same time the teenagers began to utilize the experience as a crisis that helped them grow. They had been shaken and now had to expedite the process of adolescence, which before had seemed less urgent. They would proceed a little more quickly into adulthood than their contemporaries, who had been left in a world where dependency-independency issues needed no immediate resolutions.

The Future

It is our hypothesis that a transitional period such as adolescence serves to strengthen the stability rather than threaten it. As each stage passes and the crisis becomes part of the past, stability of the character thickens. Is adolescence really a "second chance" for people to change, as the clinical literature has contended? Our data concerning our group would tend to dispute such a contention.

Stability, not change, is the overriding characteristic in the psychological patterns of reaction of these modal adolescents. This conclusion drawn from our data is in agreement with the findings of studies like those of Symonds and Jensen (1961), Masterson (1967), Escalona and Heider (1959), Bloom (1964), and Peck and Havighurst (1960). The study of Tuddenham (1959) from the Institute of Human Development at the University of California is especially relevant to our thesis. Adolescents were studied through personality ratings based on direct observations. The subjects were again studied at age thirty-three, when similar ratings were made and stability coefficients were obtained between the adolescent and adult ratings for each variable. Approximately a third of the variables yielded significant results, i.e., were stable over a period of nineteen years. This finding is impressive in view of the many potential sources for error. It is our prediction that if we followed our subjects for that length of time our findings would be similar to Tuddenham's.

A similar study by Lief and Thompson (1961) that attempted to predict behavior from adolescence to adulthood found: ". . . evidence for the persistence of behavior patterns over a decade and a half. Developed patterns were maintained and potential (latent) patterns were fully developed. The internal consistency of personality organization over time was also noted. The ego mechanisms for dealing with drives, conscience, and reality were quite consistent from adolescence to adulthood."

It would be of interest to find out whether adolescents who do go through adolescence with much *"Sturm und Drang"* do so in *every stage of development,* or at least in a significant number. We realize that such a question cannot be answered with a "yes" or "no." Many complex variables contribute to the style of one's adaptation. Nevertheless we believe that such a question should be answered by future research; and our prediction is that in the majority of cases the style of coping with crises will remain *relatively* constant throughout life.

It may well be that the ability to change the inner psychological world of people is not so easily done as it sometimes appears from reading the current social psychiatric literature (see, for example, Caplan, 1964). Psychiatrists in the past have not always accepted or realized their ultimate limitations. It is here that Hartmann's (1958) concept of the "average expectable environment" becomes meaningful, because we are dealing with the particular environment of a particular person, not a theoretical system that does not mean anything to the particular person.

What has the "average expectable environment" been for our subjects? In our day and age, when at times it seems that the expectable is the unexpectable, cultural patterns move so fast that a person must be flexible, and able to shift and change roles from one social context to the next. Our modal adolescents grew up in relatively stable social environments. Their life experiences to date took place under relatively low pressure. The mothering of the majority of our subjects had been good. The relationship between the subjects and their parents was stable, consistent, and empathic. It was crucial for the growing child in that it gave him a stable template. The parents coped with their own lives and served as an ideal for their children. The children learned to cope partially by identification.

What will happen to our subjects if they change environments and enter into unfamiliar surroundings? Will they find it difficult to cope with the new situation? We do not know the answer, but that is one of the important reasons for carrying out the follow-up study. Originally we were interested only in the high-school years. But we became more and more fascinated with the data as we realized that the questions concerning the relative health of our subjects could not be answered by the end of the high-school years, since it is not until the closing phase of adolescence, in the early twenties, that one often sees adaptive failures that were previously hidden (Blos, 1961, p. 142). Therefore we have embarked on a follow-up study that will include the first four post-high-school years. We are interested in finding out how our subjects will adapt to the new realistic demands made on them, be they in school, work, or the armed forces. How will they adjust to mature heterosexual relationships? Finally, how will they separate from their parents?

The follow-up study of the modal adolescent is now in midstream. Most of our subjects are sophomores in college, and we have found no reason to change our statement concerning their successful adaptation. We have follow-up information on more than 90 per cent of our subjects. The majority of our students have continued in their studies after high school. Eighty per cent went to college, 12 per cent joined the armed forces, and 8 per cent went directly to work. Of the students who have gone to college, 90 per cent were accepted in schools that were their first choices. Most of the students entered state universities in the Middle West. Three students dropped out of college during their freshman year. The rest are doing from fair to excellent. Four students complain of strong feelings of loneliness and rejection and three of the four received short-term counseling in college. As far as we know, however, there have been no serious disturbances that required hospitalization or prolonged treatment. We conclude that, at least for the first two years following high school, our students are functioning approximately as well as they did in high school.

Who, then, are the youth of today? How do they cope with their psychological and environmental worlds? In this book, we have presented data on one group of adolescents and concluded that there is more than one route from adolescence to young adulthood. Our subjects are experiencing a relatively long period of adolescence. They proceed through it slowly, mastering its various tasks gradually. As a result, they evidence comparatively little turmoil. In brief, gradualism, as contrasted to volcanic eruptions, best describes the development of our modal adolescent sample.

PART IV

Appendixes

APPENDIX I

The Self-Image Questionnaire

Construction of the Self-Image Questionnaire

In the development of the questionnaire we relied, in part, on Engel's (1959) Q-sort and on our own Q-sort developed for another study (Marcus, Offer, Blatt, and Gratch, 1966). In the writing of many items we were also influenced by the following works: N. Garmezy, A. R. Clarke, and C. Stochner (1957), J. S. Coleman (1961), E. H. Erikson (1950), A. Freud (1946 and 1958), E. Z. Friedenberg (1960), G. Gardner (1959), H. A. Murray (1938), R. F. Peck (1958), S. K. Polka (1954), H. L. Raush and B. Sweet (1961), W. R. Rosengren (1961), E. J. Shoben (1949), and E. Silber *et al.* (1961). In addition to using these sources, we relied on our own clinical experience with adolescents. Combining our own experience with the experience of others, we concluded that the following eleven areas were important in the psychological life of the teen-ager:

1. Impulse control
2. Emotional tone
3. Body and self-image

4. Social relations
5. Morals
6. Sexual attitudes
7. Family relations
8. External mastery
9. Vocational and educational goals
10. Psychopathology
11. Superior adjustment

It was our expressed purpose to construct a Self-Image Questionnaire that would allow the adolescent to describe his various feeling states in each of the above eleven areas.

The Self-Image Questionnaire, as can be seen below, (pp. 239–246), was divided into 11 scales and contained 130 items. Each item was to be answered on a six-point scale from "Describes me very well" on one end of the scale to "Does not describe me at all" on the other end. Half of the items are written positively and the other half negatively. "The items were scored in one direction and the score of the positive items was reversed so that the lower the score the better the adjustment. The highest possible score on an item was 6, which connotes inferior adjustment. The lowest possible score on an item was 1, meaning superior adjustment. The score of any scale is the sum of its positive and negative items. The possible score of scale 1, for example, which has 10 items, could range from 10 (superior) to 60 (inferior).

Once the questionnaire was completed, we reviewed each of the individual items with four different teen-agers to make sure that the items were understandable. We also asked the subjects in our pilot study, to be described below, to tell us whether any of the items were unclear. Several changes in wording were suggested.

We administered the original form of the questionnaire to a group of 40 adolescent boys as a check on scale reliability and validity before conducting our selection of a modal sample. Ten of these subjects were seriously disturbed patients undergoing psychiatric treatment, five as inpatients and five as outpatients. The questionnaire was individually administered to these 10 subjects by a clinical psychologist who was a staff member at the

Psychosomatic and Psychiatric Institute, where these adolescent patients were in treatment. The psychiatric diagnosis of this patient subgroup were: anxiety neurosis (2), character disorder with anxiety and depression (3), borderline character (2), and schizophrenia (3). The other 30 subjects were "normal" adolescent boys drawn from three different area high schools. None of these subjects had ever been under any psychiatric care. Both the teachers and the parents of these 30 teen-agers considered them to be "normal"—i.e., average in adjustment if not well adjusted. The tests were administered to them in a group at our Institute by the psychologist.

The internal consistency reliability of the 11 Self-Image Questionnaire scales was computed, through use of the generalized alpha formula; these reliability coefficients for the pilot sample are presented in Table 1A–1.

TABLE 1A–1

Reliability of the Self-Image Questionnaire Scales

SCALE	NUMBER OF ITEMS	SAMPLE	
		Pilot	Selection
1. Impulse control	10	.71	.65
2. Emotional tone	10	.80	.72
3. Body and self-image	10	.70	.60
4. Social relations	10	.73	.73
5. Morals	10	.70	.52
6. Sexual attitudes	10	.73	.68
7. Family relations	20	.80	.86
8. External mastery	10	.80	.56
9. Vocational-educational	10	.79	.69
10. Psychopathology	15	.57	.63
11. Superior adjustment	15	.73	.65
N		40	326

In order to determine whether the questionnaire would be sensitive to the differences in clinical status (that is, adjustment) known to exist between the two subgroups in the teen-age sample, means and variances were computed for the "patients" and "normals" separately. Since the variances for the disturbed subgroup tended to be two or three times larger than those of the normal subgroup, we used the nonparametric median test to test the hypothesis that the normal subjects would score higher (be better adjusted) than the disturbed subgroup. The prediction was confirmed for 8 of the 11 scales.

TABLE 1A-2

Median Tests for the Pilot Sample on the Original Self-Image Questionnaire Scales

| | ABOVE MEDIAN | | |
	Normal	Disturbed	χ^2
Impulse control	19	1	8.53**
Emotional tone	20	0	13.33**
Body and self-image	18	2	4.80*
Social relations	19	1	8.53**
Morals	17	3	2.13
Sexual attitudes	15	5	0.00
Family relations	18	2	4.80*
External mastery	18	2	4.80*
Vocational-educational	18	2	4.80*
Psychopathology	15	5	0.00
Superior adjustment	20	0	13.33**
N	30	10	

* $p \leq .05$; ** $p \leq .01$.

We also compared the results for the three Self-Image Questionnaire scales (Family Relationships, Social Relationships, and Emotional Tone) with those for the three conceptually parallel scales of the Bell Adjustment Inventory. Product-moment correlations were calculated between performance on each of the three scales of the Bell and the corresponding Self-Image Scale. Since the correlations were in the predicted direction, it is taken to mean that the three scales of the two tests do tap the same area but are not identical.

To summarize, our aim has been to construct a Self-Image Questionnaire for adolescent boys that would focus on the intrapsychic processes of the teen-ager. We constructed items for 11 different content areas on the basis of our clinical knowledge of

TABLE 1A–3

Pearson Product Moment Correlations between Parallel Scales on the Bell Adjustment Inventory and the Self-Image Questionnaire

	r°	p†
Family	—.64	.01
Emotional	—.61	.01
Social	—.31	n.s.

° A low score on the SIQ scales and a low score on the Bell scales indicate greater adjustment.
† N = 19: 10 subjects from the disturbed subgroup and 9 from the "normal" subgroup.

adolescence and our survey of the literature on the psychology and psychopathology of adolescents. The scales were checked for clarity, reliability, and validity. As a result of our findings, one scale (Psychopathology) was significantly altered, and a second scale (Sexual Attitudes) was not used in the selection of our modal group. Throughout the questionnaire, items were rewritten or replaced, particularly items in three scales (Family Relations, Psychopathology, and Superior Adjustment).

Finally, since we wanted to utilize our instrument to select a group of modal adolescents, we performed a "dry run" on our "normal" pilot group. The standard deviation was calculated for each subscale, and on the basis of our results we selected a "modal group" from our pilot group in the same way that the eventual modal group was to be selected. Thirteen teen-agers were selected. Five of the total normal pilot group (30 subjects) appeared clinically as having mild social and psychological problems. None of the five fell in the modal group as designated by the questionnaire.

Selection of the Modal Group

As stated above, the purpose for constructing the Self-Image Questionnaire (SIQ) was to provide a screening instrument that would enable us to select a group of typical or modal adolescents from among a larger teen-age population by statistical means. We

TABLE 1A-4

Means, Variances, and t-Test for the Self-Image Questionnaire Scales for the Total Sample

Scale	HIGH SCHOOL A (N = 181)		HIGH SCHOOL B (N = 145)		TOTAL (N = 326)		t
	Mean	Variance	Mean	Variance	Mean	Variance	
1. Impulse control	25.30	48.30	24.95	39.99	25.14	44.50	−0.46
2. Emotional tone	22.10	42.15	23.16	49.77	22.57	45.67	1.39
3. Body and self-image	25.16	45.05	25.82	45.63	25.45	45.27	0.88
4. Social relations	21.22	43.86	22.41	56.41	21.75	49.64	1.51
5. Morals	22.96	42.44	23.20	33.42	23.07	38.33	0.35
6. Sexual attitudes	30.20	64.16	29.65	46.95	29.96	56.42	−0.66
7. Family relations	42.84	192.82	45.22	214.71	43.90	203.33	1.50
8. External mastery	24.05	36.69	24.29	33.79	24.16	35.30	0.35
9. Vocational and educational	18.53	32.33	18.88	32.41	18.69	32.24	0.55
10. Psychopathology	37.54	69.88	38.34	76.07	37.90	72.51	0.84
11. Social adjustment	37.92	81.34	38.75	67.35	38.29	75.06	0.86

were interested in studying teen-agers who fell within the average range in their psychological self-awareness and who were not grossly disturbed. We therefore defined the modal population as those students who fell within one standard deviation from the mean in at least 9 out of 10 scales. Since there were no significant differences between the two high-school groups on all scales, we could combine the groups for the selection of our experimental (modal) group. There were 44 students in the modal position in all 10 scales and 62 students were in the modal position on 9 out of 10 scales, for a total of 106 modal adolescents out of a sample of 326. They were evenly distributed between the two schools. There is a remote possibility that our selection might have been biased by the fact that many of the individual item distributions were slightly skewed to the right (the high-adjustment end). A counterindication would be that the scale scores that were actually used in the selection did not show statistically significant skewness or kurtosis, so that our assumptions regarding normal distributions of scale scores are met reasonably well.

The results for the sexual-attitude scale differed from those for other scales. The sexual-attitude scale did not correlate consistently or strongly with the other scales. The different performance of the sexual-attitude scale may suggest that the scale was not well constructed or at least not as well as the other scales. It was the only scale that differentiated significantly between our two student modal populations in the two high schools which we studied. Although it was not used to select the study sample, this finding will be studied further in future tests of the SIQ. We found no significant difference between the two schools on the other 10 scales for the modal adolescents.

Validity of the Selection

As has been noted, our selection procedure is heavily dependent on the adequacy of the adolescent subjects' self-descriptions. It is our contention that the modal group is highly accurate in their

TABLE 1A-5

Means and Variances for the Self-Image Questionnaire Scales for the Modal
Adolescents from the Two High Schools

Scale	HIGH SCHOOL A (N = 44) Mean	HIGH SCHOOL A Variance	HIGH SCHOOL B (N = 29) Mean	HIGH SCHOOL B Variance	t
1. Sexual attitudes	31.84	34.14	29.14	28.69	2.00*
2. Impulse control	24.65	14.14	24.86	22.20	−0.20
3. Emotional tone	21.81	9.13	21.31	12.01	0.66
4. Body and self-image	24.25	15.17	24.03	9.89	0.25
5. Social relations	20.50	14.07	20.48	12.04	0.20
6. Morals	22.93	19.69	23.45	21.83	−0.48
7. Family relations	41.36	65.77	41.93	81.42	−0.28
8. External mastery	24.25	9.08	24.41	9.89	−0.22
9. Vocational-educational	19.07	11.46	18.41	10.47	0.82
10. Psychopathology	36.32	20.04	38.14	23.19	−1.65
11. Superior adjustment	37.61	24.01	39.31	18.79	−1.51

* $p < .05$, two-tail test.

capacity to evaluate themselves and to report these self-evaluations. It could be argued that an important source of potential distortion in self-description influencing our selection would be the activation of the social-desirability response set (Edwards, 1967). The importance of social desirability, which can be defined as the tendency to endorse statements presenting a favorable characterization of oneself and to reject statements presenting an unfavorable characterization, is by no means an accepted and clear-cut concept (Heilbrun, 1964; Cattell, 1965). However, our selection procedure avoids the inclusion of people at either extreme of the potential score range on each of the 10 scales. If social desirability were a potent response strategy for any *one* subject, it would, given the nature of the construction of the Self-Image Questionnaire, uniformly push his level score toward the upper extreme (that is, most adjusted); using as our cutoff point one standard deviation above the mean on each of 9 of the 10 content scales should exclude any such subject. If *all* the subjects were greatly motivated to respond primarily in terms of the ascription of socially desirable characteristics, it is to be anticipated that there would be much higher mean scores, more restricted variances. It should be noted that we have used a six-step fixed-response choice situation, whereas the concept of social desirability in responding to questionnaire items was originally developed for tests using a two- or three-choice response format; increasing the range of permitted favorable and unfavorable responses may negate the onus of the admission of undesirable characteristics and allow more realistic self-evaluation. Further analytic and empirical tests of the role of social desirability in responding to the Self-Image Questionnaire are being undertaken and will be published separately.

Our selection procedure, by which subjects at both extremes of the adjustment-response continuum are eliminated, should thus succeed in avoiding the inclusion of modal adolescent sample subjects who describe themselves either too positively or too negatively for reasons that are either substantive (superior adjustment, health, versus poor adjustment, illness) or strategic (social-

TABLE 1A–6

*Intercorrelation of the Self-Image Questionnaire Scales for the Total Sample**

	1	2	3	4	5	6	7	8	9	10	11
1. Impulse control											
2. Emotional tone	0.54										
3. Body and self-image	0.36	0.56									
4. Social relations	0.50	0.68	0.54								
5. Morals	0.53	0.38	0.22	0.32							
6. Sexual attitude	−0.06	0.10	0.21	0.30	−0.19						
7. Family relations	0.42	0.42	0.41	0.42	0.49	−0.20					
8. External mastery	0.46	0.56	0.54	0.50	0.41	0.12	0.48				
9. Vocational-educational	0.42	0.35	0.34	0.39	0.45	−0.01	0.49	0.55			
10. Psychopathology	0.54	0.62	0.55	0.57	0.38	0.10	0.43	0.56	0.32		
11. Superior adjustment	0.46	0.37	0.35	0.44	0.42	0.06	0.40	0.60	0.57	0.42	

* Coefficients greater than 0.148 are significant at the 0.01 level.

desirability response set, faking good versus faking bad, acquiescence, etc.).

We intercorrelated the 11 scales, which showed that there was, in general, a positive relationship between the performance of each of the students on each of the scales, but the correlations were not so high as to suggest that the scales were testing exactly the same thing.

The Factor Analysis of the Self-Image Questionnaire

For a further understanding of the properties of the rationally constructed Self-Image Questionnaire, we factor-analyzed the matrix of intercorrelations among the 10 scales that were utilized in the selection of our modal group.

Factor analysis is a statistical method employed to discover whether there are pervasive underlying sources of common variance in a given set of variables, or tests; the major goal is to reduce a larger number of variables to a smaller, more easily

TABLE 1A–7

Rotated Factor Loadings for the Factor Analysis of Self-Image Questionnaire

Scale Number	Loading		I	II	III
		Factor I: Feeling State			
2	.80	Emotional tone		.12	.33
3	.78	Body and self-image		.32	−.04
4	.74	Social relationships		.23	.26
9	.74	Psychopathology		.17	.34
		Factor II: Mastery			
8	.81	Vocational-educational	.13		.28
10	.77	Superior adjustment	.22		.25
7	.67	Mastery of external environment	.52		.13
		Factor III: Interpersonal Relations			
5	.83	Morals	.09	.29	
1	.71	Impulse control	.41	.16	
6	.52	Family relationships	.31	.39	

manageable and comprehensible set of variables but with a minimal loss of information. A factor analysis of the intercorrelations for the 10 satisfactory Self-Image Questionnaire scales was undertaken to discover if there was such an empirically determinable structure of meaningful common sources of influence underlying these rationally derived scales.

Although factor analysis itself is a mathematical operation, its application and procedures involve considerable subjective judgment and interpretation. At present, there are no completely accepted, definitive procedures, but rather a number of procedures and assumptions that can yield differing factor solutions. Since there can be no unique solution to a factor analysis, the procedure used reflects the purposes for which the analysis has been undertaken. The analytic procedure followed here maximizes the possibility of finding common factors, while insuring that the properties of the correlational matrix that make a factor analysis possible (that is, yield real rather than imaginary factors) are maintained. The choice of the final solution is based on both an analytic criterion and a criterion of psychological meaningfulness (Harman, 1960; Howard and Gordon, 1963).

The matrix of Pearson product-moment correlations among the 10 scales calculated for the total sample of 326 male high-school students was factor-analyzed by use of the principal-components method, with 1.0 in the diagonal.* Four factors, accounting for 76.56 of the total variance, were extracted and rotated using the Varimax method. Since the fourth rotated factor appeared to be a specific factor (with only one scale having its highest loading on this factor), the first three factors were rotated and this solution retained.

---

* The factor-analytic procedure followed a sequence outlined by K. Howard. Factor extraction is halted when two of the principal component factors have latent roots (eigenvalues) below 1.00. The extracted factors are then rotated with the use of Varimax, and a search for specific factors is made. If a specific factor (a factor having the highest loading of only one variable, Howard and Gordon, 1963) is found, the rotation is repeated with one less factor. This rotation procedure is continued until there are no specific factors.

The questionnaires were rescored for three second-order scales, each consisting of those scales which had their highest rotated factor loading on that factor (see Table 1A–6). Each scale was given unit weight. The specific results of this factor analysis are further discussed in Part II, Results. The relationships of the three SIQ-factor scales to the interview data were also investigated and are further discussed in Part II.

The Self-Image Questionnaire for Adolescent Boys†

When the questionnaire was introduced to the student, the first page was worded in the following way:

TO THE STUDENT:

This is a confidential self-image questionnaire. It is used only for scientific research purposes. There are no right and/or wrong answers. Please answer all items. After each statement you will have a choice of six answers. Please circle only one for each statement.

For example: I am a high-school student.	*Describes* *me very* *well* (1)	*Describes* *me* *well* 2	*Describes* *me fairly* *well* 3	*Does not* *quite de-* *scribe me* 4	*Does not* *really de-* *scribe me* 5	*Does not* *describe* *me at all* 6

Scale 1: Impulse Control

Item	Original Item No.	Mean	Variance
1. When I get very angry at a person, I let him (her) know about it	101	3.16	2.31
2. I keep an even temper most of the time	69	3.62	1.68
3. Usually I control myself	123	2.13	1.18
4. Even under pressure I manage to remain calm	59	2.95	1.69
5. I can take criticism without resentment	34	3.12	2.18
6. I carry many grudges (−)	1*	2.34	1.44
7. I "lose my head" easily (−)	8*	2.67	2.48

† The questionnaire was given, in the fall of 1962, to 350 entering freshman boys in two local suburban high schools; 326 questionnaires were completed by students and were utilized for our selection process. The means and variances for the total sample as well as the items are presented here. An instruction booklet for scoring and interpreting the Self-Image Questionnaire can be obtained by writing to the author: Daniel Offer, M.D., Institute for Psychosomatic and Psychiatric Research and Training, Michael Reese Hospital and Medical Center, 29ᵗʰ Street and Ellis Avenue, Chicago, Illinois 60616.

8. I fear something constantly (—)	81*	2.28	2.21
9. I get violent if I don't get my way (—)	50*	1.98	1.21
10. At times I have fits of crying and/or laughing that I seem unable to control (—)	17*	1.90	2.17

* Reflected as keyed.

Scale 2: Emotional Tone

Item	Original Item No.	Mean	Variance
1. Most of the time I am happy	32	2.16	1.15
2. I enjoy life	68	1.76	1.17
3. I feel relaxed under normal circumstances	44	1.91	1.23
4. Even when I am sad I can enjoy a good joke	100	2.21	1.53
5. I am so very anxious (—)	54*	3.49	2.58
6. I feel tense most of the time (—)	12*	2.30	1.63
7. I frequently feel sad (—)	130*	2.36	1.92
8. I feel inferior to most people I know (—)	23*	1.99	1.55
9. My feelings are easily hurt (—)	38*	2.57	1.90
10. I feel so very lonely (—)	66*	1.82	1.34

* Reflected as keyed.

Scale 3: Body and Self-Image

Item	Original Item No.	Mean	Variance
1. I am proud of my body	57	2.80	1.98
2. I feel strong and healthy	99	2.14	1.45
3. I am not afraid to use my hands when necessary for work	18	2.04	2.43
4. The recent changes in my body have given me some satisfaction	6	2.94	2.21
5. The picture I have of myself in the future satisfies me	42	2.34	1.78
6. I frequently feel ugly and unattractive (—)	90*	2.79	2.11
7. When others look at me they must think that I am poorly developed (—)	94*	2.27	1.90
8. I seem to be forced to imitate the people I like (—)	72*	2.78	2.40
9. In the past year I have been very worried about my health (—)	27*	1.93	1.91

10. Very often I think that I am not at all the person I would like to be (—)	82*	3.43	2.74

* Reflected as keyed.

Scale 4: Social Relationships

Item	Original Item No.	Mean	Variance
1. I enjoy most parties I go to	124	2.08	1.46
2. I do not have a particularly difficult time in making friends	113	2.39	1.86
3. I think it is important to have at least one good friend (to confide in)	47	1.61	1.08
4. Being together with other people gives me a good feeling	88	1.99	1.10
5. I do not mind being corrected, since I can learn from it	65	2.41	1.64
6. I find it extremely hard to make friends (—)	62*	1.93	1.54
7. I usually feel out of place at picnics and parties (—)	13*	2.36	2.20
8. I prefer being alone (than with other kids my age) (—)	75*	2.24	2.51
9. I think that other people just do not like me (—)	52*	2.17	1.73
10. If others disapprove of me I get terribly upset (—)	86*	2.56	1.81

* Reflected as keyed.

Scale 5: Morals

Item	Original Item No.	Mean	Variance
1. For me, good sportsmanship in school is as important as winning a game	74	2.19	1.82
2. I would not like to be associated with those kids who "hit below the belt"	120	2.73	3.16
3. I would not hurt someone just for the "heck of it"	5	1.94	2.40
4. Eye for an eye and tooth for a tooth does not apply to our society	116	3.22	3.29
5. I like to help a friend whenever I can	83	1.96	0.89
6. I do not care how my actions affect others as long as I gain something (—)	67*	2.09	1.69

7. I would not stop at anything if I felt I
   was wrong (—)   30*   2.48   2.32
8. I blame others even when I know that I
   am at fault too (—)   40*   2.51   1.98
9. If you confide in others you ask for
   troubles (—)   92*   2.40   1.67
10. Telling the truth means nothing to
    me (—)   48*   1.53   1.06

* Reflected as keyed.

Scale 6:   Sexual Attitudes

Item	Original Item No.	Mean	Variance
1. Having a girl friend is important to me	119	3.16	2.62
2. I think that girls find me attractive	77	3.63	1.72
3. Sexual experiences give me pleasure	117	3.58	2.60
4. I often think about sex	122	3.25	2.16
5. Dirty jokes are fun at times	28	3.25	2.66
6. Thinking or talking about sex frightens me (—)	97*	1.82	1.25
7. The opposite sex finds me a bore (—)	10*	2.42	1.94
8. It is very hard for a teen-ager to know how to handle sex in a right way (—)	16*	2.78	2.45
9. Sexually I am way behind (—)	91*	1.92	1.12
10. I do not attend sexy shows (—)	80*	4.16	3.32

* Reflected as keyed.

Scale 7:   Family Relationships

Item	Original Item No.	Mean	Variance
1. I can count on my parents most of the time	26	2.40	2.58
2. Most of the time my parents are satisfied with me	112	2.32	1.51
3. My parents are usually patient with me	71	2.30	1.95
4. I feel that I have part in making family decisions	64	2.84	2.20
5. Most of the time my parents get along well with each other	51	2.00	2.19
6. Usually I feel that I am a bother at home (—)	85*	2.39	2.23

7. I try to stay away from home most of the time (—)	102*	2.47	2.13
8. Very often I feel that my father is no good (—)	21*	1.74	1.83
9. Very often I feel that my mother is no good (—)	118*	1.55	1.18
10. Parents should shower children with praise even if they don't deserve it (—)	33*	1.88	1.61
11. I think that I will be a source of pride to my parents in the future	4	2.37	1.55
12. I like one parent much better than the other (—)	87*	2.08	2.61
13. When my parents are strict, I feel that they are right, even if I get angry	55	2.94	2.44
14. Understanding my parents is beyond me (—)	24*	2.33	1.87
15. When I grow up and have a family, it will be in at least a few ways similar to my own	60	2.58	2.14
16. My parents are ashamed of me (—)	95*	1.53	1.01
17. My parents will be disappointed in me in the future (—)	15*	1.63	1.24
18. I have been carrying a grudge against my parents for years (—)	106*	1.56	1.18
19. My parents are almost always on the side of someone else, e.g., my brother and/or sister (—)	9*	2.71	3.18
20. Very often parents do not understand a a person because they had an unhappy childhood (—)	73*	2.60	2.71

* Reflected as keyed.

Scale 8: *Mastery of the External World*

Item	Original Item No.	Mean	Variance
1. Most of the time I think that the world is an exciting place to live in	3	2.67	2.25
2. When I decide to do something, I do it	76	2.44	1.20
3. I feel that I am able to make decisions	105	2.25	1.31
4. If I put my mind to it, I can learn almost anything	19	1.96	1.31
5. My work, in general, is at least as good as the work of the guy next to me	35	2.84	2.56
6. I am fearful of growing up (—)	128*	1.84	1.37

7. I find life an endless series of problems—without solution in sight (−)	103*	2.24	1.83
8. I feel that I have no talent whatso-ever (−)	109*	2.01	1.70
9. When I want something, I just sit around wishing I could have it (−)	41*	2.47	1.89
10. I repeat things continuously to be sure that I am right (−)	129*	3.44	2.11

* Reflected as keyed.

Scale 9:   Vocational-Educational Goals

Item	Original Item No.	Mean	Variance
1. A job well done gives me pleasure	70	1.47	0.66
2. At times I think about what kind of work I will do in the future	58	1.74	1.04
3. At times I feel like a leader and feel that other kids can learn something from me	104	2.85	1.81
4. I feel that there is plenty I can learn from others	79	1.86	0.94
5. I am sure that I will be proud about my future profession	37	1.77	0.96
6. School and studying mean very little to me (−)	115*	1.81	1.37
7. I would rather sit around and loaf than work (−)	46*	2.44	2.17
8. I would rather be supported for the rest of my life than work (−)	63*	1.90	1.75
9. Only stupid people work (−)	20*	1.17	0.36
10. I feel that working is too much responsi-bility for me (−)	14*	1.69	1.22

* Reflected as keyed.

Scale 10:   Psychopathology

Item	Original Item No.	Mean	Variance
1. The size of my sex organs is normal	31	2.06	1.43
2. I often blame myself even when I am not really at fault (−)	29*	2.81	2.22
3. Most people my age have scary dreams once in a while	7	4.77	2.13
4. I often feel that I would rather die than go on living (−)	61*	1.86	1.93

5. I believe I can tell the real from the fantastic 96 2.05 1.57
6. When I am with people I am bothered by hearing strange noises (−) 111* 1.68 1.23
7. When I enter a new room, I have a strange and funny feeling (−) 108* 2.73 2.56
8. I do not have many fears which I cannot understand 126 2.49 1.73
9. I am confused most of the time (−) 22* 2.01 1.35
10. I am afraid that someone is going to make fun of me 2* 2.30 1.81
11. Other people are not after me to take advantage of me 78 2.92 2.66
12. Sometimes I feel so ashamed of myself that I just want to hide in a corner and cry (−) 36* 2.44 2.54
13. I feel empty emotionally most of the time (−) 45* 2.30 2.01
14. No one can harm me just by not liking me 127 2.58 2.10
15. Even though I am continuously on the go, I seem unable to get things done (−) 93* 2.90 2.34

* Reflected as keyed.

Scale 11: Superior Adjustment

Item	Original Item No.	Mean	Variance
1. Dealing with new intellectual subjects is a challenge for me	125	2.43	1.78
2. I tend to do things even if there is some danger in them	98	3.02	2.12
3. Our society is a competitive one, and I am not afraid of it	49	2.40	1.75
4. I am a superior student in school	43	3.88	2.09
5. If I know that I will have to face a new situation, I will try in advance to find out as much as possible about it	84	2.31	1.40
6. Worrying a little about one's future helps to make it work out better	121	2.66	2.17
7. Whenever I fail in something, I try to find out what I can do in order to avoid another failure	89	2.22	1.39

8. When a tragedy occurs to one of my friends, I feel sad too	39	2.41	1.68
9. I do not rehearse how I might deal with a real coming event (—)	110*	3.02	2.37
10. I do not like to put things in order and make sense of them (—)	25*	1.88	1.62
11. Working closely with another fellow never gives me pleasure (—)	56*	2.20	2.15
12. I do not enjoy solving difficult problems (—)	114*	2.88	2.44
13. I find it very difficult to establish new friendships (—)	53*	2.27	2.22
14. If I should be separated from all people I know, I feel that I would not be able to make a go of it (—)	11*	2.84	2.93
15. I am certain that I will not be able to assume responsibilities for myself in the future (—)	107*	1.87	1.77

* Reflected as keyed.

APPENDIX II

The Interview Schedules
for the
Modal Adolescent Project

*First Psychiatric Interview**
Introduction to the Study
Spring 1963

In this interview we introduce the adolescent to the study. Here he becomes acquainted with the interviewer and is helped to relieve any tension or anxiety he may have about seeing a psychiatrist. The interview should be semi-structured, but in this interview, as in others, the interviewer should always follow the various leads of the subject and explore in some depth areas that are of concern

This outline of instructions was developed prior to the beginning of the project; it was followed by the interviewers throughout the study.

* Offer interviewed 85 per cent of the students and Marcus 15 per cent. Each student was followed by the same psychiatrist from the beginning to the end.

to the subject. The adolescent should have a feeling that he would want to come back and talk more to "the understanding man." The first interview is divided into four different stages:

I. The interviewer starts by introducing himself and the study. He asks if the student remembers when he took the questionnaire (in November of 1962), and explains our method of selection. We point out our twofold interest in adolescents: (1) Through our own work with the disturbed adolescent and the feeling that by knowing more about the normal adolescent we shall be better able to help the disturbed. (2) That adults' understanding of adolescents is limited. Many adults have written books about the teen-ager and what he thinks, but few of them have actually asked the teen-ager directly. Therefore, we would like to know from him what he thinks about himself, his world, and his problems. We stress here that these problems do not necessarily have to be deep ones but anything that he considers of importance. Then we tell the subject that we are psychiatrists and tell him a little about our own background. At this point in the interview we stop and ask the student if he has any questions.

II. Next we want to find out what the teen-agers think of the project. This can be done best by asking them how their parents told them about the project. Some parents show the students the letter we sent. Some just tell them that there are tests to be taken in school, and some do not tell them anything.

III. Once we have finished the first two stages, we proceed to asking specific questions—the family situation, how many siblings, what the parents do—and make appropriate comments. For instance, when the subject says he has an older brother or younger sister we would ask him how he likes to be in a "sandwich position." We ask the student what his favorite subject is in school and which is his favorite sport, and again make appropriate comments. Although there is little time left unstructured, we let the interview develop in the direction to which the student has led us.

IV. In closing the interview, we again ask the students how they felt about the interview, how they liked it. We tell them about the future of the project. We tell them that we will see them about once every three months for about three years and talk just the way we talked today. We tell them that they will get a postcard from us approximately 10 days before their next interview and they should let us know by return mail or by phone if they cannot make it.

Survey Interview
Background Information
Summer and Fall 1963

The aim of this interview is to get an overall picture concerning the background of the subjects. The interviewer (Marlene Simon) had the questionnaire before her and filled in the answers during the interview.

The interview had four different sections:

I. Detailed development history from the subject's point of view. (See Appendix III for Results.)

II. Open-ended questions concerning the Home Environment. (See Table 4–4 for Results.)

III. Family interaction scale. See below.

IV. Each subject was asked to write down three typical early memories. (These memories were analyzed separately and the results are not included in this book.)

Family Interaction Scale

(BASED ON THE PRINCIPLE OF THE OSGOOD SEMANTIC DIFFERENTIAL)
Each scale has been completed by each family 6 times.

For subject:
   (1) My mother is
   (2) My father is

For parents:
   (3) In the company of my son, I am (for mother)
   (4) In the company of my son, I am (for father)
   (5) In the company of my son, my wife is (for husband)
   (6) In the company of my son, my husband is (for wife)

Check two in each line.

	not at all	slightly	fairly	very		not at all	slightly	fairly	very
1. encouraging	—	—	—	—	discouraging	—	—	—	—
2. permissive	—	—	—	—	authoritative	—	—	—	—
3. rewarding	—	—	—	—	punishing	—	—	—	—
4. sympathetic	—	—	—	—	antagonistic	—	—	—	—
5. warm	—	—	—	—	cold	—	—	—	—
6. close	—	—	—	—	distant	—	—	—	—
7. active	—	—	—	—	passive	—	—	—	—
8. relaxed	—	—	—	—	tense	—	—	—	—
9. consistent	—	—	—	—	inconsistent	—	—	—	—
10. attractive	—	—	—	—	unattractive	—	—	—	—
11. grateful	—	—	—	—	resentful	—	—	—	—
12. assertive	—	—	—	—	submissive	—	—	—	—
13. secure	—	—	—	—	fearful	—	—	—	—

Second Psychiatric Interview
General Problem Areas
Winter 1964

In this interview we cover general issues of significance to adolescents. As in all the other interviews, we begin by asking the subjects to tell us if anything special has happened to them since we last saw them. Is there anything they would like to tell us? Or do they have any questions for us? We bring in any significant current event (e.g., the 1963 civil-rights march on Washington) and ask how they feel about it.

In each interview we attempt to pursue areas that seem to be of interest to the teen-ager (such as current relationship with a girl friend). We intersperse the areas to be covered within the interview situation.

(1) Delinquency: Its causes, how society can combat it; does subject know any delinquents and if yes, his feelings about them.

(2) The dropout problem: Cause and cure.

(3) Smoking and drinking during adolescence.

(4) Three major problems that an adolescent has to master during the high-school years.

(5) Three wishes.

(6) What would he do with a million dollars?

(7) Whom would he like to be with on a desert island?

(8) Why is it difficult for an adolescent to get his first date?

Third Psychiatric Interview
Affects and Relationship with Adults
Spring and Summer 1964

In this interview we specifically explore the subject's experience with four major feeling states. We define each feeling state for the subject and then ask him for personal examples (or experiences). We inquire into the intensity of the feeling state: How does the feeling manifest itself (example: in anxiety is it palpitation, sweating, etc.)? How long does it last? What does the subject do to cope with the feeling? Finally, how successful is the subject in coping with the feeling (e.g., does the depressive feeling disappear after hours, days, or weeks)? The four feeling states and the examples we gave the subject are:

(1) Anxiety (feeling before exams).
(2) Depression (sadness, when someone dies).
(3) Shame (failing to live up to expectation).
(4) Guilt (did something wrong).

In addition to the above, we explore the kind of daydreams the subject has. When do they occur? How frequent are they? And, specifically, does he daydream about girls?

Toward the end of the interview we bring the student back to a more neutral subject. We ask him to tell us in detail his picture of the (1) ideal teacher, (2) ideal father, (3) ideal mother. After he describes each person, we ask him how close these descriptions are to the real figures in his life.

At the end of the interview we again, as always, ask for the subject's feelings about the interview and the project. We especially explore further any negative feelings expressed.

Psychological Testing
Between Fall 1964 and Spring 1965*

The procedure for testing was followed routinely, but with some flexibility for each subject. The examiner telephoned each boy one to three days before the appointment. She introduced herself and identified her relationship with the senior investigator, asking whether he had mentioned that she would be calling. She then commented that she was seeing each of the boys for an hour or

* Conducted by Sara Lee Futterman.

so and set up an appointment. If the boy was unable to meet that time, either another time was set up or the boy was told he would be called later. When the new appointment was set up for more than a week in advance, a postcard was sent as a reminder several days prior to the appointed day. On those occasions that the boy was not home to receive the initial call, an appointment was usually set up through the mother, with a request that the boy telephone the examiner if the appointment time was inconvenient for the boy.

The testing session itself began with small talk. The examiner then remarked that the subject had been told of the project psychiatrists' interest in studying normal boys and comparing their successful handling of problems with the unsuccessful efforts of patients. The tests were then described along similar lines—as an additional source of information about the boys, with the emphasis on their use as a confirmation about what is known about the boys from the interviews. They were also told of the project psychiatrists' interest in the tests themselves and that this afforded an unusual opportunity to see what the tests of normal people are like. They were then asked what they knew about psychological tests (almost every subject said he knew nothing) and if they had heard of or seen the ink-blot test (about a third had seen it on television); the examiner said she would be giving them this test as well as some others, but that they would start with a short vocabulary test. She pointed out that after that she would tell them more about the other tests since they are quite different from the vocabulary test. She stressed that the other tests to come were not tests of knowledge.

The examiner explained that some of the words on the vocabulary test were very easy, others very hard, and that she didn't expect them to know all the words. The standard instructions, "Tell me the meaning of these words," were given. At the end of the series the examiner stated, "That was very good," or words to that effect, and would ask each boy what his career interests were.

At this point the examiner repeated that the remaining tests were not tests of knowledge. She described the vocabulary test as one in which there is a right answer and in which one tries to come as close to that answer as one can. She contrasted this with the remaining tests, saying that they shouldn't really be called tests at all, and describing them rather as efforts to learn more about how the boys see things and think about things.

The Rorschach was then administered by means of the procedure outlined by Schafer (1954) and Rapaport (1946). The subject was asked: "What could this look like? What might it be? Tell me everything you see." When the subject finished his responses to a card—the free association—the examiner conducted the inquiry about those responses, with the card not exposed. The inquiry was given thus after each card. When the entire set of ink cards was completed, the examiner asked what the boy thought of the test, but the reply was generally brief and noncommittal.

The instructions for the Thematic Apperception Test were as follows: "I'm going to show you some pictures. I'd like you to make up a story about each one. Tell me what's going on in the picture, what led up to it, what's going to happen, and what the characters are thinking and feeling. Make it as dramatic as you like but don't go too fast because I want to write down everything you say." When the six stories were completed the examiner commented that those were good stories.

Finally, the boys were asked what they thought of the tests, and the examiner discussed their reactions with them. She mentioned the discomfort of the boy's not knowing what was found out from these tests. She explained that she had written down everything he had said and how he had said it, and that this information would add dimension to the data obtained from the interviews. Frequently, directly, or indirectly, the boys asked whether their responses were like those of other people. The boys were then told that they would soon be seen for an interview.

The Rorschachs were scored by the Beck method of scoring

(1961). A psychologist with several years of Rorschach experience scored all the tests. Her scoring was then reviewed by Singer, and the few disagreements that arose were settled by the two psychologists discussing the issue until a consensus was obtained. Thus, although reliabilities are not computed, the tests were all scored under the same frame of reference, with opportunity for checks built in.

Fourth Psychiatric Interview
Sexuality and Vocation
Spring and Summer 1965

In this interview we explore two rather different subjects: (1) "The sexual feelings and behavior of our subjects, and (2) their vocational and educational goals. We begin by asking them about:

1. Vocational and educational plans.
2. Present working situation (Earning money now?).
3. What kind of work gives them pleasure now?

When introducing the subject of sex, we begin by telling the adolescents that although these sexual feelings are very private and personal, they are nonetheless an important part of everyone's life. We therefore want to know what their experience has been. We also tell them that we shall be glad to answer any questions they may have.

We start the questions by asking them whether they think it is important for teen-agers to have girl friends. If they say "no" emphatically and add that they have not yet gone out with girls, we do not proceed to ask them all the other questions. We go easy with these (inhibited?) teen-agers. When the answer is "yes" we ask them to elaborate on their answer: Why is it important for teen-agers to have a girl friend? What has been their experience, and do they have a girl friend? If they do have a girl friend, how do they get along with her and what kind of arguments (or problems) do they have with her?

From the above we proceed to ask more general questions. What does he think of sex? Has he had any sexual experiences? If the answer is "yes," had the sexual experiences given him pleasure? How easy is it for him to get a date, and does he feel that girls find him attractive? Finally, we ask him what he thinks of sexual education and what his experiences with it have been in the school, in church, or at home.

At the end of the interview we ask the subject to tell us who outside of his immediate family he considers great. In addition to exploring general feelings toward the study, we also ask the subjects how they liked the psychological testing.

Fifth Psychiatric Interview
The Study in Retrospect
Fall 1965 and Winter 1966

1. Review of material from first interview concerning parents and siblings. Have his feelings and impressions changed? If so, in what way? Why?

2. What is the basic difference between a fourteen-year-old and a seventeen-year-old? (That is, what has he learned in the past three years, or how much has he changed?)

3. The study in retrospect:

    (a) What difficulties did they have in relating to us as adults?

    (b) What was their parents' orientation toward the study?

    (c) What was their friends' orientation toward the project?

    (d) Speculating, what percentage of their friends would be willing to participate in such a study?

    (e) Which of the seven interviews was most helpful and why?

    (f) Which of the seven interviews was most disturbing and why?

    (g) Any suggestions, criticisms, or comments.

4. The subject's plans for the future.

The Parents' Interview
Summer 1965 and Spring 1966*

  I. Explain to the parents the general philosophy of the project and thank them for their cooperation. Explain briefly the reason for the interview (to validate certain of our observations and to correlate them with studies of parents of disturbed populations). Assure them of the confidential nature of the interview. Insert the possibility of seeing them again, remote though it may be.

  II. Detailed developmental history (both parents together). The same one which was given to their sons during the second interview.

III. Separate parents, if both are present. Give one the two rating scales to complete (in another room) and interview the other. Then reverse.

THE INDIVIDUAL INTERVIEW

  (a) Description of their son:
His outstanding characteristics
His assets
His shortcomings; if the parent cannot think of any, ask him if he could change a particular trait, which one would he like to see changed?

  (b) The parents' feelings about their son.
Satisfaction (elaborate and document).
Dissatisfaction or disappointments (why?)

  (c) How does their son compare to their other son(s) or sons of friends?

  (d) Is there mutual understanding between them and their son?

* Conducted by Joanne Miller.

(Document. Example: When you are moody, does your child leave you alone? Can you share his troubles?)

(e) Parents' own adolescence:

(1) Are teen-agers of today similar to or different from what they used to be one generation ago?

(2) Feelings about teen-agers of today (What are they like? More or less delinquency? What do they lack? How does their son's adolescence compare to others today?).

(3) How does their son's adolescence compare to their own?

(4) First memory of parent from high-school years.

(5) What else do they remember from their own adolescence?

(f) What do they feel about research in the high schools: advantages; safeguards.

What about our project?

Did it affect their children? If "yes," how?

Any questions, comments, or criticism.

IV. Family Interaction Scale (each parent separately). See Second Interview.

V. The Self-Image Questionnaire. Each parent takes the questionnaire separately and tries to predict son's answer on 40 select items from the SIQ. The results are discussed in Chapter 4.)

Sixth Psychiatric Interview
The High School in Retrospect
Spring 1966

1. Establish the continuity from last year. Special experiences in past year, etc.
2. Plans after high school (college, Army, career choice).
3. Special comments. (Has subject thought about the project dur-

ing the past year? If so, in what connection? Any questions of us? How did parents react to their interview? The high-school years in retrospect.)
4. The future of the project, with willingness to cooperate in follow-up project.

The last two interviews were less structured. We explored in more detail any previous material which the teen-agers had brought up and which seemed unclear to us. We also assumed that by then most of the teen-agers would have developed considerable trust in us and would be more willing and able to bring up confidential material of their own.

ANALYSIS OF INTERVIEW DATA

The data analysis itself can be seen as proceeding in three phases: (1) reliability, (2) description, and (3) associations. The first phase involved a check of the reliability (interrater agreement) of the coding and rating of the interview material. One judge rated all 73 subjects on the sentence-completion items, symptom-rating scale, parents' interview material, and psychiatrist's ratings; a second judge, working independently, rated at random 20 per cent of the subjects. For any item, if the agreement was greater than 70 per cent, the first judge's ratings were used. If agreement fell below 70 per cent, the item was dropped.

The second phase of the analysis was simply to describe the sample's response to each of the items. Frequency counts (percentages) for the interview schedules are presented and discussed wherever appropriate in Part II: Results, and in Appendix III.

The third phase of the analysis involved seeking associations among interview items and between interview items and test variables. This search was guided by two major considerations: (1) the nature of the obtained frequency distributions, and (2) theoretically relevant questions. First, the distributions for a number of the items were too skewed or limited in variance to provide meaningful relationships; whenever possible the original categories were combined to provide sufficient and meaningful variance. Such combinations will be indicated when the analysis is presented. Second, a series of questions was posed, identifying a subgroup of important independent variables whose relationship with the other items might have theoretical significance. These variables included dating pattern, geographic mobility, socioeconomic status, class standing, participation in delinquent behavior, character structure, cooperativeness, symptoms manifested, teachers' ratings, and psychiatrists' ratings of interview behavior.

Both continuous and categorical variables are represented, as well as some (for example, socioeconomic status) that may be considered either categorical or continuous, in line with the assumptions one may wish to make. Pearson product-moment correlations and point biserial correlations as well as the analysis of variance and chi square are each used where appropriate.

Several special analyses were also undertaken, such as a factor analysis of the symptom rating scales; these special analyses are described in more detail in Chapter 9.

In a study in which a large amount of data has been gathered about a relatively small, select sample of subjects, it is always necessary to take notice of possible questions about the interpretation of the results. In our study, two areas of special concern are the level of significance chosen and the generalizability of the findings.

Throughout the study, the .05 level of significance has been used; two-tailed tests were applied unless a specific unidirectional hypothesis is presented. However, we tend to use as our basic criterion for discussion and inference the consistency and theoretical significance of our findings rather than the numerical estimate of the level of statistical significance. There are many problems in adopting a strictly statistical criterion for inference from our data; the vast number of explicit and implicit comparisons in such a rich (and even yet not completely analyzed) data pool makes very difficult the task of setting the a priori level of significance at .05, .01, or even .001. The judgment whether a particular significant relationship could have arisen through chance alone (that is, the possibility of accepting a given result as true when it is not) in a single experiment is always difficult; we have preferred to be cautious in our interpretations of relationships, to be guided by the psychological meaningfulness of the finding, and to view future replication as necessary for confirmation. Our approach to the interpretation of the results has also been guided by our recognition that specific questions regarding the basic issues in adolescence (and our own potentially biasing, often unexpressed, personal answers) have throughout shaped our data-collection, reporting, and analysis procedures, even though no formal hypotheses were stated at the onset of our project. (The interested reader is referred to Rosenthal, 1966, where the question of the influence of the experimenter bias is discussed in detail.)

Second, concerning generalizability, our sample is a carefully screened special subgroup and not a random sample of adolescent boys. Our sampling plan (or possibly it could be called our case-finding procedure from an epidemiological viewpoint) has been based on the systematic exclusion of disturbed adolescent boys; by the use of the most restrictive definition of generalizability, then, our two-step selection procedure (modal self-description on a structured, fixed-response questionnaire, followed by a check for nonsymptomatic overt behavior) has limited the generalizability of our findings to groups selected in the same manner. On the one hand, we see this limitation as a virtue—it has been our explicit goal to describe in dynamic terms the adolescent experience of one portion of the adolescent population that the psychiatrist rarely if ever sees clinically, as well as to develop and refine the psychiatric techniques and concepts relevant to future expansion of such efforts. On the other hand, while we do not wish ourselves to fall victim to the same errors of spurious, premature generalization for which we have criticized others, we do wish to affirm our confidence that our selection procedures and interview process provide data from a base-line normative sample of male adolescents that need be taken into account when generalizing about or actually studying the adolescent.

APPENDIX III

Selected Questions and Answers
Collected in the Second Interview

	Yes	No	N.A.
1. Was being *overweight* a problem to you in childhood?	14 (19.2)	59 (80.8)	———
2. Was being *too short* a problem to you?	9 (12.3)	64 (87.7)	———
3. Was being *too tall* a problem to you?	2 (2.7)	71 (97.3)	———
4. Did you have any *difficulties walking?*	1 (1.4)	72 (98.6)	———
5. Did you have any *eating* problems?	4 (5.5)	69 (94.5)	———
6. Is *thumbsucking* a problem to you?	19 (26.0)	54 (74.0)	———
7. Was *nail biting* ever a problem to you?	44 (60.3)	29 (39.7)	———
8. Were *nightmares* ever a problem to you?	17 (23.3)	56 (76.7)	———
9. Were any *specific fears* ever a problem (e.g., fear of dark)?	28 (38.4)	45 (61.6)	———

		Yes	No	N.A.
10.	Did you have any *reading difficulties?*	19 (26.0)	54 (74.0)	———
11.	Did you have any *speech difficulties?*	18 (24.7)	55 (75.3)	———
12.	Was *stealing* ever a problem to you?	10 (13.7)	63 (86.3)	———
13.	Was *cheating* ever a problem to you?	7 (9.6)	66 (86.3)	———
14.	Was *lying* ever a problem to you?	20 (27.4)	53 (72.6)	———
15.	Is your family worried about your *eating habits?*	9 (12.3)	64 (87.7)	———
16.	Is your family worried about your *staying out late?*	16 (21.9)	55 (75.3)	2 (2.7)
17.	Is your family worried about your *going out on single dates?*	1 (1.4)	68 (93.2)	4 (5.5)
18.	Is your family worried about your *morals?*	3 (4.1)	66 (90.4)	4 (5.5)
19.	Is your family worried about your *clothes?*	15 (20.5)	58 (79.5)	———
20.	Is your family worried about your *orderliness?*	35 (47.9)	38 (52.1)	———
21.	Is your family worried about your *cleanliness?*	23 (31.5)	50 (68.5)	———
22.	Is your family worried about your *friends?*	13 (17.8)	60 (82.2)	———
23.	Is your family worried about your being *independent?*	8 (11.0)	62 (84.9)	———
24.	Is your family worried about your *not telling them everything?*	13 (17.8)	59 (80.8)	———
25.	Is your family worried about your *discipline?*	17 (23.3)	56 (76.7)	———
26.	Is your family worried about your *respect for elders?*	17 (23.3)	56 (76.7)	———
27.	Is your family worried about your *social life?*	5 (6.8)	67 (91.8)	1 (1.4)
28.	Is your family worried about *physical sports?*	14 (19.2)	59 (80.8)	———
29.	Is your family worried about your *completion of tasks?*	27 (37.0)	45 (61.6)	1 (1.4)
30.	Is your family worried about your *smoking?*	5 (6.8)	68 (93.2)	———
31.	Is your family worried about *masturbation?*	1 (1.4)	16 (20.5)	51 (78.1)

	Yes	No	N.A.
32. Is your family worried about *drinking?*	3 (4.1)	70 (95.9)	———
33. Is your family worried about *excessive use of the telephone?*	11 (15.1)	62 (84.9)	———
34. Is your family worried about your *manners?*	12 (16.4)	61 (83.6)	———
35. Is your family worried about *responsibility?*	15 (20.5)	58 (79.5)	———

	Yes	No	Don't Know	N.A.
36. Do you expect to have an active social life?	59 (80.8)	14 (19.2)	———	———
37. Do you want to have the same profession as your father?	15 (20.5)	53 (72.6)	5 (6.8)	———
38. Did parents work on projects together?	48 (65.8)	23 (31.5)	———	2 (2.7)
39. Did parents encourage you to be competitive in sports?	42 (57.5)	27 (37.0)	———	4 (5.5)
40. Father likes his work?	66 (90.4)	3 (4.1)	1 (1.4)	3 (4.1)
41. Mother likes her housework?	46 (63.0)	21 (28.8)	———	6 (8.2)
42. I enjoy studying alone.	58 (79.5)	15 (20.5)	———	———
43. I have trouble studying.	23 (31.5)	60 (68.5)	———	———
44. I hate to recite in class.	23 (31.5)	49 (67.1)	———	1 (1.4)
45. Do your parents go to church once a week?	43 (58.9)	29 (39.7)	———	1 (1.4)
46. Is your religion helpful to you?	47 (64.4)	20 (27.4)	3 (4.1)	3 (4.1)
47. Do you expect to earn more money than your father?	42 (57.5)	18 (24.7)	6 (8.2)	7 (9.6)
48. If so, will that bother you?	59 (80.8)	6 (8.2)	1 (1.4)	7 (9.6)
49. Does your father approve of your future plans?	59 (80.8)	———	2 (2.7)	12 (16.4)
50. Does your mother approve of your future plans?	57 (78.1)	2 (2.7)	2 (2.7)	12 (16.4)
51. Do you expect to marry?	67 (91.8)	5 (6.8)	———	1 (1.4)
52. Do you expect to have children?	66 (90.4)	———	1 (1.4)	6 (8.2)

53. Who was your mother's favorite?
    1. I was (subject)   19 (26.0)
    2. Sister   11 (15.1)
    3. Brother   6 (8.2)
    4. No favorites   35 (47.9)
    5. Don't know   2 (2.7)
    6. N.A.

54. What are your plans after high school?
    1. Go to college   64 (87.7)
    2. Go to the Army (or any branch of service)   3 (4.1)
    3. Work
    4. Other   6 (8.2)
    5. N.A.

55. If you do not go to college will your parents be:
    1. Satisfied   5 (6.8)
    2. Dissatisfied   61 (83.6)
    3. Don't know   3 (4.1)
    4. Neither   3 (4.1)
    5. N.A.   1 (1.4)

56. Who was your father's favorite?
    1. I was (subject)   25 (34.2)
    2. Sister   10 (13.7)
    3. Brother   6 (8.2)
    4. No favorites   29 (39.7)
    5. Don't know   1 (1.4)
    6. N.A.   2 (2.7)

57. Which one of your parents makes most of the decisions?
    1. Father   42 (57.5)
    2. Mother   13 (17.8)
    3. Both   13 (17.8)
    4. Don't know
    5. N.A.   5 (6.8)

58. Check the category that comes closest to your feelings about yourself:
    1. I don't like myself the way I am; I'd like to change completely   0
    2. There are many things I'd like to change, but not completely   33 (45.2)
    3. I'd like to stay very much the same; there is very little I would change   40 (54.8)
    4. Don't know
    5. N.A.

59. If your voice has changed, at what age did it take place?
    1. 11 years   3 (4.1)
    2. 12 years   8 (11.0)
    3. 13 years   25 (34.2)
    4. 14 years   28 (38.4)
    5. 15 years   4 (5.5)
    6. Has not changed   4 (5.5)
    7. N.A.   1 (1.4)

60. How often do you go to church?
    1. Once a week   27 (37.0)

2. Less often than once a week   15 (20.5)
3. Attend very rarely   8 (11.0)
4. Do not attend   14 (19.2)
5. N.A.   9 (12.3)

	First	*Second*	*Third*	*N.A.*
61. If you had your choice, how would you rate *being a star athlete?**	21 (28.8)	26 (35.6)	24 (32.9)	2 (2.7)
62. How would you rate *being a real scholar?**	35 (47.9)	24 (32.9)	13 (17.8)	1 (1.4)
63. How would you rate *being a social leader?**	16 (21.9)	21 (28.8)	34 (46.6)	2 (2.7)
64. How would your parents rate *being a star athlete?**	2 (2.7)	30 (41.1)	39 (53.4)	2 (2.7)
65. How would your parents rate *being a real scholar?**	57 (78.1)	13 (17.8)	2 (2.7)	1 (1.4)
66. How would your parents rate *being a social leader?**	13 (17.8)	28 (38.4)	30 (41.1)	2 (2.7)

67. Ego ideal ("Who, outside of your close family, do you think is really great?"):
    1. Political figure (e.g., President, Governor)   23 (32.0)
    2. Scientist (e.g., Einstein)   2 (2.7)
    3. Artist (e.g., writer, painter, musician)   3 (4.1)
    4. Sports hero   4 (5.5)
    5. Personal friend or relative (peer)   4 (5.5)
    6. Girl friend   4 (5.5)
    7. Older relative or friend of parents   13 (17.8)
    8. Other   12 (16.4)
    9. N.A.   8 (11.0)

* These questions are taken from Coleman (1961).

Bibliography

Ackerman, N. W. 1958. *The Psychodynamics of Family Life.* New York: Basic Books, Inc.

Ackerman, N. W. 1966. *Treating the Troubled Family.* New York: Basic Books, Inc.

Adelson, J. 1964. "The Mystique of Adolescence." *Psychiatry,* XXVII, 1–5.

Alden, P., and Benton, A. L. 1951. "Relationship of Sex of Examiner to Incidence of Rorschach Responses with Sexual Content." *Journal of Projective Techniques,* XV, 230–234.

Ames, L. B., Metraux, R. W., and Walker, R. N. 1958. *Adolescent Rorschach Responses.* New York: Paul B. Hoeber, Inc.

Arieti, S. 1966. "Creativity and Its Cultivation: Relation to Psychopathology and Mental Health." In Arieti, S., ed., *American Handbook of Psychiatry,* Vol. III, 722–741. New York: Basic Books, Inc.

Ausubel, D. P. 1954. *Theory and Problems of Adolescent Development.* New York: Grune and Stratton.

Baittle, B., and Offer, D. 1969. "On the Nature of Adolescent Rebellion." Unpublished manuscript.

Barglow, P., and Bornstein, M., *et al.* 1968. "Pregnancy in Early Adolescence." *American Journal of Orthopsychiatry,* 38,4:672–687.

Barron, F. 1963. *Creativity and Psychological Health.* Princeton, New Jersey: D. Van Nostrand.

Baughman, E. E. 1951. "Rorschach Scores as a Function of Examiner Differences." *Journal of Projective Techniques,* XV, 243–249.

Beck, S. J., Beck, A. G., Levitt, E. E., and Molish, H. B. 1961. *Rorschach's Test. I. Basic Processes.* New York: Grune and Stratton.

Benedek, T. 1967. "On the Psychic Economy of Developmental Processes." *American Medical Association Archives of General Psychiatry,* XVII, 271–276.

Bernstein, L. 1956. "The Examiner as Inhibiting Factor in Psychological Testing." *Journal of Consulting Psychology,* XX, 287–290.

Bibring, G. 1961a. "A Study of the Psychological Processes in Pregnancy and of the Earliest Mother-Child Relationship: I. Some Propositions and

Comments." *Psychoanalytic Study of the Child*, XVI, 9–24.

Bibring, G. 1961b. "A Study of the Psychological Processes in Pregnancy and of the Earliest Mother-Child Relationship: II. Methodological Considerations." *Psychoanalytic Study of the Child*, XVI, 25–72.

Bloom, B. J. 1964. *Stability and Change in Human Characteristics*. New York: John Wiley and Sons, Inc.

Blos, P. 1961. *On Adolescence*. New York: The Free Press of Glencoe.

Blos, P. 1967. "The Second Individuation Process of Adolescence." *Psychoanalytic Study of the Child*, XXII, 162–187.

Borowitz, G. 1969. *Parent Loss and Alcoholism*. Unpublished manuscript.

Bowlby, J. 1960. "Grief and Mourning in Infancy and Early Childhood." *Psychoanalytic Study of the Child*, XV, 9–52.

Brown, F. 1961. "Depression and Childhood Bereavement." *Journal of Mental Science*, CVII, 754–777.

Caplan, G. 1964. *Principles of Preventive Psychiatry*. New York: Basic Books, Inc.

Caplan, G. and Grunebaum, H. 1967. "Perspectives on Primary Prevention." *American Medical Association Archives of General Psychiatry*, XVII, 331–347.

Cattell, R. B. 1965. *The Scientific Analysis of Personality*. Baltimore, Maryland: Penguin Books, Inc.

Census Tracts: Chicago, Illinois. 1962. U.S. Censuses of Population and Housing: 1960, Final Report, PHC (1), 26. Washington, D.C.: U.S. Department of Commerce.

Coelho, G. V. 1959. *Changing Images of America; A Study of Indian Students' Perception*. Glencoe, Illinois: The Free Press.

Coelho, G. V., Hamburg, D. A., and Murphey, E. B. 1963. "Coping Strategies in a New Learning Environment." *American Medical Association Archives of General Psychiatry*, IX, 433–443.

Coleman, J. S. 1961. *The Adolescent Society*. New York: The Free Press of Glencoe.

Coles, R. 1967. *Children of Crisis; A Study of Courage and Fear*. Boston: Little, Brown and Company.

Conference on Normal Behavior. 1967. *American Medical Association Archives of General Psychiatry*, XVII, 258–330.

Cooper, A. M., Karush, B., Easser, R., and Swerdloff, B. 1965. "The Adaptive Balance Profile and Prediction of Early Treatment Behavior." In Goldman, G. S. and Shapiro, D., eds., *Developments in Psychoanalysis*, 51–61. New York: Hafner Publishing Company.

Cronbach, L. J. 1949. "Statistical Methods Applied to Rorschach's Scores: A Review." *Psychological Bulletin*, XVI, 393–429.

Davis, A. 1944. "Socialization and Adolescent Personality." In *Adolescents*, Forty-third Yearbook, Part I. Chicago Society for the Study of Education.

Davis, K. 1940. "The Sociology of Parent-Youth Conflict." *American Sociological Review*, V, 523–535.

Deutsch, H. 1967. *Selected Problems of Adolescence*. New York: International Universities Press.

DiMascio, A., Boyd, R. W., and Greenblatt, M. 1957. "Physiological Correlates of Tension and Antagonism During Psychotherapy." *Psychosomatic Medicine*, XIX, 99–127.

Douvan, E. and Adelson, J. 1966. *The Adolescent Experience*. New York: John Wiley and Sons, Inc.

Edwards, A. L. 1957. *The Social Desirability Variable in Personality Assessment and Research*. New York: The Dryden Press.

Eisenberg, L., and Neubauer, P. B. 1965. "Mental Health Issues in Israeli Collectives: Kibbutzim." *Journal of the American Academy of Child Psychiatry*, IV, 426–442.

Eissler, K. R. 1958. "Notes on Problems of Technique in the Psychoanalytic Treatment of Adolescents." *Psychoanalytic Study of the Child*, XIII, 223–254.

Elkin, F., and Westley, W. A. 1955. "The Myth of Adolescent Culture." *American Sociological Review*, XXIII, 680–683.

Engel, M. 1959. "The Stability of the Self-Concept in Adolescence." *Journal of Abnormal and Social Psychology*, LVIII, 74–83.

Epstein, N. B., and Westley, W. A. 1960. "Grandparents and Parents of Emotionally Healthy Adolescents." In Masserman, J. H., ed., *Science and Psychoanalysis, Volume 3: Psychoanalysis and Human Values*, 181–188. New York: Grune and Stratton.

Erikson, E. H. 1950. *Childhood and Society*. New York: W. W. Norton and Company, Inc.

Erikson, E. H. 1956. "Ego Identity and the Psychosocial Moratorium." In *New Perspectives for Research on Juvenile Delinquency*, 1–23. Washington, D.C.: Children's Bureau, U.S. Department of Health, Education, and Welfare.

Erikson, E. H. 1959. "Identity and the Life Cycle." *Psychological Issues*, I, 1–171.

Erikson, E. H. 1968. *Identity: Youth and Crisis*. New York: W. W. Norton and Company.

Eron, L. D. 1950. "A Normative Study of the Thematic Apperception Test." *Psychological Monographs*, LXIV, No. 9.

Escalona, S., and Heider, G. M. 1959. *Prediction and Outcome*. New York: Basic Books, Inc.

Esecover, H., Malitz, S., and Wilkens, B. 1961. "Clinical Profiles of Paid Normal Subjects Volunteering for Hallucinogen Drug Studies." *American Journal of Psychiatry*, CVII, 10–24.

Fine, P., and Offer, D. 1965. "Periodic Outbursts of Anti-social Behavior." *American Medical Association Archives of General Psychiatry*, XIII, 240–254.

Fisher, C. 1953. "Studies on the Nature of Suggestion, Part II." *Journal of the American Psychoanalytic Association*, I, 406–437.

Fisher, C. 1956. "Dreams, Images and Perception." *Journal of the American Psychoanalytic Association*, IV, 5–48.

Fiske, D. W. 1959. "Variability of Responses and the Stability of Scores and Interpretations of Projective Protocols." *Journal of Projective Techniques*, XXIII, 263–267.

Fiske, D. W., and Baughman, E. E. 1953. "Relationships Between Rorschach Scoring Categories and the Total Number of Responses." *Journal of Abnormal Social Psychology*, XLVIII, 25–32.

Fleming, J., and Benedek, T. 1966. *Psychoanalytic Supervision*. New York: Grune and Stratton.

Fountain, G. 1961. "Adolescent into Adult: An Inquiry." *Journal of the American Psychoanalytic Association*, IX, 417–433.

Freud, A. 1958. "Adolescence." *Psychoanalytic Study of the Child*, XVI, 225–278.

Freud, A. 1946. *The Ego and the Mechanisms of Defense* (1936). New York: International Universities Press.

Freud, A. 1946. *The Psycho-analytical Treatment of Children*. London: Imago Publishing Company, Ltd.

Freud, S. 1959. "Analysis Terminable and Interminable (1937)" In *Collected Papers of Sigmund Freud*, Vol. V. New York: Basic Books, Inc.

Freud, S. 1961. "Negation" (1925). *The Standard Edition*, XIX, 235–242. London: Hogarth Press.

Friedenberg, E. Z. 1959. *The Vanishing Adolescent*. Boston: Beacon Press.

Friedenberg, E. Z. 1965. *Coming of Age in America*. New York: Random House.

Gardner, G. 1957. "Present-day Society and the Adolescent." *American Journal of Orthopsychiatry*, XXVII, 508–517.

Gardner, G. 1959. "Psychiatric Problems of Adolescence." In Arieti, S., ed., *American Handbook of Psychiatry*, 870–894. New York: Basic Books, Inc.

Garmezy, N., Clarke, A. R., and Stochner, C. 1957, not published. "Child Rearing Attitudes of Mothers and Fathers as Reported by Schizophrenic and Normal Control Patients." Duke University.

Geleerd, E. R. 1961. "Some Aspects of Ego Vicissitudes in Adolescence." *Journal of the American Psychoanalytic Association*, IX, 394–405.

Gesell, A., Ilg, F., and Ames, L. 1956. *Youth: The Years from Ten to Sixteen*. New York: Harper and Row.

Gibbons, T. L. N. 1963. *Psychiatric Studies of Borstal Lads*. London: Oxford University Press.

Gibby, R. G., Miller, D. R., and Walker, E. L. 1953. "The Examiner's Influence on the Rorschach Protocol." *Journal of Consulting Psychology*, XVII, 425–428.

Gitelson, M. 1962. "Curative Factors in Psychoanalysis." *International Journal of Psycho-analysis*, XLIII, 194–205.

Goodman, P. 1962. *Growing Up Absurd*. New York: Vintage Books.

Goodrich, W., Ryder, R. G., and Raush, M. L. 1966. "Patterns of Newlywed Marriage." Presented at the Annual Meeting of the American Psychiatric Association, Atlantic City, New Jersey.

Greenson, R. 1965. "The Working Alliance and the Transference Neurosis." *Psychoanalytic Quarterly*, XXXIV, 155–181.

Grinker, R. R., Sr. 1963. "A Dynamic Story of the Homoclite." In Masserman, J., ed., *Science and Psychoanalysis*, Volume 6: *Violence and War*, 115–134. New York: Grune and Stratton.

Grinker, R. R., Sr. 1968. Personal communication.

Grinker, R. R., Sr., Grinker, R. R., Jr., and Timberlake, J. 1962. "A Study of 'Mentally Healthy' Young Males (Homoclites)." *American Medical Association Archives of General Psychiatry*, VI, 405–453.

Grinker, R. R., Sr., Macgregor, H., Selan, K., Klein, A., and Kohrman, J. 1961. *Psychiatric Social Work*. New York: Basic Books, Inc.

Grinker, R. R., Sr., and Spiegel, J. 1945. *Men Under Stress*. New York: McGraw-Hill Book Company, Inc.

Gustin, J. C. 1961. "The Revolt of Youth." *Psychoanalysis and Psychoanalytic Review*, XLVIII, 78–90.

Hall, G. S. 1916. *Adolescence; Its Psychology and Its Relations to Physiology, Anthropology, Sociology, Sex, Crime, Religion and Education* (1904). New York: D. Appleton and Company.

Hamburg, D. A., *et al.* 1953. "Adaptive Problems and Mechanisms in Severely Burned Patients." *Psychiatry*, XVI, 1–20.

Hamburg, D. A., and Adams, J. E. 1967. "A Perspective on Coping Behavior." *American Medical Association Archives of General Psychiatry*, XVII, 277–284.

Harman, H. H. 1960. *Modern Factor Analysis*. Chicago: University of Chicago Press.

Harris, I. D. 1950. *Normal Children and Mothers*. Glencoe, Illinois: The Free Press of Glencoe.

Hartmann, H. 1958. *Ego Psychology and the Problems of Adaptation*. New York: International Universities Press.

Hathaway, S. R., and Monachesi, E. D. 1963. *Adolescent Personality and Behavior*. Minneapolis: The University of Minnesota Press.

Heath, D. H. 1965. *Explorations of Maturity*. New York: Appleton-Century-Crofts.

Heilbrun, A. B. 1964. "Social Learning Theory, Social Desirability and the MMPI." *Psychological Review*, LXI, 377–387.

Hendin, H., Gaylin, W., and Carr, A. 1965. *Psychoanalysis and Social Research*. New York: Doubleday.

Hendricks, I. 1943. "The Discussion of the 'Instinct to Master.'" *Psychoanalytic Quarterly*, XII, 561–574.

Hertz, M. R. 1951. *Frequency Tables for Scoring Responses to the Rorschach Ink-blot Test*. 3rd edition. Cleveland: Western Reserve University Press.

Hertzman, M., and Margulies, H. 1943. "Developmental Changes as Reflected in Rorschach Test Responses." *Journal of Genetic Psychology*, LXII, 189–215.

Hess, R. D. 1964. Personal communication.

Hilgard, J. R., Newman, M. F., and Fisk, F. 1960. "Strength of Adult Ego Following Childhood Bereavement." *American Journal of Orthopsychiatry*, XXX, 788–798.

Hollingshead, A. de B. 1949. *Elmtown's Youth, the Impact of Social Classes on Adolescents*. New York: John Wiley and Sons, Inc.

Hollingworth, L. S. 1928. *The Psychology of the Adolescent*. New York: Appleton-Century.

Holmes, D. 1964. *The Adolescent in Psychotherapy*. Boston: Little, Brown and Company.

Holtzman, W. H. 1952. "The Examiner as a Variable in the Draw-a-person Test." *Journal of Consulting Psychology*, XVI, 145–148.

Howard, K. I., and Diesenhaus, H. I. 1965. "Personality Correlates of Change-seeking Behavior." *Perceptual and Motor Skills*, XXI, 655–664.

Howard, K. I., and Gordon, R. A. 1963. "Empirical Note on the 'Number of Factors' Problem in Factor Analysis." *Psychological Reports*, XII, 247–250.

Hurlock, E. B. 1955. *Adolescent Development*. New York: McGraw-Hill.

Hsu, F. L. K. 1961. "Culture Patterns and Adolescent Behavior." *International Journal of Social Psychiatry*, VII, 33–53.

Hyman, H. H. 1954. *Interviewing in Social Research*. Chicago and London: University of Chicago Press.

Jacobson, E. 1961. "Adolescent Moods and the Remodeling of Psychic Structures in Adolescence." *Psychoanalytic Study of the Child*, XVI, 164–183.

Josselyn, I. M. 1952. *The Adolescent and His World*. New York: Family Service Association of America.

Josselyn, I. M. 1967. "The Adolescent Today." *Smith College Studies in Social Work*, XXXVIII, 1–15.

Jourard, S. M. 1964. *The Transparent Self*. Princeton, New Jersey: D. Van Nostrand.

Kagan, J. 1964. "American Longitudinal Research in Psychological Development." *Child Development*, XXXV, 1–32.

Kagan, J., and Moss, H. 1962. *Birth to Maturity*. New York: John Wiley and Sons, Inc.

Kahn, R. L., and Cannell, C. 1957. *The Dynamics of Interviewing*. New York: John Wiley and Sons, Inc.

Keniston, K. 1962. "Social Change and Youth in America." *Daedalus*, XCI, 53–74.

Keniston, K. 1965. *The Uncommitted: Alienated Youth in American Society*. New York: Harcourt, Brace and World.

Kiell, N. 1964. *The Universal Experience of Adolescence*. New York: International Universities Press.

Koch, H. L. 1955. "Some Personality Correlates of Sex, Sibling Position and Sex of Sibling Among Four- and Six-Year-Old Children." *Genetic Psychology Monograph*, LII, 3–50.

Koch, H. L. 1960. "The Relation of Certain Formal Attributes of Siblings to Attitudes Held Toward Each Other and Toward Their Parents." *Society for Research in Child Development*, XXV, 78.

Koestler, A. 1960. *The Lotus and the Robot*. London: Hutchinson.

Korchin, S. J., and Ruff, G. 1962. *Personality Characteristics of Mercury Astronauts*; A Paper Presented Before the American Association for the Advancement of Science, Philadelphia.

Krause, M. S. 1965. "Role Deviant Respondent Sets and Resulting Bias, Their Detection and Control in the Surrey Interview." *Journal of Social Psychology*, LXVII, 163–183.

Kroeber, T. C. 1963. "The Coping Functions of the Ego Mechanisms." In White, R. W., ed., *The Study of Lives*, 213–220. New York: Atherton Press.

Kubie, L. S. 1953. "The Problem of Specificity in the Psychosomatic Process." In Deutsch, F., ed., *The Psychosomatic Concept in Psychoanalysis*, 63–81. New York: International Universities Press.

Laufer, M. 1966. "Object Loss and Mourning During Adolescence." *Psychoanalytic Study of the Child*, XXI, 269–294.

Lederer, W. 1964. "Dragons, Delinquents and Destiny." *Psychological Issues*, IV, 3.

Lief, H. I., and Thompson, J. 1961. "The Prediction of Behavior from Adolescence to Adulthood." *Psychiatry*, XXIV, 32–38.

Linn, L. 1958. "Psychoanalytic Contributions to Psychosomatic Research." *Psychosomatic Medicine*, XX, 88–98.

Malmo, R. B., Boag, T. J., and Smith, A. A. 1957. "Physiological Study of Personal Interaction." *Psychosomatic Medicine*, XIX, 105–119.

Marcus, D., Offer, D., Blatt, S., and Gratch, G. 1966. "A Clinical Approach to the Understanding of Normal and Pathologic Adolescence." *American Medical Association Archives of General Psychiatry*, XV, 569–576.

Masling, J. M. 1960. "The Influence of Situational and Interpersonal Variables in Projective Techniques." *Psychological Bulletin*, LVII, 65–85.

Masterson, J. F., Jr. 1967. *The Psychiatric Dilemma of Adolescence*. Boston: Little, Brown & Company.

Mead, M. 1954. *Coming of Age in Samoa* (1928). New York: New American Library.

Mead, M. 1961. "The Young Adult." In Ginzberg, E., ed., *Values and Ideals of American Youth*, 15–23. New York: Columbia University Press.

Murphy, L. B., and associates. 1962. *The Widening World of Childhood*. New York: Basic Books, Inc.

Murray, H. A. 1938. *Explorations in Personality*. New York: Oxford University Press.

Murray, H. A. 1943. *Manual for the Thematic Apperception Test.* Cambridge: Harvard University Press.

Murstein, B. I. 1960. "Factor Analyses of the Rorschach Test." *Journal of Consulting Psychology,* XXIV, 262–275.

Muslin, H., Friedberg, S., and Fisher, L. 1966, not published. "The Teaching Alliance."

Neubauer, P. B. 1965. *Children in Collectives.* Springfield, Illinois: Charles C Thomas.

Nixon, R. E. 1962. *The Art of Growing; A Guide to Psychological Maturity.* New York: Random House.

Offer, D. 1967. "Studies of Normal Adolescents." *Adolescence,* I, 305–321.

Offer, D., and Barglow, P. 1960. "Adolescent and Young Adult Self-mutilation Incidents in a General Psychiatric Hospital." *American Medical Association Archives of General Psychiatry,* III, 194–204.

Offer, D., and Sabshin, M. 1963. "The Psychiatrist and the Normal Adolescent." *American Medical Association Archives of General Psychiatry,* IX, 427–432.

Offer, D., and Sabshin, M. 1966. *Normality: Theoretical and Clinical Concepts of Mental Health.* New York: Basic Books, Inc.

Offer, D., and Sabshin, M. 1967. "Research Alliance Versus Therapeutic Alliance: A Comparison." *American Journal of Psychiatry,* CXXIII, 1519–1526.

Offer, D., Sabshin, M., and Marcus, D. 1965. "Clinical Evaluations of Normal Adolescents." *American Journal of Psychiatry,* CXXI, 864–872.

Paulsen, A. 1943. "Personality Development in the Middle Years of Childhood." *American Journal of Orthopsychiatry,* XXIV, 336–350.

Pearson, G. H. J. 1958. *Adolescence and the Conflict of Generations; An Introduction to Some of the Psychoanalytic Contributions to the Understanding of Adolescence.* New York: W. W. Norton and Company.

Peck, R. F. 1958. "Family Patterns Correlated with Adolescent Personality Structure." *Journal of Abnormal and Social Psychology,* LVII, 347–350.

Peck, R. F., and Havighurst, R. J. 1960. *The Psychology of Character Development.* New York: John Wiley and Sons, Inc., Science Editions.

Perlin, S., Polin, W., and Butler, R. N. 1958. "The Experimental Subject: 1. The Psychiatric Evaluation and Selection of a Volunteer Population." *American Medical Association Archives of Neurology and Psychiatry,* LXXXVI, 65–70.

Petersen, W. 1961. "Rock 'n' Roll"; a review of Coleman, J. S., *The Adolescent Society. Science,* CXXXIV, 1061–1062.

Pfeffer, A. Z. 1961. "Follow-up Study of a Satisfactory Analysis." *Journal of the American Psychoanalytic Association,* IV, 698–718.

Pfeffer, A. Z. 1963. "The Meaning of the Analyst After Analysis." *Journal of the American Psychoanalytic Association,* XI, 229–244.

Polka, S. K. 1954, not published. "The Influence of Temporally Projected Goals of Present Behavior." Ph.D. Thesis. University of Kansas.

Pollock, G. H. 1962. "Childhood Parent and Sibling Loss in Adult Patients." *American Medical Association Archives of General Psychiatry*, VII, 87–97.

Rabin, A. I. 1965. *Growing Up in the Kibbutz*. New York: Springer Publishing Company, Inc.

Rabin, I. E., and Beck, S. J. 1950. "Genetic Aspects of Some Rorschach Factors." *American Journal of Orthopsychiatry*, XX, 595–599.

Rapaport, D. 1946. *Diagnostic Psychological Testing*, Vol. II. Chicago: The Year Book Publishers, Inc.

Raush, H. L., and Sweet, B. 1961. "The Preadolescent Ego: Some Observations of Normal Children." *Psychiatry*, XXIV, 122–132.

Reiser, M. F., Reeves, R. B., and Armington, J. 1955. "Effect of Variation in Laboratory Procedure and Experimentor Upon the Ballistocardiogram, Blood Pressure, and Heart Rate in Healthy Young Men." *Psychosomatic Medicine*, XVII, 185–199.

Reiss, I. L. 1961. "Sexual Codes in Teen-Age Culture." *Annals of the American Academy of Political and Social Sciences*, CCCXXXVII, 53–63.

Richardson, S. A., Dohrenwend, B. S., and Klein, D. 1965. *Interviewing, Its Forms and Functions*. New York: Basic Books, Inc.

Richmond, J., and Waisman, H. 1955. "Psychological Aspects of Management of Children with Malignant Diseases." *American Journal of Disturbed Children*, LXXXIX, 42–61.

Rochlin, G. 1965. *Griefs and Discontents: The Forces of Change*. Boston: Little, Brown and Company.

Rogers, C. 1961. *On Becoming a Person*. New York: Houghton Mifflin Company.

Rosenberg, M. 1965. *Society and the Adolescent Self-Image*. Princeton, New Jersey: Princeton University Press.

Rosengren, W. R. 1961. "The Self in the Emotionally Disturbed." *American Journal of Sociology*, LXVI, 113–127.

Rosenthal, R. 1966. *Experimenter Effects in Behavioral Research*. New York: Appleton-Century-Crofts.

Sanford, N., ed. 1962. *The American College*. New York: John Wiley and Sons, Inc.

Schachtel, E. G. 1966. *Experiential Foundations of Rorschach's Test*. New York: Basic Books, Inc.

Schafer, R. 1954. *Psychoanalytic Interpretation in Rorschach Testing*. New York: Grune and Stratton.

Shakow, D. 1967. "Understanding Normal Psychological Function." *American Medical Association Archives of General Psychiatry*, XVII, 306–319.

Shoben, E. J. 1949. "The Assessment of Parental Attitudes in Relation to Child Adjustment." *General Psychology Monographs*, XXXIX, 101–148.

Silber, E., et al. 1961a. "Adaptive Behavior in Competent Adolescents." *American Medical Association Archives of General Psychology*, V, 359–365.

Silber, E., et al. 1961b. "Competent Adolescents Coping with College Decision." *American Medical Association Archives of General Psychology*, V, 517–528.

Solomon, F., and Fishman, J. R. 1964. "Youth and Peace: A Psychosocial Study of Student Peace Demonstrators in Washington, D.C." *Journal of Social Issues*, XX, 54–73.

Spranger, E. 1955. *Psychologie des Jugendalters*, 24th edition. Heidelberg: Quelle and Meyer.

Srole, L., Langer, T., Michael, S. T., Opler, M. D., and Rennie, T. A. C. 1963. *Mental Health in the Metropolis*. New York: McGraw-Hill.

Steiner, J. 1951. "The Rorschach Test." In Frank, L. K., *et al. Personality Development in Adolescent Girls*, 34–59. Monograph of Social Research and Child Development, XVI.

Sterba, R. 1934. "The Fate of the Ego in Psycho-Analytic Therapy." *International Journal of Psycho-Analysis*, XV, 117–126.

Stone, L. J., and Church, J. 1957. *Childhood and Adolescence*. New York: Random House.

Strauss, A., Schatzman, L., Bucher, R., Ehrlich, D., and Sabshin, M. 1964. *Psychiatric Ideologies and Institutions*. New York: The Free Press of Glencoe, Collier-Macmillan Ltd.

Suares, N. 1938. "Personality Development in Adolescence." *Rorschach Research Exchange*, II, 2–12.

Sullivan, H. S. 1954. *The Psychiatric Interview*. New York: W. W. Norton, Inc.

Symonds, P. M. 1949. *Adolescent Fantasy*. New York: Columbia University Press.

Symonds, P. M., and Jensen, A. R. 1961. *From Adolescent to Adult*. New York: Columbia University Press.

Tuddenham, R. D. 1959. "The Constancy of Personality Ratings Over Two Decades." *General Psychology Monographs*, LX, 3–29.

van Krevelen, A. 1954. "A Study of Examiner Influence on Responses to MAPS Test Materials." *Journal of Clinical Psychology*, X, 292–293.

Visotsky, H. M., Hamburg, D. A., Goss, M. E., and Lebovits, B. Z. 1961. "Coping Behavior Under Extreme Stress." *American Medical Association Archives of General Psychiatry*, V, 423–448.

Webster New Twentieth Century Dictionary, 2nd edition. 1956. New York and Cleveland: The World Publishing Company.

Westley, W. A. 1958. "Emotionally Healthy Adolescents and Their Family Backgrounds." In Galdston, I., ed., *The Family in Contemporary Society*, 131–147. New York: International Universities Press.

White, R. W. 1960. "Competence and the Psychosexual Stages of Development." *Nebraska Symposium on Motivation*, 97–138. University of Nebraska Press.

White, R. W. 1966. *Lives in Progress: A Study of the Natural Growth of Personality*, 2nd edition. New York: Holt, Rinehart and Winston.

White, R. W., ed. 1963. *The Study of Lives*. New York: Atherton Press.

Wolfenstein, M. 1966. "How Is Mourning Possible?" *Psychoanalytic Study of the Child*, XXI, 93–127.

X, Malcolm. 1964. *The Autobiography of Malcolm X*. New York: Grove Press, Inc.

Zetzel, E. R. 1956. "Current Concepts of Transference." *International Journal of Psycho-analysis*, XXXVII, 369–376.

Index

abortion, 158
academic achievement: dating and, 82–83; depression and, 98; emphasis on, 67; satisfaction with, 90, 219
Ackerman, N. W., 194–197
acting out: adolescent turmoil and, 189, 191, 192; delinquent, 77; of impulses, 178
Adams, J. E., 209, 216
adaptation, 7–9, 95, 209; definition of, 209–210; studies on, 210–212
Adelson, J., 9, 181, 184, 186, 196, 197
Adolescence, 174
adolescence: biogenetic theory of, 174–175; normal developmental process of, 176–177; normative crises of, 182–185; psychic structure and, 175, 177–179, 190; psychoanalytical theory of, 177–178; "*Sturm und Drang*" theory, 174–175, 181, 222; transitional stage, 175, 184
adolescent psychology, 8
adolescent rebellion, *see* rebellious behavior
Adolescent Society, The, 198–200
adolescent subculture, 197–200
adolescent turmoil, 5, 6, 174–193; acting out and, 189, 191, 192; anxiety and, 175, 176, 189, 191; clinical conceptions of, 176–182; definition of, 5 n., 174–176; depression and, 174, 175, 189–191; guilt and, 108; as internal process, 180, 192; level of, 184, 190–191; mood swings and, 178, 189–190;

normative-crisis concept and, 182; onset of puberty and, 214; rebellious behavior and, 179, 180, 185–189; shame and, 108, 191; strength of, 179–180
adolescent value system, 197–200, 205–207
adult double standards, 78
affect(s), 96–109; anger, 101–102, 109, 213; anxiety, *see* anxiety; coping with, 97–103, 108–109, 189–192, 220; depression, *see* depression; guilt, 100–101, 103, 108, 109, 158, 168, 191; pleasurable, 103–105, 109, 134–135; shame, 99–100, 103, 108, 109, 191; symptom rating scale, 105–109
aggressive impulses: coping with, 69, 73–77, 190, 212–213; ego strength and, 178; sports activities and, 77, 213; upsurge of, 175
Alden, P., 114
alliance, definition of, 149
altruism, 174, 189, 190, 217
ambiguous sexual identifications, 116
ambivalence, 75, 94, 115–117, 135, 153, 194, 202
Ames, L. B., 123–125, 150, 186, 212, 220
analytic situation, 149
anger, coping with, 101–102, 109, 213
antisocial behavior, *see* delinquent behavior
anxiety: adolescent turmoil and, 175, 176, 189, 191; coping with, 97, 109, 189, 220; about dating, 80–82, 85, 108; defenses against, 176;

dormant, revival of, 183; over examinations, 97, 102; facilitative, 97; separation, 91, 117; over sports activities, 67, 97, 102
anxiety neurosis, 229
apathy, 174
Arieti, S., 217
"as if" personality, 175, 177
asceticism, 197
athletics, see sports activities
Ausubel, D. P., 181
authority, parental, see parental authority
autonomy: loss of, 186; parental independence and, 195
average expectable environment, concept of, 223

Baittle, B., 185 n.
Barglow, P., 83 n.
Barron, F., 210
Barron ego-strength scale, 210
Basch, M., 158 n.
Baughman, E. E., 114, 128
Beck, S. J., 123 n., 124, 125
Beck scoring method, 254–255
behavioral-science research, 149, 150
Bell Adjustment Inventory for Adolescents, 12, 230
Benedek, T., 149, 216
Benton, A. L., 114
Bernstein, L., 114
Bibring, G., 210
bickering, 186
Blatt, S., 57, 66, 204–205, 227
Bloom, B. J., 222
Blos, P., 176–178, 183, 184, 187, 189, 217, 223
Boag, T. J., 150
borderline character, 229
Bowlby, J., 210
Boyd, R. W., 150
Butler, R. N., 11

Cannell, C., 18
Caplan, G., 8, 223
Carr, A., 150
cathexis, quantitative changes in, 177, 184–185
Cattell, R. B., 235

Census Tracts report (1962), 27 n., 48 n.
change-seeking behavior, 218
character disorder, 229
charity-orientation, 215
Children of Crisis, 212
Church, J., 181
civil rights, attitudes toward, 58–59, 206
Clarke, A. R., 227
clinical depression, 98
closeness: fear of, 84, 203; need for, 75, 93, 115
Coelho, G. V., 210
cognitive stereotype, 196
Coleman, J. S., 9, 194, 196–200, 207, 227
Coles, R., 201, 212
community psychiatry, 6, 8, 193
competence: definition of, 210; "pure" pleasure involved in, 218
compromise, 93
Conference on Normal Behavior (1967), 6 n.
conformity, 186; interpersonal, 196
conservatism, 191
consistency, patterns of, 180, 190, 191, 222
contraceptives, 85
Cooper, A. M., 210
coping, 7, 67, 209–224; with aggressive impulses, 69, 73–77, 190, 212–213; with anger, 101–102, 109, 213; with anxiety, 97, 109, 189, 220; assessment of, 210–212; definitions of, 209–210; with depression, 98–99, 102–103, 109, 189, 220; ego strength and, 184; with environment, 217; goal-directed behavior and, 216–218; with guilt, 100–101, 103, 108, 109; with hostile impulses, 212–213; self-observation and, 218–220; with sexual impulses, 190, 213–215; with shame, 99–100, 103, 109; social action and, 215–216; with special crises, 89–95, 221
counseling, 18
creativity, stimulation of, 217
crises, special, coping with, 89–95, 221

crisis, definition of, 182
Cronbach, L. J., 126, 128

dating: academic achievement and, 82–83; anxiety over, 80–82, 85, 108; attitudes toward, 80–85, 103–104, 116, 153, 213
Davis, A., 181
Davis, K., 194
death, reactions to, 91, 93–95, 98, 221
Dedalus, Stephen, 181 *n.*
defensive energy, waste of, 183
delinquent acting out, 77
delinquent behavior, 69, 70, 73–76; depression and, 98; guilt and, 100; mass media and, 204; rebellious behavior and, 76, 186
denial, 189, 214, 220
dependency wishes, 188
dependent behavior, 60, 153, 187–188
depression: academic achievement and, 98; adolescent turmoil and, 174, 175, 189–191; clinical, 98; coping with, 98–99, 102–103, 109, 189, 220; delinquent behavior and, 98; obsessive-compulsive, 107–109
depth psychology, 177, 180
Deutsch, H., 177, 178, 214, 215
Diesenhaus, H. I., 10 *n.*, 218
DiMascio, A., 150
discipline: parental, feelings about, 53, 57, 202–204; self-, 182
displacement, 190, 210
dissociation, 107, 108, 191
distortion(s), 107, 108, 147, 148, 154, 157, 191, 215
Dohrenwend, B. S., 18, 19
Don Carlos, 174 *n.*
dormant anxiety, revival of, 183
double standards, adult, 78
Douvan, E., 9, 181, 184, 186
draft-card burning, attitudes toward, 58
drive regression, 183

Easser, R., 210
Edwards, A. L., 235
effectance motivation, 218
ego defenses, 177

ego psychology, 212
ego repression, 183
ego resiliency, 95
ego strength, 95, 96, 175, 178, 183, 184
ego-syntonic experiences, 178, 192
egotism, 191
ego weakness, 177
Eisenberg, L., 187 *n.*
Eissler, K. R., 175
Elkin, F., 181, 197, 200
emancipation, concept of, 185–188
enthusiasm, 174, 189–190
environment: average expectable, 223; coping with, 217
environmental conditioning, 182
epidemiological surveys, 18–19
Epstein, N. B., 200
Erikson, E. H., 71, 176–177, 182–183, 188, 204, 216, 227
Eron, L. D., 140
Escalona, S., 222
Escover, H., 11
examinations, anxiety over, 97, 102
experiencing ego, 178
experimental situations, 149–150

facilitative anxiety, 97
family communication, 65–68, 194, 200–202, 204–205; breakdown of, 156, 195, 204
family integrity, 200–204
Family Interaction Scale, 21, 23, 65, 71, 258
family isolation, 195
fantasy, 78, 83, 84, 179, 212, 217
feelings: intensity and volatility of, 175–176; sexual, *see* sexual feelings
femininity, negation of, 217
fighting, attitudes toward, 58, 71
Fisher, C., 150
Fisher, L., 149
Fishman, J. R., 200
Fisk, F., 210
Fiske, D. W., 128, 140
Fleming, J., 149
fluctuant behavior, adolescent turmoil and, 179, 189–190
Fountain, G., 176
Freud, A., 175–177, 184–185, 189, 227

Freud, S., 187, 215
Friedberg, S., 149
Friedenberg, E. Z., 9, 42, 79, 181, 184, 196, 227
Futterman, S. L., 22

Gardner, G., 176, 195, 227
Garmezy, N., 227
Gaylin, W., 150
Geleerd, E. R., 178
generalized perception of input, 218
generation gap, 156, 195, 204
genital sexuality, sublimation of, 214
Gesell, A., 150, 181, 186, 211, 220
Gilby, R. G., 114
Gitelson, M., 149
goal-directed behavior, 95, 216–218
Goethe, Johann von, 174 n.
Goodman, P., 189, 196
Goodrich, W., 210
Gordon, R. A., 238
Goss, M. E., 210
Gratch, G., 57, 66, 204–205, 227
gratification(s): postponement of, 215; search for, 175–176, 188, 218
Greenblatt, M., 150
Greenson, R., 149
Grinker, R. R., Sr., 9, 19, 20, 180, 181, 210, 211, 216; quoted, 20
Grunebaum, H., 8
guilt, 158, 168, 191; and adolescent turmoil, 108; coping with, 100–101, 103, 108, 109; delinquent behavior and, 100
Gustin, J. C., 188

Hall, G. Stanley, 174–175, 181
Hamburg, D. A., 209, 210, 216
Harman, H. H., 238
Harris, I. D., 38 n.
Hartmann, H., 223
Hathaway, S. R., 12 n.
Havighurst, R. J., 212, 222
Heath, D. H., 9, 209–210
Heider, G. M., 222
Heilbrun, A. B., 235
helping relationship, 158–159, 167
Hendin, H., 150
Hertz, M. R., 123, 124
Hertzman, M., 123 n.

Hess, R. D., 11 n.
heterosexual behavior, 78–88, 116–117, 215, 224
Hilgard, J. R., 210
hippies, 188–189, 195, 200
hobbies, 94, 103
Hollingshead, A. de B., 41, 200
Hollingworth, L. S., 181
Holmes, D., 152
Holtzman, W. H., 114
homosexuality, 83
hostile impulses, coping with, 212–213
hostility, 101–102
Howard, K. I., 106, 218, 238
Hsu, F. L. K., 181
humor, 104, 130–132, 141, 220
Hurlock, E. B., 181
Hyman, H. H., 18

id forces, 177
idealism, 174 n., 191, 196, 197, 215, 217
identity: loss of, 186; negative, search for, 196
identity formation, process of, 183
ideology, lack of involvement in, 196
Ilg, F., 150, 186, 212, 220
impulses: acting out of, 178; aggressive, see aggressive impulses; hostile, coping with, 212–213; inability to control, 175, 213; sexual, see sexual impulses
impulsiveness, 93; concern over, 117–118
inadequacy, feelings of, 92
incorporation, capacity for, 132
independence, desire for, 118, 215
industrial revolution, psychological implications of, 195
inferiority complex, 36
infighting, 186
information-seeking behavior, 216
inner realities, willingness to face, 219
Institute of Human Development (University of California), 222
intensity of feelings, 175–176
intercourse, sexual, attitudes toward, 83–85
interpersonal conformity, 196

isolation, 189, 220; family, 195; psychosocial, 183
Israel, adolescent rebellion and, 187 *n*.

Jacobson, E., 178, 189
Jensen, A. R., 150, 222
Johnson, Lyndon B., 206
Josselyn, I. M., 176, 178, 189, 194
Jourard, S. M., 219

Kagan, J., 150, 211, 212
Kahn, R. L., 18
Karush, B., 210
Keniston, K. 181, 184, 186, 195–197
Kennedy, John F., 98, 206
kibbutz adolescents, rebellion of, 187 *n*.
"kicks," search for, 175–176
Kiell, N., 181 *n*.
Klein, A., 9, 19
Klein, D., 18, 19
Koch, H. L., 210
Koestler, A., 217
Kohrman, J., 9, 19
Korchin, S. J., 217
Krause, M. S., 19
Kroeber, T. C., 210
Kroll, Felix, 181 *n*.
Kubie, L. S., 150

Langer, T., 15, 19
Laufer, M., 178, 189
learning alliance, 149
Lebovits, B. Z., 210
Lederer, W., 203–204
Lief, H. I., 222
Linn, L., 150
loneliness: fear of, 117; feeling of, 220
looseness of thinking, 175
LSD, 188–189

Macgregor, H., 9, 19
Malcolm X, 42 *n*.
Malitz, S., 11
Malmo, R. B., 150
Marcus, D., 17, 22, 57, 66, 104–105, 204–205, 227, 247 *n*.
Margulies, H., 123 *n*.
marriage, attitudes toward, 81
masculine identity, need for, 36, 43, 217

Masling, J. M., 114
mass media, delinquent behavior and, 204
Masterson, J. F., Jr., 9, 176, 181, 183, 222
masturbation, 83
Mead, Margaret, 181, 196, 197
Michael, S. T., 15, 19
military draft, attitudes toward, 58
Miller, D. D., 114
Miller, Joanne, 22, 257 *n*.
miniaturized transference neurosis, 8
Minnesota Multiphasic Personality Inventory (MMPI), 12
Modal Adolescent Project: analysis of interview data, 259–261; characteristics of subjects, 47–48; data-collection procedure, 16–23; demographic variables of subjects, 22, 31, 32, 46–47; detachment-involvement approach, 152–154; geographic mobility of subjects, 47; home environment of subjects, 46–68; inception of, 3–9; individual attitudes toward, 167–173; interview sample, characteristics of, 14–15; interview schedules, 247–261; parent interviews, 21, 22, 30, 48, 52, 60–68, 257–258; parental attitudes toward, 193–194; purpose of, 3, 10; research alliance, 147–149, 151–173; research interviews, 18–21; resistance to, level of, 159–163; school environment of subjects, 27–45; seduction-rejection approach, 154–159; selected questions and answers in second interview, 262–264; selection of subjects, 10–14; social-class status and, 48–51; subjects' responsiveness to, 163–165, 167; teachers' ratings and, 33–42, 165–167; *see also* Self-Image Questionnaire
Monachesi, E. D., 12 *n*.
mood swings, adolescent turmoil and, 178, 189–190
morality, concern about questions of, 75, 118
Moss, H., 150, 212
Murphy, L. B., 210
Murray, H. A., 112, 227

Murstein, B. I., 128
Muslin, H., 149

nakedness, shame and, 99
National Opinion Research Center, 48
negation, 187; of femininity, 217
negative dependence, 187
negative identities, search for, 196
negative transference, 155
Neubauer, P. B., 187 n.
neurotic crises, 183
Newman, M. F., 210
Nixon, R. E., 210, 211
normality, functional perspectives of, 4
Normality: Theoretical and Clinical Concepts of Mental Health, 4–5, 10, 177
normative crises, adolescent, 182–185
normative theory, 7

observing ego, 149
obsessive-compulsion: adolescent turmoil and, 191; depression and, 107–109
oedipal feelings, 203
Offer, D., 4, 10, 17, 21–22, 57, 66, 91, 94, 151, 177, 186 n., 204–205, 227, 239 n., 247 n.
Opler, M. D., 15, 19
optimism, 189
Osgood-Semantic differential, 65

parental authority: decrease in, 195; inspiring of respect for, 203–204; rebellious behavior and, 119–120, 185–188
parental discipline, feelings about, 53, 57, 202–204
parental independence, 195
parental objects, emancipation from, 185–188
parental uncertainty, 195
parental values: acceptance of, 118–119, 186–187; adolescent value system and, 197–200, 205–207; challenging of, 194–195; inspiring of respect for, 203–204; lack of commitment to, 195–196

parent interviews, 21, 22, 30, 48, 52, 60–68, 257–258
parents: communication with, 65–68, 156, 194, 195, 200–202, 204; students' opinions of, 51–60, 202–204
passivity, femininity and, 217
Paulsen, A., 123 n.
Pearson, G. H. J., 178, 187, 189, 194
Pearson product-moment correlations, 106, 230, 231, 238, 260
Peck, R. F., 212, 222, 227
Perlin, S., 11
personality ratings, 222
Petersen, W., 197
Pfeffer, A. Z., 7–8
phobia, 107, 108, 191
pleasurable affect, 103–105, 109, 134–135
police force, attitudes toward, 59
Polin, W., 11
political standards, 205, 206
Polka, S. K., 227
positive self-image, 218
positive therapeutic outcome, 8
power, hunger for, 182
pregnancy, fear of, 83–85
premarital sexual intercourse, attitudes toward, 83–85
Promethean enthusiasm, 174
prostitution, venereal diseases and, 87
psychiatric clinical research methods, 6
psychiatry, 155, 156; community, 6, 8, 193; coping and, 7; recent changes in, 8
psychic structure, adolescence and, 175, 177–179, 190
psychoanalysis, 18
psychoanalytic situation, 7
psychoanalytic theory, 175, 181–182
psychological conditioning, 182
psychological development, longitudinal studies of, 211
psychological disequilibrium, 179
psychological norms, 12
psychopathology, 7, 9, 147, 176–177, 183–185, 195, 212
psychosocial isolation, 183
psychosocial moratorium, 71, 188, 202

psychotherapy, 18, 73, 152, 154–159, 169–170
psychotic crises, 183
puberty, onset of, adolescent turmoil and, 214

Rabin, I. E., 123 *n.*, 187 *n.*
Rapaport, D., 254
rationalization, 131–132, 135, 189
Rausch, H. L., 227
realities, inner, willingness to face, 219
reality, control over, 180
reality-oriented experiences, 178
reality testing, 175
rebellion, definition of, 185
rebellious behavior: adolescent turmoil and, 179, 180, 185–189; delinquent behavior and, 76, 186; healthiness of, 186; institutionalized, 214–215; parental authority and, 119–120, 185–188; pathology of, 186; romanticizing of, 188–189
regression(s), 133–134, 157, 180; drive, 183
Reich, Wilhelm, 215
Reiser, M. F., 150
Reiss, I. L., 83
rejection, 158; feeling of, 98
religious values, 52–53, 71, 206
Rennie, T. A. C., 15, 19
repression: ego, 183; of sexual impulses, 214
Richardson, S. A., 18, 19
Richmond, J., 210
Rochlin, G., 210
Rogers, C., 158, 220
romanticism, 174 *n.*
romanticizing of rebellious behavior, 188–189
Rorschach Test, 21, 23, 111–113, 121–136, 138–143, 254–255
Rosenberg, M., 11
Rosengren, W. R., 227
Rosenthal, R., 19, 150, 261
Ruff, G., 217
Ryder, R. G., 210

Sabshin, M., 4, 10, 151, 177
Sanford, N., 210
Schachtel, E. G., 114

Schafer, R., 254
Schiller, Johann von, 174 *n.*
schizophrenia, 229
scholarship, adolescent values and, 198, 199, 207
Selan, K., 9, 19
self-alienation, sense of, 196
self-assertion, negation of femininity and, 217
self-awareness, assessment of, 148, 220
self-control, 175, 182
self-criticism, 133, 141; and self-esteem, 219
self-discipline, 182
self-esteem, self-criticism and, 219
self-image, positive, 218
Self-Image Questionnaire, 12–15, 23, 65; for adolescent boys, 239–246; administration of, 13–14; construction of, 227–231; factor analysis of, 237–239; reliability of scales (table), 229; selection of modal group for, 231–237; teachers' ratings and, 33–38
self-observation, capacity for, 218–220
self-observing ego, 178
separation anxiety, 91, 117
sexual adequacy, concern over, 116
sexual closeness, fear of, 84
sexual education, 86–88
sexual feelings, 32; denial of, 214; obtaining data about, 78–80, 255–256
sexual identifications, ambiguous, 116
sexual impulses: coping with, 190, 213–215; ego strength and, 178; repression of, 214; upsurge of, 175
sexual intercourse, attitudes toward, 83–85
Shakow, D., 217–218
shame: adolescent turmoil and, 108, 191; coping with, 99–100, 103, 109
Shoben, E. J., 227
sibling rivalry, 66, 120, 210, 220
Silber, E., 9, 38 *n.*, 210, 211, 219, 227
Simon, Marlene, 249

Singer, P. R., 110
Smith, A. A., 150
smoking, attitudes toward, 71–73, 161
social action, 215–216
social-action clubs, 77
social clubs, participation in, 77
social-desirability response set, 235
social norms, 12
social-psychological factor, 12
social-science research, 18, 19
social workers, 30–31
Solomon, F., 200
special crises, coping with, 89–95, 221
Spiegel, J., 210
sports activities: adolescent values and, 198, 199; aggressive impulses and, 77, 213; anxiety over, 67, 97, 102; depression and, 98; emphasis on, 42–43; 67; and masculinity, 217; pride in, 90
Spranger, E., 181–182
Srole, L., 15, 19
Steiner, J., 123 n.
Sterba, R., 149
Stochner, C., 227
Stone, L. J., 181
studying, enjoyment in, 103
"Sturm und Drang," 174–175, 181, 222
Suares, N., 123
sublimation, 213–215
success-oriented behavior, 196
Sufferings of Young Werther, The, 174 n.
Sullivan, H. S., 19
supervisory alliance, 149
suspicion, 191
Sweet, B., 227
Swerdloff, B., 210
Symonds, P. M., 11 n., 150, 212, 222

teachers: ratings by, 33–42, 165–167; student opinions of, 42–45
"Teaching Alliance, The," 149
television, delinquent behavior and, 204

Thematic Apperception Test, 21, 23, 112–121, 140, 141
therapeutic alliance, 149, 155, 164, 169
therapeutic contract, absence of, 161
therapeutic wish, 157
thinking, looseness of, 175
Thompson, J., 222
threat, minimizing of, 135–136, 221
transference, 154, 157, 180; negative, 155
transference neurosis, miniaturized, 8
Tuddenham, R. D., 222
turmoil, definition of, 178; see also adolescent turmoil

Uncommitted, The, 196
undoing, 93
unpredictable behavior, 179
Universal Experience of Adolescence, The, 181 n.

value stasis, 196
values: adolescent, 197–200, 205–207; parental, see parental values; political, 205, 206; religious, 52–53, 71, 206
Van Krevelan, A., 114
Varimax method, 107, 238
venereal diseases, prostitution and, 87
Vietnam war, attitudes toward, 58
Visotsky, H. M., 210
vocational choices, 218–219
volatility of feelings, 175–176

Waisman, H., 210
Walker, E. L., 114
Wechsler Adult Intelligence Scale, Vocabulary Subtest, 21, 112, 113, 136–140
Westley, W. A., 181, 197, 200
White, R. W., 9, 150–151, 210, 211, 218
Wilkins, B., 11
withdrawal, 98, 180
Wolfenstein, M., 94

X, Malcolm, 42 n.

Zetzel, E. R., 149

Date Due